Expressibility and the Problem of Efficient Text Planning

Linguistics: Bloomsbury Academic Collections

This Collection, composed of 19 reissued titles from The Athlone Press, Cassell and Frances Pinter, offers a distinguished selection of titles that showcase the breadth of linguistic study.

The collection is available both in e-book and print versions.

Titles in Linguistics are available in the following subsets:

Linguistics: Communication in Artificial Intelligence

Linguistics: Open Linguistics

Linguistics: Language Studies

Other titles available in Linguistics: Communication in Artificial Intelligence include:

New Concepts in Natural Language Generation: Planning, Realization and Systems, Ed. by Helmut Horacek and Michael Zock

Evolutionary Language Understanding, Geoffrey Sampson

Text Knowledge and Object Knowledge, Annely Rothkegel

Linguistic Issues in Machine Translation, Ed. by Frank Van Eynde

User Modelling in Text Generation, Cécile L. Paris

Expressibility and the Problem of Efficient Text Planning

Marie Meteer

Linguistics: Communication in Artificial Intelligence
BLOOMSBURY ACADEMIC COLLECTIONS

Bloomsbury Academic
An imprint of Bloomsbury Publishing Plc

B L O O M S B U R Y

LONDON • NEW DELHI • NEW YORK • SYDNEY

Bloomsbury Academic
An imprint of Bloomsbury Publishing Plc

50 Bedford Square
London
WC1B 3DP
UK

1385 Broadway
New York
NY 10018
USA

www.bloomsbury.com

BLOOMSBURY and the Diana logo are trademarks of Bloomsbury Publishing Plc

First published in 1992 by Pinter Publishers Limited

This edition published by Bloomsbury Academic 2015

British Library Cataloguing-in-Publication Data
A catalogue record for this book is available from the British Library.

ISBN: HB: 978-1-4742-4656-9
ePDF: 978-1-4742-4657-6
Set: 978-1-4742-4692-7

Library of Congress Cataloging-in-Publication Data
A catalog record for this book is available from the Library of Congress

Series: Bloomsbury Academic Collections, ISSN 2051-0012

Printed and bound in Great Britain

Expressibility and the Problem of Efficient Text Planning

Expressibility and the Problem of Efficient Text Planning

Marie W. Meteer

Pinter Publishers, London

Distributed exclusively in the United States and Canada by St. Martin's Press, New York

First published in Great Britain in 1992 by
Pinter Publishers Limited,
25 Floral Street, London WC2E 9DS

Distributed exclusively in the United States and Canada by
St. Martins Press, Inc.,
175 Fifth Avenue, New York, NY 10010, USA

British Library Cataloguing in Publication Data
A CIP catalogue record for this book is available from
the British Library.

ISBN 1 85567 022 5

Library of Congress Cataloging-in-Publication Data
A CIP catalog record for this book is available from
the Library of Congress

Printed and bound in Great Britain by Billing and Sons Ltd., Worcester

Contents

List of Figures

Foreword

Natural language generation is an unusual field. It requires its researchers to start from something they can know nothing about: the nature of human thought. As a cognitive science using the methodologies of computational linguistics and artificial intelligence, generation is trying to understand the processes by which people conceive and produce utterances ("texts"), using as its tools computer programs that model both the processing and the mental faculties that dictate what can be said and how it is conceptualized and represented. But unlike its sister field of language understanding, where the starting point is a text, generation starts with a mental state–something that cannot be directly studied.

Faced with this dilemma, people working in generation have to depend upon carefully articulated principles to guide their research. There are too many possible ways that mental structures and the intermediate representations of the generation process could be formed just to pick one arbitrarily. Instead, one must adopt a set of principles to govern what a theory of generation must account for and what it can be like computationally. Such principles constrain what can be a possible structure or procedure, and make it possible to evaluate theories and test them empirically, since their design choices are no longer arbitrary but must conform to the criteria that the principles impose.

Principles have not always been important in generation. In the early days of the field it was sufficient just to accomplish something–to produce a text that was fluent regardless of how it was done. But young fields go through a natural evolution. Once people have gained experience and begun to get some perspective on the options open to them, they become dissatisfied with arbitrary accounts. They seek out generalizations and broad principles that can provide explanations and guide their design decisions.

Marie Meteer's work is an key step in this progression. She confronts the problem of the unknown mental source for a text by working backwards from careful analyses of what we do know, actual texts themselves. Emerging from her analysis is a genuinely new principle: that of *expressibility*, a requirement on the early stages of the generation process–those that select and organize what is to be said–that the decisions they make actually be able to lead to an utterance, ie that the information chosen be able to be expressed.

While it seems obvious, this principle is no small matter. People only rarely "talk themselves into a corner", starting a sentence only to stop part way through because there is no way to express what they want to say. The fact that this kind of mistake in text planning occurs so rarely requires an explanation:

what is it about the computational architecture of the human language generation process that enables it to satisfy this principle of expressibility? More concretely, what representations and procedures can be employed in a theory of generation that would make expressibility *inescapable*, ie not something that a designer stipulates by carefully choosing the rules to be used but rather a property that follows from the rule-writing formalism itself such that a rule that might violate expressibility simply cannot be written.

Meteer's own answer to these questions, in this book that has emerged out of her dissertation, is grounded in thorough corpus analysis. Her early work was on the question of how a generator might incorporate a "revision" component, making additional passes over a text to improve it after it is first drafted, as people do when writing. To support this investigation, she went through professionally edited scientific papers, comparing the wording of initial and subsequent drafts. What emerged was an appreciation that the kinds of changes being made were in fact beyond the state of the art for current generators: how is a generator to appreciate the need for a change if it has no motivation for its initial choice of constructions?

This led to a redirection of her research to the question of how to increase a generator's expressiveness so that it could begin to approach human fluency. Following the work of linguists such as Len Talmy, she developed a system of types which categorizes communicable information into semantic classes, each with a specific realization in language. These types provide abstractions that encapsulate the surface linguistic details of the realizations, while exposing and emphasizing those details that bear on the distinctions that were pivotal in her corpus. In addition, the semantic types provide a crucial theoretical function in that they are the only route by which the generator is permitted to produce a text: all information selected by the text planning process must be couched in terms of these types and deployed in her 'Text Structure' level of representation where constraints on their combination and configuration are enforced. It is this level of her generator's computational architecture that enforces the principle of expressibility and makes it truly inescapable–her generator cannot talk itself into a corner because it cannot formulate what it wants to say except in terms of a linguistically coherent system of types for expression.

It is true, of course, that the problem now regresses to how a text planner is to get to this system of semantic types from whatever embodiment the information and intentions have in the speaker's mind. Compounding the problem is the additional goal to meet a principle deriving from my own work, that of efficiency, which in its strongest form requires that all decisions be indelible, disallowing any form of backup or generate-and-test. But a set of strong principles is actually an aid in this process since it reduces the space of possible designs that could be considered. The principles provide a disciplined means of projecting backwards from what can be observed and analyzed: the texts that people actually produce, to what we can otherwise only guess about: their source in the mind.

Meteer's work is a step along this path, one that is not only rigorous theoretically but also tested in the implementation of her generation system 'Spokesman'. Spokesman is a full system that starts with the data structures of the application program in whose service it is producing the text. It uses a set of declarative rules to select units of information from those structures, give them a realization in terms of her abstract linguistic types and organize them as a text by placing the typed units at legal positions in her Text Structure level of representation. From this level, other mapping rules incrementally construct a linguistic specification for successive portions of the text structure, realizing the linguistic abstractions as concrete, surface-level lexical and syntactic constructs formalized in a Tree Adjoining Grammar. The specification is then passed to my surface generator, Mumble, for linearization as a surface structure and the imposition of surface grammatical constraints as the words of the text are uttered.

As a running program whose text output can be examined for sensibility and cohesion, Spokesman provides a context for making theoretical designs concrete and testable. This is crucial methodologically, since in generation, as in any aspect of research into artificial intelligence, the best work is in equal parts a study of the engineering of computational systems and a probe into the possible mechanisms underlying intelligent human behavior. Meteer's Spokesman program is solid engineering, working as it has with seven different applications in four representations, and meeting difficult standards of robustness and real time operation. It is at the same time a thorough and persuasive exemplification of her theory of expressibility, illustrating the new intermediate abstract linguistic level of Text Structure and the semantic types that populate it.

This combination of careful theorizing, text analysis and implementation makes Meteer's work an important milestone in generation research, where for the first time in generation we have a computationally motivated linguistic level of representation more abstract than surface structure and yet more concrete and more carefully constrained than the conceptual structures that have been hypothesized *a priori* as sources for the generator. It is a vivid and firm foundation for further work, pushing back the curtain a little more and giving us confedence that generation research really will provide a window on the mind.

David D. McDonald
Arlington, Massachusetts
February 1992

1 The Generation Gap

Natural language generation is the deliberate production of text to meet the communicative goals of some underlying application program. It consists of the following major activities: (1) determining what information is to be communicated, (2) imposing a suitable order on the elements of this information consistent with the constituent structure of language and expressing the relative salience and newness of the elements, and (3) determining what wording and syntactic constructions to use. The first two of these activities are generally considered "text planning" and its output is the "plan". The third activity is "realization" and generally handles all of the linguistic decision making. While it is recognized that this division is problematic (Hovy *et al.* 1988), nearly all generation systems today make this division. One of the chief accomplishments of this work has been to bridge the gap between these two activities through the introduction of a new representational level that both provides the choices necessary for the text planner to take advantage of the expressiveness of natural language and prevents it from composing an utterance that is not expressible in the language.

Most state-of-the-art text planning systems follow a common design (see for example McKeown 1985, Derr & McKeown 1984, Paris 1987, or Hovy 1988 discussed in more detail in Chapter Seven). They start from a set of propositions, each typically verb-based and able to be realized independently as a simple sentence. Then they organize the propositions into a coherent discourse by combining them according to the dictates of predefined "schemas" representing plausible discourse relationships. Subsequent choices of surface resources[1] are all local to the propositions and not sensitive to the schemas or other context, except for the discourse-level connectives used in combining the propositions into complex sentences and occasionally a shallow discourse history governing the use of pronouns.

In these approaches to natural language generation there is a gap between the plan, usually represented in the terms of the application program, and the resources that must be used by the realization component to carry out that plan, the resources of language. The gap occurs in most current systems because the text planner selects units from the application program and organizes them without consideration for what linguistic resources are available for expressing them. Such systems ensure the plan is realizable by accepting limits to their expressive competence, e.g. each atomic unit in the plan is required to be a

[1] The surface linguistic resources are all the syntactic structures, words, and grammatical features of the language available to the speaker.

proposition and thus can always be realized as a clause. Each unit can be independently translated into language using the linguistic realization component since there are few restrictions on the connection between clauses. Clauses can be connected with coordinate or subordinate conjunctions (e.g. "and", "because") or simply made into separate sentences.

However, this approach does not take advantage of the full expressive power of language, in which units can be much more tightly composed. In order to exercise the full expressiveness of language, text planning needs to address the *internal* composition of clauses and not just their organization into larger structures. Clauses in actual texts reflect a combination of multiple atomic units. Systems that ignore this and begin with units that are inevitably realized as kernel clauses (e.g. Mann & Moore 1981, McKeown 1985, Hovy 1988) have two major deficiencies: (1) they are presuming underlying programs have units of this size that may be simply selected for inclusion in the message and then realized intact, and (2) they are under-utilizing the power of natural language, which can use complex noun phrases, nominalizations, adverbial phrases, and other adjuncts to pack information from multiple units into one clause.

Moreover, the process of composing multiple units into one clause is a much more complex problem than simply ordering propositions in a text plan. What compositions are possible depend on what linguistic resources are available to realize the units involved. For example, an Army battalion that has been assigned a defensive mission can be said to be "defending", but if we say that a battalion that has been assigned an offensive mission is "offending" we mean something very different. There is no comparable resource available to fit that textual niche and either a different, more complex resource must be used or the whole text changed. Furthermore, different types of resources have different constraints on their composition: one can "make an important decision", but one cannot "decide importantly".

In order to plan complex utterances and ensure they are expressible in language, i.e. can be realized as a grammatical utterance, the text planning process must know (1) what realizations are available to an element, that is what resources are available, (2) the constraints on the composition of the resources, and (3) what has been committed to thus far in the utterance which constrains the choice of resource. This work provides the theoretical apparatus required to supply this information, centering on a new representational level which I call *Text Structure*.

1.1 Overview

In this initial chapter, I define the problem, first by placing it within the framework of a computational model of natural language generation. I use Marr's notion of the three levels of a computational account in order to put this model of a cognitive process on theoretically sound ground. Then in the second half of the chapter, I look particularly at the problems of composing linguistic resources for text planning and ensuring expressibility and expressiveness.

In the second chapter, I present an overview of the terminology of natural language generation and the modularization of the process. I also discuss several important issues, such as the place of content delimitation and lexical selection, the role of revision, and different views of text structure.

In Chapter Three, I present motivations for my new representational level, Text Structure, from the two directions the research has taken throughout: the analysis of actually occurring texts, and the design and construction of a generation system that produces text from real application programs. Since my original interests were in revision, the analysis of revised texts provided a great deal of the motivation for this work. The variation between the initial and revised texts provides insights into the kinds of decisions a generator must be able to make. Generalizations over the data can help to define a vocabulary for describing those decisions. I also discuss how the model presented in this work can account for the generation of the initial texts and the need to revise them. In the second part of this chapter, I motivate the Text Structure level from a text planning perspective, focusing on the disparity between a representation designed for reasoning in an application and the appropriate language for realizing it.

Chapter Four returns to the problem of expressibility and how the Text Structure representation provides a solution. I look at Text Structure from a linguistic perspective and demonstrate its adequacy for capturing significant linguistic abstractions necessary for composing linguistic resources and also at the representation of Text Structure in my Spokesman generation system and show its importance for text planning

In Chapter Five, I describe the Text Structure as implemented in the text planner of Spokesman. I present the details of how the text planner constructs the Text Structure and then uses it to construct the linguistic specification that is the input to the linguistic realization component. In the sixth chapter, I show Text Structure in action by walking through a full example of the system, describing events from the Main Street simulation program (Abrett *et al.* 1989).

In Chapter Seven, I contrast this work with other architectures for generation, focusing in particular on how they handle the problem of expressibility. I look at three approaches: (1) those that simply organize kernel clauses (as described above, e.g. Mann & Moore, McKeown, Paris, Hovy), thereby limiting the competence of their generation systems; (2) approaches that relax some of the processing constraints adopted in my approach, in particular efficiency, and let the system backtrack and change decisions (e.g. Nirenburg, Gabriel); and (3) those that are not necessarily concerned with modeling the process at all but rather focus on achieving competence, in particular, the systemic approaches (e.g. Mann & Matthiessen, Bateman, Patten).

Finally, in Chapter Eight I summarize the accomplishments, adding some directions for the future of the work.

1.2 Defining the problem

Marr, in his introduction to *Vision* (Marr 1982), stresses the importance of understanding the nature of a computational problem—simply solving an instance of the problem is inadequate as a basis for a theory. In particular he warns against equating an implementation of an information processing task with a model of that process. In the approach he lays down, he posits three levels of description that must be understood before one can be said to understand a process. The most abstract level is the *computational theory* which addresses *what* the process does and *why* it does that rather than something else. The second level of analysis is comprised by the representations and algorithms by which one describes *how* the process works. We will call this second level the *computational model* of the process. The third level is that actual *implementation* of those representations and algorithms in some physical device (e.g. a Lisp machine or a brain). While these levels are related, they are not strictly dependent on each other. For a single computational theory, there may be many representations and algorithms that meet its constraints, and similarly, there may be many implementations of the representations and algorithms.

Following Marr, I will define the problem I am addressing in terms of these three levels. I first introduce the computational theory by exploring the nature of the generation process. Next, I define the constraints that are inescapable parts of generation as a computational problem to be solved. I then describe the representations and algorithms I propose to meet the constraints of this theory. It is this level, that of the **computational model**, that is the focus of my work and is expanded on in the rest of this document. Finally, I briefly describe the implementation of this computational model in the Spokesman generation system.

1.2.1 *Key properties of the generation process*

In this section, I define what I see to be the most important properties of natural language generation, using the characteristics of language production in people as a guide.

People are very *fluent* text producers. They rarely make grammatical mistakes; they rarely begin an utterance they cannot complete. They can continue speaking seemingly indefinitely, adding more as they go, rarely needing to stop while deciding what to say next. Many will talk as long as their audiences will listen or until they themselves become hungry or tired. People are also capable of saying something on almost any topic: while the depth of the content may vary a great deal, the rate of speech and grammaticality of the text are relatively stable.

However, while fluent, people are *rarely high quality* text producers. In order to produce what is deemed "good" text, people must rehearse; this rehearsal is usually in the form of writing drafts and then reading and revising those drafts, although mental rehearsals are also common, such as trying out different wordings to yourself before asking your boss for a raise.

These qualities suggest characteristics that our computational model of natural language generation must account for:

- A generator must be *efficient*. Given today's processor speeds, it should at least be able to produce text as fast and continuously as people can talk. Therefore, the algorithm should be closer to linear than exponential.
- A generator must be able to *produce continuous, connected text*. Therefore, it must be able to begin uttering words before all of the details of the entire utterance have been determined.
- A generator must be able to produce text that is *grammatical and understandable*; and it must be competent in the language. While it need not have the complete coverage of the language (it's not clear any individual has such coverage, or that we even know what it is), it must be capable of a large subset.
- However, the text it produces need not be optimal text. The generator can use a revision component to assess its own output and decide how to improve it and revise it by regenerating the text.
- The generator should be independent of the application program. The same mechanisms should work regardless of the topic of the text being produced or the particular application program the generator is working with. (This is not to say we cannot establish minimal requirements for an application program for generation.)
- The same architecture must be capable of working in written or spoken mode; that is, it should be able to both generate competent text in a single pass and revise that text to produce quality written text.

1.2.2 *The computational problem of generation*

A computational problem can be identified uniquely by the constraints it has to satisfy. We begin by defining natural language generation (NLG) and then define the necessary constraints on the process that any model must meet.

NLG is the process of going from a representation of a situation to a textual expression of some relevant portion of that situation in a natural language, such as English or German. A situation is the state of the program or individual (complete with the intentions and goals) at the time of the utterance. A situation can be the representation of the world in a simulator that is describing its actions, or a person's mental state and physical surroundings as she answers the phone. Some "relevant portion of the situation" will contribute to the message that will be expressed. The utterance, the textual expression of the message, is a composition of resources in some natural language and must obey the constraints of that language. An utterance consists of serially ordered constituents, ultimately words.

There are three inescapable facts about the process that any model of generation must account for: compositionality, grammaticality, and the limited resources of language. We look at each in turn.

- NLG must be *compositional*. Situations are composites. If they were not, then we could associate a single utterance with each situation and make NLG a table lookup process (this is in fact the case with programs that use print statements). Since new situations can always be composed of known pieces (or pieces of known types), a NL generator must be able to build a new text that expresses the relevant portion of that situation.[2] Furthermore, utterances themselves are compositional. They are compositions of the resources of the language.

- The utterance produced must be *grammatical*, that is the composition of linguistic resources must be in accordance with the rules of composition in the language.
- The individual resources of language are *limited*. There are not words available to describe every object or action uniquely and words do not necessarily participate in the full paradigm of variation (for example, a *runner* is someone who runs, but a *skipper* is someone who captains a boat, not someone who skips).

These three constraints suggest a corollary, which is the problem addressed here:

- The message, the relevant portion of the situation to be communicated, must be *expressible* in natural language, that is that there must be linguistic resources available to realize the elements of the message.

In this work, I provide a non-stipulative account of expressibility in natural language generation in which the representation language the message is composed in ensures expressibility by embodying the resources of language and the constraints on their composition. This is in contrast to a stipulative account in which an outside process or rule set ensures the message can be expressed.

1.2.3 *The computational model*

We have identified a computational problem in natural language generation in terms of the necessary constraints and properties of the process we are trying to model. We now look at what these properties have contributed to the design of the algorithms and representations that make up the computational model. The computational model must primarily meet the constraints that define the problem. However, those constraints do not necessarily fully define a particular model. Many different representations and algorithms might meet the same computational theory. Therefore, we further constrain the model by adopting the properties of natural language generation outlined in §1.2.1.

The model of natural language generation proposed here retains the division of the generation process into text planning and linguistic realization. However, I introduce multiple levels of representation into both text planning and linguistic realization so that the generation process becomes a series of small

[2] This notion of compositionality of situations is related to Chomsky's notion of creativity in language, namely that there are infinitely many sentences in a language and that this is an important fact that must be accounted for (Chomsky 1957). The classic argument for creativity uses the idea that one can continually add further adjuncts to sentences to establish that there can be no longest sentence and therefore no finite number of sentences. However, this argument is overly strained: who has actually heard a 500-word sentence (even children eventually get bored with "this is the cat that ate the rat that..."). A far more reasonable and

steps through progressively more linguistically based representations, rather than the work of two separate, internally homogeneous components. This makes an overall division into two components a convenience, rather than theoretically significant, and is useful for fitting my work into the literature. The representational level that I focus on in this work is called the *Text Structure*. It is the central representation in the text planner and plays two important roles:

(1) It provides an intermediate level between the structures of the application program and the linguistic structures needed by the Linguistic Realization Component.

(2) It constrains the planning process to ensure that what is planned is *expressible* in language.

Text Structure is represented as a tree capturing the following kinds of information:

- constituency: each node in the tree is a complete constituent of the utterance.[3] A constituent may range in size from a paragraph to a single word;
- structural relations among constituents (head-argument, matrix-adjunct, coordinates);
- the information expressed by the constituent;
- the semantic type of that information (e.g. event, property, object).

The necessity of this representational level falls out of the basic constraints of the generation process itself: that situations and utterances are compositional, utterances must be grammatical, and that the resources of language are limited.

In section 1.3, we return to this representation and show why this particular representation is appropriate for ensuring expressibility. Before that, we look at what aspects of my computational model meet the other criteria we have set out, in particular of efficiency and the role of revision. Finally, we look at Marr's third level, the implementation of the model.

1.2.3.1 *Efficiency* One of the most important properties of language generation is that it must be efficient in order to produce continuous fluent text at the rate of speech. If our only concern were speed, we could address efficiency at the level of the implementation (e.g. letting it run on a Cray); however, speech is continuous, which means the algorithm itself must be linear or at most geometric.

Since NLG is a decision making process, we can measure efficiency in terms of decisions along two dimensions:

- the number of decisions a generator must make to produce an utterance;

commonsense demonstration of creativity is to observe that one continually uses new utterances because one is continually faced with new situations.

[3] "Utterance" is a general term for what is being produced ("uttered") by the generator. The utterance is represented at various levels of abstraction throughout the generation process from the objects specified by the application program to the text itself.

- the amount of computation required to make a single decision.

One way of limiting the number of decisions the generator must make is to require that the decisions are *indelible*, that is once made, they cannot be changed. The alternative would be to allow the system to backtrack and remake decisions, increasing the overall number of decisions made. (Direct comparisons with these alternative architectures are made in Chapter Seven.) Note that this strategy of indelibility does not come without a cost: the generator must be certain that each decision is correct, which may increase the amount of computation required to make the decision. We can state this requirement that is imposed by indelibility as *expressibility*: at all points in the generation process, the generator must make sure that the representation of the utterance it has built is realizable in the language, that is that it is "expressible".

There are three other aspects of the model which support efficiency: modularity, use of progressive refinement, and message driven processing.

In generation, the amount of computation required to make a decision can be reduced by organizing decisions according to the kind of reference knowledge they use, thereby allowing that knowledge to be given a very efficient representation, simplifying the effort required to make a decision. This leads to multilevel designs, particularly a division between the resource knowledge used in planning and that used in linguistic realization. The tradeoff here is that more independent levels may increase the overall number of decisions made, though each one will be made with less effort.

Multiple levels of representation contribute to the use of *progressive refinement*, wherein the text planner begins by building an abstract representation of the utterance, and then fills in details conservatively. The advantage of progressive refinement is that it is efficient: the system never has to backtrack and remake the same decisions it has already made; it just makes them successively more detailed. A disadvantage is that the terms in which the planning is done must now do more work. They must serve to constrain the decisions in such a way that no choice is ever made that will ultimately lead to the failure of the plan. It is well recognized that progressive refinement alone is inadequate for general purpose planning (Cohen & Feigenbaum 1982). However, in generation, a text planner is not solving problems in general: its target is language, and we know a great deal about the structure of language—far more than we know about planning for all the possible contingencies in some real world situation—for example a planner in a military domain has to account for all the possibilities that could occur in a real battle.

Another factor in the efficiency of an algorithm is its method of control. Control in a computational system is the determination of the sequence in which a set of actions will be taken. We distinguish between two general modes of control:

- control lies in the reference knowledge, that is it is governed by some predetermined body of tests that gate and order actions;
- control lies in the input itself, which is interpreted by some general control loop within the process.

We argue in McDonald, Meteer, & Pustejovsky (1987) that the latter mode, termed *message directed* processing, is more efficient, as the action sequence has already been implicitly determined by the process that built the input structure and consequently no effort needs to be expended on control decisions. The alternative, in which control is in the reference knowledge (termed *grammar directed* processing), expends an appreciable amount of activity as "overhead" that does not contribute to the real goals but is rather spent determining which of the possible sequences is appropriate in the situation at hand. Most systemic grammar systems are examples of grammar directed control (e.g. NIGEL, Mann & Matthiessen 1985).

One point in all generation systems where this control difference is apparent is at the interface between the application program and the generator. In a message driven system, the structures of the application program themselves direct what is to be said. The events in the application program that trigger the "urge to speak" also provide the structures that determine the content of what is to be communicated. This is in contrast to systems where the application program only provides a "communicative goal" and the generator searches the knowledge base of the application for information to fulfil the goal using a schema or other structure internal to the generator to control the search (e.g. McKeown 1985).[4]

1.2.4 *The implementation*

The third of Marr's levels is the implementation of the computational model on some device. Again, there may be any number of implementations for a particular computational model as there may be many models for a particular theory. The model presented here is implemented in a system called Spokesman. It is implemented in Common Lisp and the examples in this book were run on a Symbolics 3600 series computer, though versions of the system also run on a Macintosh and SUN4. In this section I briefly describe the system, particularly focusing on those aspects that meet the constraints posed by the model described in the previous section. This description serves as a summary of many of the points made thus far and an introduction to the specific representations employed.

The Spokesman generation system produces natural language text for an underlying application program. The application program is the planning system, simulator, expert diagnostician, cooperative database, etc. that the human users want to talk with; it is developed independently of the generator *per se*. Events within this underlying program will determine the goals the generator's utterances are to achieve and initiate the generation process. SPOKESMAN produces text for a number of different application programs, including a military tactical planning system (the MOVES system on the AirLand Battle Management Program), two different simulation systems (Semi-automated Forces and Main Street), and a Navy database as part of the

[4] Data driven approaches are becoming more common in generation systems as application programs become more active. In early generation work, where the only programs available were static data bases, search was the only option.

Janus Interface. (These applications are described in more detail in Chapter Seven.)

Spokesman is composed of two major components: the *text planner* and the *linguistic realization component*. The text planner selects the information to be communicated explicitly (or omitted), determines what perspectives and rhetorical organization the information should be given, and chooses a mapping for the information on to the linguistic resources that the language provides (e.g. open-class words and syntactic constructions). The linguistic realization component is MUMBLE-86 (McDonald 1984; Meteer *et al.* 1987). It carries out the planner's specifications to produce an actual text. It ensures that the text is grammatical and handles all of the syntactic and morphological decision making.

Both components use multiple levels of representation, beginning with objects from the application program through progressively more linguistic representations to the final text. Each representational level is a complete description of the utterance. Furthermore, while a level is being built, it provides constraints and context for the further decisions that go into its construction. This is an essential part of planning by successive refinement because the representation must constrain the planner so that it is not allowed to make decisions it will later have to retract.

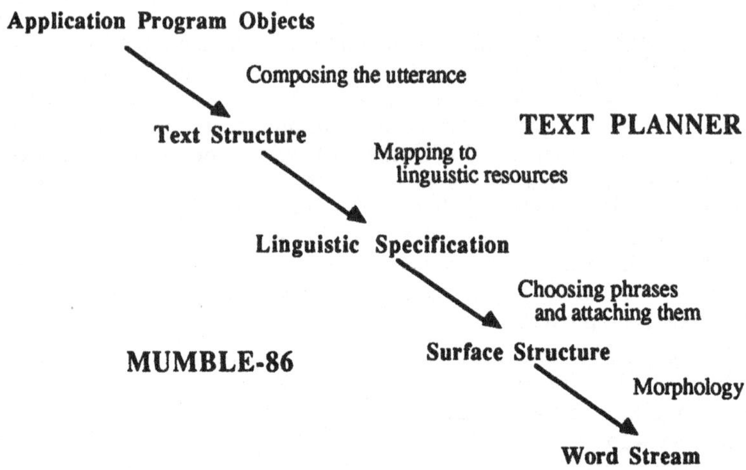

Figure 1.1 Spokesman

Since the control is message directed, the representational levels also control the order of the decisions. As I described in the previous section, this multi-leveled, message directed architecture makes the processing efficient, since it simplifies the decision making and constrains the reference knowledge needed at each level. The components and levels of representation in SPOKESMAN are shown in Figure 1.1. Examples of the structures are shown in Figure 1.2.

TEXT STRUCTURE

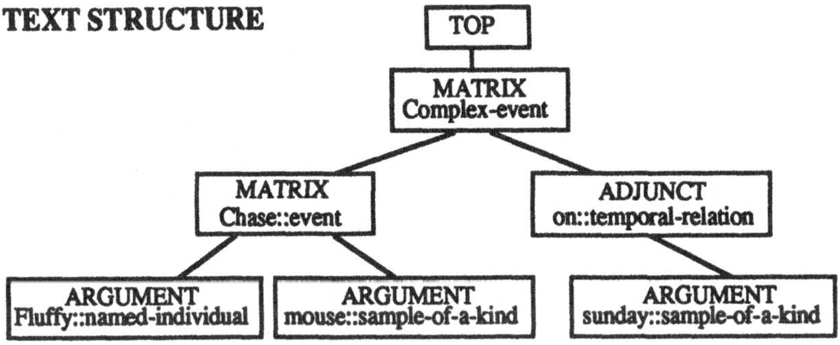

LINGUISTIC SPECIFICATION

```
DISCOURSE-UNIT
 head: GENERAL-CLAUSE
        head: realization-function: CHASE+TRANSITIVE-TWO-ARGS
              arguments: GENERAL-NP
                          head: realization-function: PROPER-NAME
                                arguments: "Fluffy"
                          accessories: <number SINGULAR>
                         GENERAL-NP
                          head: realization-function: NP-COMMON-NOUN
                                arguments: "mouse"
                          accessories: <number PLURAL>
        accessories: <tense-modal PRESENT> <UNMARKED>
        further-specifications:
           attachment-function: CLAUSAL-ADJUNCT
           specification: head: realization-function: PP+ON
                                arguments:  GENERAL-NP ....Sunday
```

SURFACE STRUCTURE

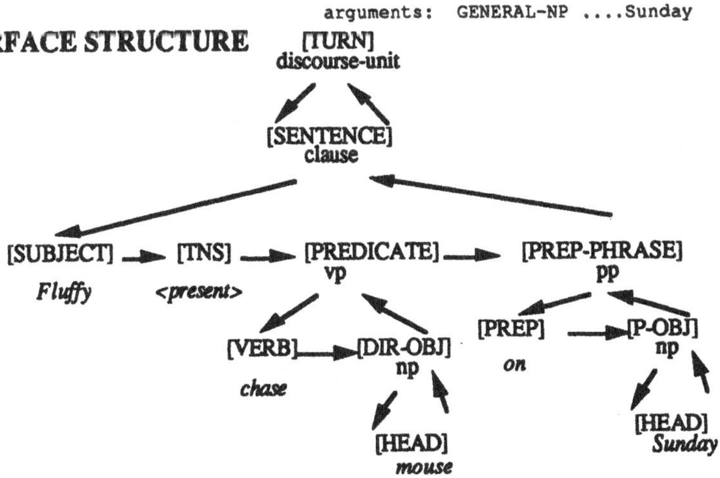

WORD STREAM *Fluffy chases mice on Sundays.*

Figure 1.2 Examples of the representational levels in Spokesman

The first level of representation (not shown in Figure 1.2) is the specification of the utterance in the terms of the application program. The system uses an object-oriented approach which predefines mappings from objects[5] to the routines that know how to process those objects (or can choose among different routines depending on the context). The efficiency of using predefined mappings for known types comes from drastically reducing or entirely eliminating search; the decisions available to a type are defined by the developer, rather than presenting all options at all times and letting a search procedure find the best one.

The Text Structure is the central representation in the text planner. Text Structure is a tree capturing relationships between the subparts of the utterance (its *constituent* structure). Each node in the tree represents a constituent and contains information about it, such as what information it expresses and its relation to its parent. Text Structure nodes also contain discourse information, such as what entities have been previously referenced. The application objects directly drive the process that builds the Text Structure through mappings associated with their types. In addition, the Text Structure itself plays a role in the construction process by providing a representation of the decisions made so far and constraining further decisions. For example, the Text Structure can constrain where additional information may be added (e.g. additional adjuncts may only be added to a matrix, for instance a matrix based on the word "operations" can be made more specific as "covering force operations" and even as specific as "offensive covering force operations"; or, more obviously, in an incremental pipeline architecture, information can only be added ahead of the point of speech).

Once the Text Structure has been built, it is traversed, top down and left to right, to build the *linguistic specification* for the utterance (the input to MUMBLE-86). The linguistic specification acts as a transition between the more conceptual and structural vocabulary of the text planner to the strictly linguistic vocabulary of the realization component. The Text Structural representational level must completely specify the information to be expressed by the utterance. During the mapping to the linguistic specification, the final choice of the lexical heads (content words) is made and the classes of syntactic structures are chosen (this constrains the final decisions of syntactic structure while leaving open the final linearization, which will be decided by the linguistic realization component using the context of the surface structure). In addition, the mapping to the linguistic specification ensures that all the necessary linguistic information is present. For example, if the specification is for a clause and no temporal information has been specified, a default tense is assigned. The specification for a noun phrase must be marked singular or plural, and if it is to be realized as a pronoun, it must have gender (masculine, feminine, or neuter) to correctly produce "he", "she", or "it".

[5] In general we use OBJECT to refer to any structure that can be manipulated independently of its context. OBJECT can refer to both instances and types from the application program and to instances and types defined within the text planner.

MUMBLE-86 uses the linguistic specification of the message to build the *surface structure*, which linearizes the words and phrases within each constituent. As the surface structure is created, MUMBLE uses the context of the structure already built to make decisions about what syntactic structure to use. As it is built, the structure is traversed and other syntactic and morphological decisions are made, such as subject/verb agreement, placement of gaps ("the book that Susan bought <trace>"), and syntactically required pronominalization ("Peter bought himself a book").

MUMBLE's grammar is based on a Tree Adjoining Grammar ("TAG", Joshi 1985) defined in terms of elementary trees and rules for their composition. This type of grammar is particularly appropriate for our compositional approach to language generation and, together with the explicit representation of the surface structure, allows the system to generate complex syntactic constructions, such as complex noun phrases and adjunct clauses: "Peter bought a book *to read on the plane*" (Huettner, Meteer & McDonald 1987).

1.3 Text Structure: an intermediate level of representation for text planning

I have defined the generation process as going from an underlying program's representation of a particular situation with a set of communicative goals to some appropriate text intended to accomplish those goals in that situation. This definition emphasizes the fact that the generation process involves a change in the terms in which information is expressed: the situation is represented in the terms of the application program; the final utterance must be in the terms of the surface language.

The approach I have taken to traversing the distance between these two very different representations is to provide an intermediate level of representation that both captures the resources of the language and provides constraints on the composition of those resources. In designing such a representation, it is essential to work from both sides: (1) the underlying representation of the knowledge to be communicated and (2) the actual resources of the language.

These two approaches highlight different aspects of the problem and add to the richness of the design. In working from an underlying representation to a text, the change in representation highlights the problem of *expressibility*: as the text planner composes the message to be expressed, it needs to know that there are resources in the language available for realizing that message and what their properties are. In working from a target text backwards, we face the problem of *expressiveness*, that is what distinctions must a text planner be capable of making in order to take advantage of the full expressive power that the language provides. This bi-directional approach is seen throughout this work, from the motivations for the work described in Chapter Three to the implementations described in Chapter Six.

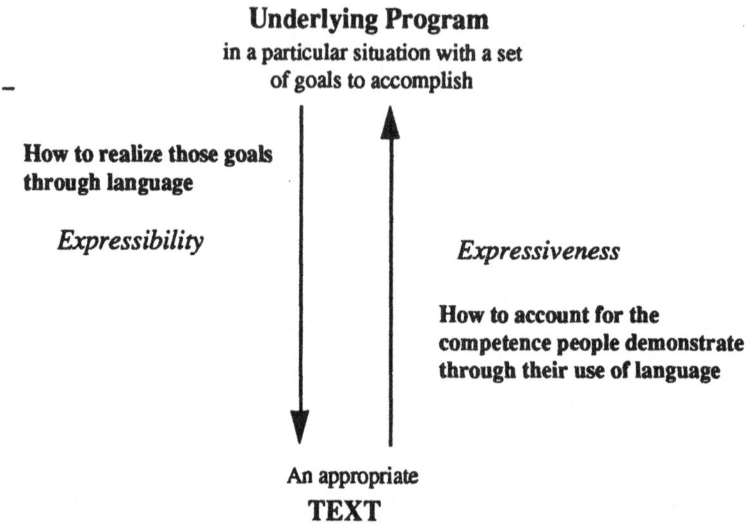

Figure 1.3 Bi-directional approach to generation research

The design of the intermediate level of representation, in particular the choice of terms and expressions, is crucial to its effectiveness in providing the necessary constraints for the text planner. Since it is the representation itself that is doing the work, the design must fit the task, as stated by Marr:

> *Any particular representation makes certain information explicit at the expense of information that is pushed into the background and may be quite hard to recover. This issue is important, because how information is represented can greatly affect how easy it is to do different things with it.*[6]

In the next section, I give some examples of Text Structure and a brief overview of the kinds of considerations that went into its design. I elaborate on the design in Chapter Four.

1.3.1 *A preview of Text Structure*

Figure 1.4 shows an example of the Text Structure representation for a relatively simple utterance. We look at this example again in more detail in Chapters Four and Six.

[6] Marr, 1982, p.22.

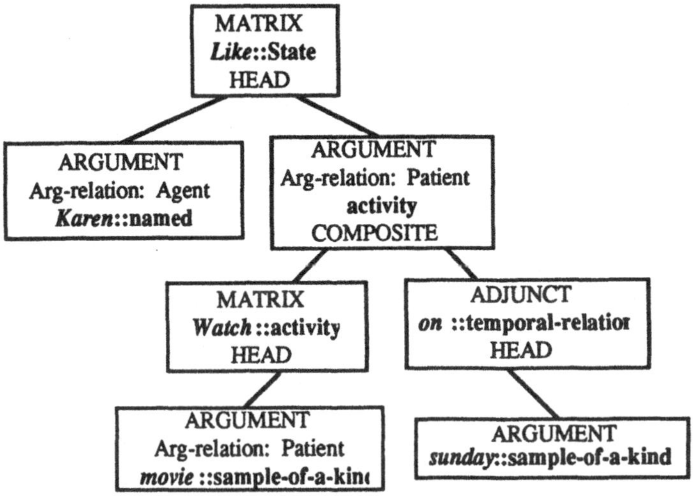

Figure 1.4 Text Structure for "Karen likes watching movies on Sundays"

The following information is shown in the Text Structure diagram:

Constituency: The nodes in the Text Structure tree reflect the constituency of the utterance.

Structural relations among constituents: Each node is marked with its structural relation to its parent (the top label) and to its children (the bottom label on nodes with children).

Semantic category: the constituent expresses: The labels in the center of the node (in bold) show the lexical head (in italics) and the semantic category the constituent expresses.

The Text Structure representation is in abstract linguistic terms, which were derived by looking at the concrete resources the language provides.

Constituency is present in language from the level where individual words form phrases to that of whole paragraphs contributing to a text. The Text Structure is designed to capture constituency and other structural relations that can be found at *all* levels of text. Consequently, it does not make the traditional distinctions between syntactic relations below the level of the sentence and discourse relations above that level. This allows Text Structure to capture general notions that appear both within sentences and between them, such as constituents where one element is special and the rest support it. Furthermore, the very same mechanisms can be used at different levels (e.g. adding elaboration information into a paragraph or a noun phrase). Figure 1.5 shows an automatically generated Text Structure graph for a partial description of a person from the Main Street simulation program.

Karen is at International Conglomerate, which is at 1375 Main Street. Her skills are cooking and managing. Karen likes reading books...

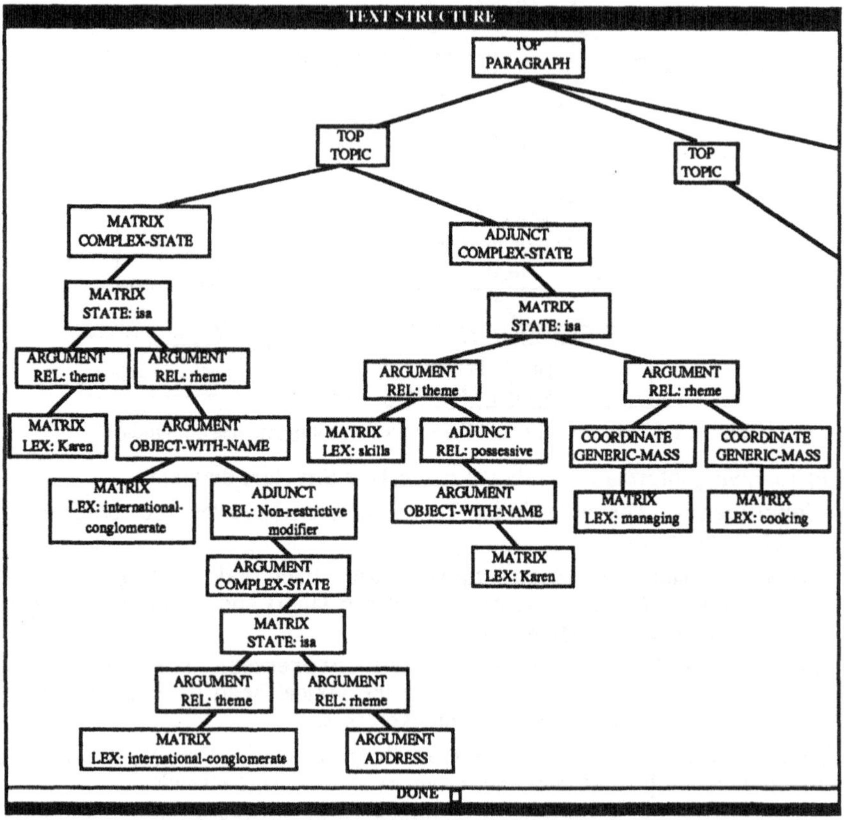

Figure 1.5 Partial Text Structure graph for paragraph

The **semantic category** expressed by the constituent is a central part of the Text Structure representation. To arrive at a vocabulary that captures the most useful set of abstract semantic categories that reflect the concrete linguistic resources, we must look to the language itself. A great deal of linguistic analysis has already been done that can help define the set of linguistic and grammatical resources and a vocabulary for describing them at a conceptual level. I briefly preview some of these analyses here; they are described in detail in Chapter Four.

Jackendoff (1983) makes the following claim about the relationship between language structure and meaning: "Each contentful major syntactic constituent of a sentence maps into a conceptual constituent in the meaning of the sentence." Included in his vocabulary of conceptual categories are Thing, Path, Action, Event, and Place.

Talmy's extensive cross linguistic analyses (1987) have yielded a vocabulary of the kinds of notions which are expressed grammatically in language. He identifies categories including matter/action, uniplex/multiplex, bounded/unbounded, and discrete/continuous. A lexical item may be prespecified for values in these categories (for example, *furniture* inherently has values matter, discrete, unbounded, multiplex). A value may be changed by an operator for that category (the uniplex operator over *furniture* yields *a piece of furniture*).

Pustejovsky's work on Event Structure (1988, 1991) and Grimshaw's work on nominals (1988, 1991) can help define conceptual object types which convey particular perspectives on events. Pustejovsky's three-way distinction between event types (state, process, and transition) applies to both primitive types for lexical items and composition types for complex phrases. Grimshaw's distinction between two types of nominalizations—process nominals and result nominals—predicts some grammatical features and constrains composition.

1.3.2 *Using the Text Structure for text planning*

In designing a text planner we need to be concerned not only with the objects that are reflected in the constituency of the utterance being planned and the function of those objects in the structure of the message but also with the actual process of composing the message. The abstract linguistic terms of our message vocabulary can provide constraints on the composition of the message to ensure that it will continue to be expressible as we add more information.

The semantic category of a constituent can constrain the kind of information that can be composed into that constituent. Consider the following examples:

(1) a. Michael decided to go to college. It was the most important decision of his life.
b. Michael made an important decision: he decided to go to college.
c. * Michael importantly decided to go to college.

(2) a. Dan decided to join the National Guard. It was the quickest decision of his life.
b. Dan made a quick decision: he decided to join the National Guard.
c. Dan quickly decided to join the National Guard.

The sets of sentences above, (1) and (2), differ in whether the RESULT of the event is modified, as in set (1), or the EVENT itself is modified, as in set (2). In the (a) and (b) sentences of both sets, the event and the result are both expressed, but in different kernel clauses, so the modification is easily composed in both. However, when we attempt to compose the modification into a single clause where only the event is available (the (c) examples), it is only allowable in (2c) where the manner of the event is modified, and not in (1c) where the result is modified. The two structures shown in Figure 1.6 below capture this difference in the types of the objects.

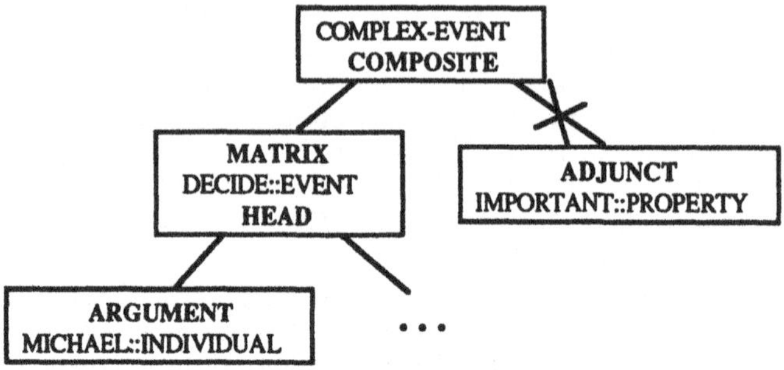

"Michael decided ..."

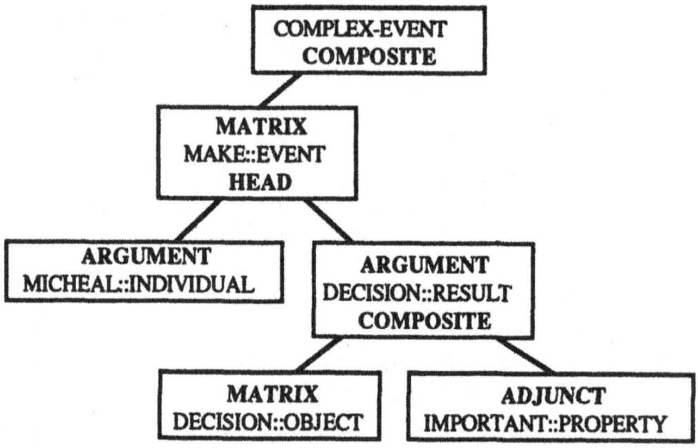

"Michael made an important decision"

Figure 1.6 Text Structures for "decided" vs. "made a decision"

In summary, the Text Structure can constrain the following types of decisions within the text planner:

- where additional information may be added (e.g. structure can only be added at leaves and nodes of type COMPOSITE; furthermore, in an incremental pipeline architecture such as this, information can only be added ahead of the point of speech)
- what functions and positions are available for the elements being added in (e.g. matrix or adjunct)
- what form the added element must be in (e.g. an object of type *property* can be added to a *thing* but not to an *event*)[7]

[7] The constraints on particular types here are merely examples and not meant to be claims about properties of such types in general.

- what parameters are set and which need to be set (e.g. an object of type *kind* may be marked inherently indefinite/plural, "dogs"; an object of type *event* needs temporal information).

In Chapter Four, I describe the Text Structure and the methodology of its design in detail and in Chapter Five I show how Spokesman's text planner uses the Text Structure to compose the utterance. First, however, I look at some basic terminology and issues in Chapter Two and the motivations of Text Structure from data analysis and from a generation viewpoint in Chapter Three.

2 Terminology and Issues

A problem in comparing NL architectures is that researchers use the same words to mean different things: "text planning", "revision", "lexical selection", "text structure" are all commonly used to mean different things. Even the term "generator" is sometimes used to mean only the linguistic realization component, as in "the text planner and the generator" (although this usage is rare among those in the field; an exception is Patten, 1988). The goal of this chapter is to provide definitions of these terms and show where other researchers stand with respect to those definitions. I define a set of conventional activities of natural language generation (content delimitation, organization of units, lexical selection, choice of syntactic structures, morphology and read out, and focus) and I describe the two components that traditionally make up generation systems (text planning and linguistic realization). (In Chapter Seven, I describe some particular systems illustrating how various researchers distribute the activities among the processes.)

I also address directly what I see to be some of the more contentious points among generation researchers:

- Whose responsibility is content delimitation? Is it part of text planning?
- Where does lexical selection belong: in the text planner? linguistic component? both?
- What is revision? optimization?
- What is text structure?

Another goal of this chapter is to indicate what problems I won't be addressing in this work and point to others who do address them.

2.1 The generation process

Before looking at particular issues, it is useful to define the activities that are commonly considered to make up the generation process and the two major components that comprise nearly every generation system: text planning and linguistic realization. I first briefly describe these activities and components and then return to particular issues that are relevant to this work. Since my goal is to map the territory of generation architectures, I only name researchers and systems in this section and leave complete system descriptions to Chapter Seven.

2.1.1 *The activities of generation*

Delimiting Content: Choosing what information the utterance should express. In McDonald, Meteer & Pustejovsky (1987), we more generally call this activity "identifying the relevant portion of the situation", where the situation includes the speaker's intentions, model of the user, attitudes toward the hearer and topic, as well as propositional information. In §2.2.1, I address the question of which should have responsibility for content delimitation, the application program or the generator.

Organizing Units: Determining a coherent organization of the units delimited by the above activity. This is perhaps the major activity of text planning; it is certainly the most well studied. In §2.2.4, I look at the different definitions of "text structure", which many view as the output of the organizational process. In Chapter Seven, I look at some of the better-known approaches to organizing units: McKeown's schemas and Rhetorical Structure Theory.

Lexical Selection: Choosing the content words. This aspect of generation is perhaps the least well studied. Variations in approaches stem from the perspectives of the researchers: Nirenburg & Nirenburg (1988), from a machine translation background, views lexical selection as feature matching. McDonald (1984, 1991), originator of "description directed control", has a Whorfian view where the words are intimately connected with conceptualizations in the underlying program; it is the underlying concepts that direct the selection of lexical items. Goldman (1975), working from an Conceptual Dependency representation, employed a discrimination network because the underlying representation was far too abstract to delimit word choice; for example, from a primitive such as P-TRANS his system could choose "eat" or "drink" depending on whether the object of the TRANS was food or liquid. I look more closely at the question of what component should be responsible for lexical choice in §2.2.2.

Choosing Syntactic Structures: Choosing the syntactic structures in effect linearizes the syntactic constituents of the text. There are a wide range of different approaches to syntax in generation, due in part to the variety of linguistic approaches that have spawned them.[8] The two best known systems for making syntactic choices are NIGEL, in the systemic tradition (Mann & Matthiessen 1985), and MUMBLE (McDonald 1980) and MUMBLE-86 (Meteer *et al.* 1987).

Morphology and Read Out: Producing the actual text from a syntactic representation with lexical items inserted. The main function of this process is to produce the correct morphological forms for the words. In systems that have an explicit representation of the surface structure,

[8] Unfortunately, as commented in Meteer (1989a) many of these approaches are only concerned with grammatical competence and not when a particular choice should be made–they are literally "generative" grammars, in the sense used by linguists, (e.g. Block 1988, Horacek 1988, Bunt 1988).

whether it be in terms of features or phrases, the reading out of morphologically correct words is deterministic and rarely gets any attention. In contrast, systems that attempt to produce a stream of words without the benefit of linguistic context (e.g. Cullingford 1986) must go to great efforts to accomplish relatively straightforward morphological operations, such as subject-verb agreement and avoiding putting a possessive marker on a possessive pronoun (e.g. "her's").

Focus: Determining which entities are most salient at a given moment in the discourse and the effects of that salience on the choices made in the generator.[9] Focus is rarely thought of as a separate activity in generation, as in general it intrudes on the other activities rather than standing alone. McKeown (1985) and Derr & McKeown (1984) use Sidner's (1983) model of focus for choosing the information and organizing units. Moore & Paris (1989) use Grosz & Sidner's (1986) notion of attentional state for choosing information and organizing it in explanations. Dale (1989) incorporates focus in lexical choice, particularly in subsequent reference strategies. The effects of salience on generation in general is explored by Conklin (1983).

Other researchers may cut up the pie of generation activities differently (for example, Nirenburg *et al.* 1989 separates choice of syntactic structures from constituent ordering); however, these categories provide a useful base. I argue later, though, that while they help us talk about what a generator does, they are not in and of themselves an effective way to modularize the processing.

2.1.2 *The modularization of the generation process*

Probably the most commented on aspect of text generation is its division into two parts:

- text planning / strategic / "What to say"
- linguistic realization / tactical / "How to say it".

The original terms, strategic and tactical, were coined by Thompson (1977) and brought into common usage by McKeown (1982), who used the distinction to help circumscribe her thesis work, which was on "what to say" rather than "how to say it". Since then, "text planning" and "linguistic realization" have become more common terms for the two components, and I use them here as they are more precise.

There are many arguments on whether there should be such a division and if so, what activities should be on one side or another. The recent AAAI-88 Workshop on Text Planning and Realization (Hovy *et al.* 1988) is an indication

[9] The term "focus" is perhaps an unfortunate choice for this phenomenon, though it is the common usage in generation research, since it is used in other circles to mean very different things. For example, in the modern Prague school of linguistics (e.g. Hajicova 1983), "focus" is used to mean the new portion of the sentence (similar to what previous Prague school linguists called "theme"). Their notion of "topic" (the given portion of the sentence, previously "rheme") has more in common with what is called "focus" here, though there are differences.

of the current attention focused on this problem. Despite the comment in the introduction to the proceedings that "the historically common decomposition of language generation systems into two stages—planning and realization—was widely deemed more convenient that accurate",[10] most of the researchers present upheld the distinction. Paris argues for the distinction on practical grounds:

> *Because the textual [text planning] and the tactical components of a [generator] are concerned with different linguistic abstractions, they can be seen as implementing different strata of linguistic theories. As such, they should be kept separated. The textual component needs to do work to identify what needs to be expressed in semantic and textual (discourse) terms; the realizer makes decisions based on grammatical notions. ... There are no reasons for the textual component to have to know all the tactical component knows and vice versa.*[11]

Paris advocates controlled interaction between the two components, while allowing them to influence each other's decisions, but only at predefined "windows", thus limiting the amount they need to know about each other's processing vocabulary.

McDonald argues for modularization on more theoretical grounds. He maintains that using a general, powerful architecture "would constitute a null theory of processing architecture for generation"; rather one should use the architecture to make strong theoretical statements:

> *Assuming, as I do, that one's goal is a computational theory of generation that can in principle be applied to people (work in "theoretical psycholinguistics" as it were), then it is always better to hypothesize a division into distinct stages and processing modules.... Proving a strong hypothesis wrong always leads to greater insights for the next attempt; choosing the null hypothesis from the start gains nothing.*[12]

He posits four criteria for partitioning the generation process: what is decided, what reference knowledge is used, how the results of the decisions are represented, and the representations of the information being manipulated.

While most generation systems modularize the processing into text planning and realization, some researchers have argued against this distinction, notably Dik, Appelt, and Danlos. However, even their systems still make a change at some point in the processing from an essentially semantic representation to an essentially linguistic one (though the second "component" may be merely a deterministic transducer).

Note that this division, and in particular the change in vocabulary, creates the problem of expressibility, since the essentially semantic vocabulary typically employed in the text planning component has no knowledge of the constraints

10 Hovy, McDonald, & Young, 1988, p.9.

11 Paris, 1988a, p. 58.

12 McDonald, 1988, p.96.

on how the linguistics resources can compose. We return to this point in Chapter Seven.

While there is general agreement on the activities and components described above, there is less agreement on which activities go into which components. Most agree that organizing units is part of text planning, and syntax and morphology belong in linguistic realization; however, as shown in Figure 2.1, delimiting content and lexical selection are not so regularly distributed across actual systems.

System[13]	Delimiting Content	Organizing Information	Lexical Selection	Syntax	Morphology
TEXT	TP	TP	LRC	LRC	LRC
PENMAN	?	TP	LRC	LRC	LRC
DIOGENES	?	TP	TP	TP	LRC
PAULINE	TP	TP	LRC	LRC	LRC
SPOKESMAN (with MUMBLE-86)	AP	TP	TP	LRC	LRC

TP: text planning
LRC: linguistic realization component
AP: application program

Figure 2.1 Generation system comparison

McKeown's TEXT and Hovy's PAULINE both give the responsibilities of content delimitation and organizing information to the text planner and leave lexical selection, syntax, and morphology to the realization component. Neither Mann *et.al.*'s PENMAN nor Nirenburg's DIOGENES indicate who is responsible for content delimitation, only that the input to the text planner is the delimited content. In other respects PENMAN follows TEXT and PAULINE. Nirenburg adds lexical selection and syntax to the responsibilities of the text planner, in effect giving that component all of the decision making. Spokesman (which uses MUMBLE as its linguistic component) explicitly leaves content delimitation to the application program, putting lexical selection and organization of information in the text planner; MUMBLE handles syntactic selection and morphology.

While Figure 2.1 is a simplification of how these systems organize their decision making, it is informative to see where in general they draw lines between components. In Chapter Seven, we look at these systems in more

[13] TEXT: McKeown 1982; PENMAN: Mann 1983, Hovy 1988; DIOGENES, Nirenburg *et al.* 1989; PAULINE: Hovy 1987; SPOKESMAN & MUMBLE-86, Meteer 1989b, Meteer *et al.* 1987.

detail. But first, I address some of the general issues involved in choosing where to place these activities.

2.2 Issues

This section is organized around particular questions concerning content delimitation, lexical selection, text structure, and revision. I have two goals: to indicate how these terms are used by other researchers and to show what view I take on them.

2.2.1 *Content delimitation: Whose responsibility is it? Is it a part of text planning?*

Generation systems can roughly be divided into two groups on the question of content delimitation: (1) those for which the content is a side effect of the application program (Davey, McDonald, Meteer) and (2) those who take on the responsibility of extracting the content from the application program (McKeown, Paris, McCoy, Bienkowski). The first group, in general, uses more active programs than the second, such as simulations or expert systems as compared with data bases (e.g. Davey's system played Tic-Tac-Toe as well as describing it). Generators used for machine translation and paraphrasing fall into this first group, since there is no independent application: the content is determined by the input text. The second group takes on the work of content delimitation for one of two reasons: (1) the application is static, that is it is not taking actions or retaining representations of actions that it could pass to the generator (such as a data base), or (2) the researchers are interested in studying the effects of things that are beyond the competence of today's application programs, such as user modeling,[14] discourse information (i.e. topic and focus), or pragmatic and rhetorical goals (i.e. convincing). Middle of the road systems either do both (use information from the program as a base, and then seek supplemental information (Hovy at Yale)), or they do neither (i.e. they assume some content has already been delimited without committing to what component actually did it (Hovy at ISI)).

We argue in McDonald, Meteer & Pustejovsky that the most efficient way is for the content of the utterance to be delimited as a side effect of the application; however, this is not always practical. The extreme problematic case is extracting information from a completely static program, such as a data base, which cannot delimit content (McKeown). Even programs that do provide input to the generator, such as the simulation and tactical planning systems used with SPOKESMAN (Meteer), often do not provide information in the most useful terms; for example, calculations may need to be done to describe a vector of points as "to the east" and information may have to be reorganized to produce reduced forms ("A/1 TB and A/3 TB are to the east. A/2 TB is to the north.").

[14] Tutoring and advice-giving application systems are often an exception to this as they usually focus on representing information about the student being tutored (see for example, Woolf 1984).

Mellish (1988) addresses this problem directly by including a "message optimization" phase which applies algebraic simplification rules to the applications program's plans it is trying to express, making them more palatable for a generator.

There are other reasons as well why it may be impractical to let the application do all of the work of content delimitation. Much of the work on explanation has emphasized the importance of having a model of the user in order to know what information they need and at what level of detail it should be expressed (Paris 1987, McCoy 1988, Suthers 1988). Moore & Paris's (1989) work on interactive explanations shows that a content delimitation module must also have access to a representation of the shared information in the discourse as well as a model of the user in order to provide adequate explanations interactively. In order to do effective research on user models and shared discourse information in the context of generation, it is clear that these researchers must build systems that take on the responsibility of content delimitation, since application programs in general do not have a rich enough model of the situation (including the hearer and discourse) to provide an adequate research base.

This raises a second, yet related, question: is content delimitation a part of text planning or should it be a separate component? A few systems separate content delimitation from text planning: Nirenburg *et al*. (1989) do not yet address content delimitation outside of machine translation (where the content is given); Cargano & Iordanskaja (1989) posit a separate module to do topic collection which produces the input to the text planner. However, most of those cited above as taking on content delimitation within generation consider it a part of text planning. The main problem with this classification is that it makes text planning too broad a notion. Given the enormous amount of work to be done before we can begin to understand and model the complexities of natural language generation, a finer distinction between the activities is more instructive.

What I will take to be "text planning" for the purpose of this work, is *composing* the utterance, that is planning what resources will be used to realize the communicative goals of the speaker. I will assume the content has been delimited, either by the application program, or by some independent component. I leave the interaction between these components as a topic for future research.

2.2.2 *Lexical selection: text planning, linguistic realization, or both (or neither?)*

The place of lexical choice in the generation process is one of the least agreed upon points among generation researchers. Some argue that lexical choice must be early (first in fact: McDonald 1991) or simultaneously with all the other decisions (Danlos 1987). Others, in particular feature-based systems such as systemic grammars, put lexical selection last as a "reading out" of the features. Still others, such as blackboard architectures (e.g. Nirenburg), let it mingle freely with other decisions, allowing the system to backtrack if the resulting set of decisions is incompatible.

In many respects, lexical selection is the most constraining of a generator's choices. The open class words carry the bulk of the content in language, and particular lexical items have restrictions on which of their arguments are obligatory or optional. Furthermore, there are unpredictable gaps in a language's lexical repertoire, where a derivable form of the word is taken for some specific usage, e.g. a "defensive" military unit "defends", but an "offensive" unit doesn't necessarily "offend"; similarly, a "runner" is someone who "runs", but a "skipper" isn't someone who "skips". The availability (or lack) of a lexical resource will have a significant impact on the possibilities for expression.

While this implies that lexical selection should be an early generation choice, there is the contradictory evidence that one can utter parts of a phrase without having completely selected all the lexical items (the tip-of-the-tongue phenomena—sort of), which implies lexical selection should be later than the delimitation of the content.

I argue that the problem is caused by trying to make lexical selection a single activity, rather than acknowledging that there may be multiple places where a lexicon is accessed by a generator, each place extracting different kinds of information and sometimes choosing a set of possibilities or simply appreciating constraints, rather than necessarily returning a single lexical item. There is support for this kind of approach from the psycholinguistic community: word- and sound-exchange errors suggest semantic information is accessed separately from phonemic information (Garrett 1975). Bock (1987) suggests that the multiple access of a lexicon can account for many kinds of errors while still allowing a strong levels hypothesis.

2.2.3 *What is revision and where does it go on?*

The term "revision" has been used in general to mean when a generator changes its decisions. It has been used both to mean changes within the initial generation process (Mann & Moore 1981; Gabriel 1988; Wong & Simmons 1988) and operations over finished text (Mann 1983, Meteer 1985). This second meaning is what I consider more accurately to be "revision". Yazdani (1987) uses the term to mean both changes during initial generation and changes over final text, even though he purports to follow Hayes & Flower's (1980) model of the writing process who do make a distinction between these processes: Yazdani defines reviewing as "an independent process from planning and generation, applied during and after other stages of the writing process". Hayes and Flower distinguish between "reviewing", an operation over finished text, and "editing" changes during initial generation.

It is clear that there are great differences computationally between a process that operates over intermediate levels of representation and one that only has the finished text to evaluate. In order to make that distinction clear when describing systems that use these techniques, I will call operations over intermediate levels *optimizations* and those over final text *revisions*. Optimizations are done over internal representations in the generator during initial generation. Revisions are done over text after initial generation is completed.

2.2.4 *What is "text structure"?*

Most of those who use the term "text structure" restrict it to refer to organization above the level of the clause. This view has its roots in the early definition of "text" as units larger than a sentence (e.g. Pike 1967) where a "sentence" was considered the largest unit with inherent structure. "Text" has since come to have a more operational definition as part of a large field of text linguistics (a mainly European tradition) where it can be applied to suitable units of any size, small or large, as for instance in the following definition:

> *Text is a communicative occurrence which meets the seven standards of textuality: cohesion, coherence, intentionality, acceptability, informality, situationality, and intertextuality.*[15]

However, in text planning the notion of text structure as the organization of large units (clause and sentence sized) has remained. Typical is Nirenburg's definition:[16]

> *Text structuring. The System must determine the order of propositions and the boundaries of sentences in the target language text.*

I take "text structure" to include constituents both above and below the level of the sentence. Not only are important generalities made available in this approach, as I show in Chapter Four, but this approach is necessary to provide the full expressive power of language, since the relations exhibited in actual texts are not only between clauses but often between smaller constituents within and among clauses.

The inability to capture such relations causes problems for approaches that define text structure as stopping at the clause level. This can be illustrated with Rhetorical Structure Theory (RST) which has been used at the Information Sciences Institute, where it was developed, both for the descriptive analysis of relations in text (Mann & Thompson 1987) and operationally in text planning (Hovy 1988). RST relations only hold between units of text that are clause-sized or larger. In what follows, I first give an overview of RST and then look at two examples: the first is an example of an RST analysis of an advertising text, and the second, a text generated by ISI's generation system, PENMAN. (I discuss PENMAN in more detail in §7.1.4.) I show that while RST effectively captures relations between clauses, it is not capable of capturing the same relations within clauses.

RST is perhaps the most well-defined theory of text structure in computational circles. RST is a strong descriptive formalism that has been used in analyses of an exceptionally wide range of actually occurring texts. It attempts to capture the organization of natural text through the relations that hold between parts of the text. It falls within a larger family of approaches that posit coherence relations between portions of a text, such as Grimes (1975) and

[15] Beaugrande & Dressler, 1981, p.3.

[16] Nirenburg, Nyberg, & Defrise, 1989, p. 3.

Hobbs (1982). The relations in RST are embodied in schemas which define the "structural constituency arrangements of a text". RST posits approximately thirty schemas, each of which represents an abstract (unordered) pattern of text spans and the relations which hold between them, for example solutionhood, elaboration, background, summary. The complete analysis of a text is a tree, with a single schema at the top level and clause-sized minimal units as the leaves.

The first example is a text that was excerpted from an advertisement for Maxell floppy diskettes; it was one of the texts analysed by Mann & Thompson (1987).

> *(1) Features like our uniquely sealed jacket and protective hub ring make our discs last longer. (2) And a soft inner liner cleans the ultra-smooth disc surface while in use. (3) It all adds up to better performance and reliability.*[17]

The RST analysis is shown in Figure 2.2. While this structure effectively captures the large scale rhetorical relations in the text, it says nothing about how its smaller units are organized since the leaves of the RST tree only span entire sentences. However, if we look at the information expressed in each of these leaves, we see that the same kinds of relations that exist between clauses also exist between elements within clauses.

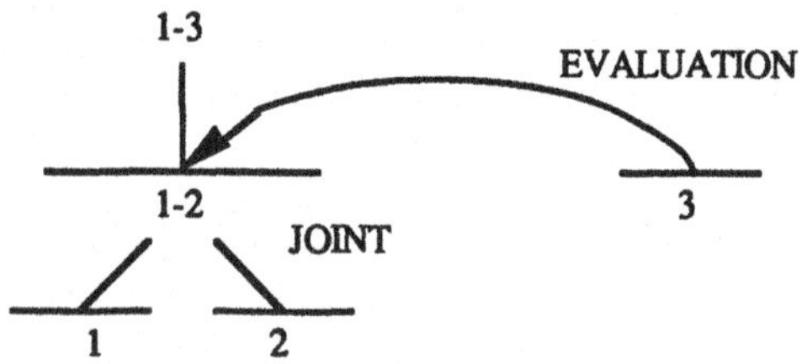

Figure 2.2 RST schema for advertising example

In RST terms, the third, summary sentence of the advertisement (*"It all adds up to..."*) is an "evaluation" of the first two: it gives an assessment of the value of the disc features described, that they make for better disc performance and reliability. This very same evaluation relation also appears within the first sentence, where it is realized by the grammatical subject–predicate relationship (*"Features ... make our discs last longer"*) rather than the paragraph–summary sentence form of the RST schema. In other circumstances, this evaluative information could also be realized as a complex sentence with a subordinate clause (e.g. *"Our discs have features like ..., so they last longer."*)

The same kind of relation can have at least three possible realizations, at least one of them below the level that RST can operate at, depending on the particular details of the information being related. In each case, the choice

[17] The numbers in parenthesis indicate minimal RST units (see Figure One) and were not in the original advertisement.

between these alternative realizations is governed by the overall goals of the text (e.g. the need for a summary sentence) and the possible realizations of the parts. Realization as a subject–predicate in the first sentence is possible because the evaluation is over only two of the features, allowing them to fit comfortably into a subject noun phrase.[18] Realization as a paragraph summary sentence is possible because the third evaluation sentence can use a pronoun to refer to all the features described in the first two sentences,[19] and by the availability of the summary phrase *"adds up to"*.

The fact that RST chooses kernel clauses as minimal units forces it to make an arbitrarily large distinction between two kinds of expressions of the same relation: one between clause and one within a single clause.

My second example of the problems that stem from using clauses as the minimal units of text structure is from a text generated by the PENMAN generation system, where RST is used operationally (Hovy 1988) in the text planner (see discussion in §7.1.4.). In this example the problem stems from treating kernel clauses as impenetrable units:

> *Knox, which is C4, is en route to Sasebo. It is at 79W 18E heading SSW. It will arrive 4/24, and will load for four days.*

In this case the kernel clause "Knox is C4" is information about the ship "Knox" as it appears as an argument in the kernel "Knox is *en route* to Sasebo". ("C4" is a readiness rating of a ship used by the Navy.) However, RST cannot represent that fact, since the arguments of a kernel clause are unavailable in the RST structure.

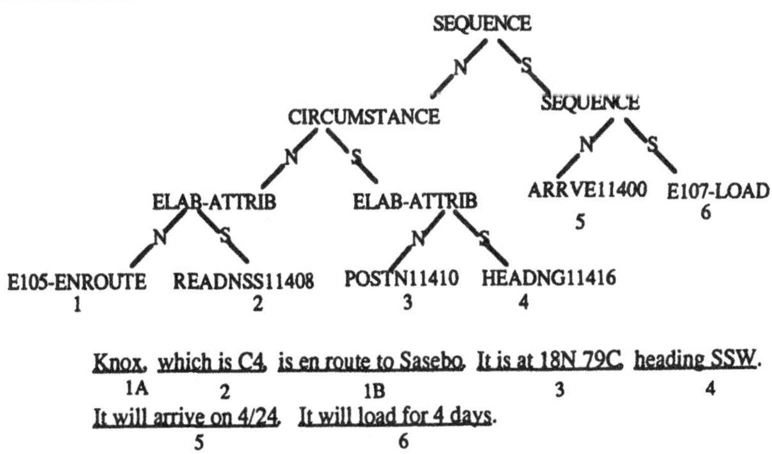

Figure 2.3 RST schema from PENMAN

18 Note, however, that the existence of more features is implied by the choice to realize the head as a sample (*"Features like x and y"*) rather than as a definite set (*"The features x and y"*).

19 Webber (1988) describes this phenomenon as an anaphoric reference to a discourse segment.

The RST representation given to this sentence[20] (shown in Figure 2.2) makes the "C4" clause an attribute of the "*en route*" clause. However, this can only be an expediency, since "C4" is an attribute of the Knox, and not of the event the Knox is participating in. Similarly, the RST analysis makes the proposition of the Knox's heading an attribute of the proposition expressing its location. Again, the correct analysis, that both location and heading are attributes of the ship, cannot be expressed in the RST notation.

The need for the ability to combine information at a finer granularity than simply combining clauses has been recognized, as exemplified by the following passage from Hovy (1991):

> *A leaf of the paragraph tree need not even always be realized as a clause, but can sometimes give rise to a grammatically simpler constituent such as an adjective. ... To handle this issue, we have had to arbitrarily stop RST structure planning at the clause level and use a number of default rules to control realization as dependent or independent clauses (for example elaboration-attribute satellites become dependent clauses instead of separate sentences, as in [Figure 4 above]).*[21]

As I discuss in detail in Chapter Four, I take a much broader view of text structure. Text Structure in my sense does not stop at the level of the clause but rather makes available all the constituents of the text, from the paragraph structure down to the minimal constituents of language, the words.

2.2.5 *Composition of linguistic resources*

When planning at a finer granularity than the clause level then the text planner must take into account the problem of the composition of the resources of language. In Chapter One, I briefly discussed the approach I take to this problem; here I discuss another approach, the Meaning Text Model (MTM). MTM, which is based on Melchuk's Meaning Text Theory (MTT) (Melchuk 1988), is a lexicon-based approach which puts the kinds of constraints Text Structure places on semantic categories on individual words in the lexicon. Generation systems based on MTM (e.g. GOSSiP, (Iordanskaja *et al.* 1991) and Joyce (Kittredge *et al.* 1991)) use an intermediate level of representation called deep syntactic representation (DsyntR) which is a network of words and the relations between them (e.g. argument, attribute). In building this representation from the underlying semantic representation for the utterance, MTM takes into account constraints on the combinations of words; for example since there is no word in English "importantly", MTM will not build a network for "Peter decided importantly", rather it will backtrack and build a "paraphrase" of it, such as "Peter made an important decision".

One important difference between MTM and the one described here is that in MTM the constraints are at the level of words. While this is effective in handling gaps in the language (e.g. "the troops are *offending*" is not the

20 Hovy, 1991, p. 92.
21 Hovy 1991, p.96.

opposite of "the troops are *defending*"), it fails to capture such generalizations as: surface events (expressed as clauses) cannot be attributed with properties and objects cannot be attributed with duration.

MTM, like RST, is a theory about language, and as such, is independent of the systems that make use of it. MTM is particularly adaptable to generation applications because one of its central concerns is to represent information about how words combine. However, the two systems that I am aware of that use an MTM-based approach have two other kinds of problems: (1) the linguistic constraints of are not part of the text planning process, so they cannot be used to constrain the selection of information, and (2) they use backtracking, which does not allow incremental generation and is inefficient.

The GOSSiP system (Iordanskaja *et al.* 1991) makes the assumption that some other process has built a sentence-sized semantic network from which it will realize a sentence. This approach has the same problems as all of those that make a strict division between text planning and linguistic realization: how does the planning process ensure that the semantic net it builds will be expressible as a sentence in natural language? GOSSiP assumes there is some realization of the network and keeps trying different paraphrases of the network until it finds one that works.

The Joyce system (Kittredge *et al.* 1991) seems to relax the constraint of making text planning produce a network for each sentence. Joyce's text planner produces a list of propositions, from which the "sentence planning" component build the deep syntactic representation. However, this still separates selection from composition. Joyce's use of domain specific schemas ("domain communication knowledge") to control selection may make expressibility less of a problem since what pieces can be composed are known in advance; however, the effect of this is to limit the competence of the system.

3 Motivations from Language and Applications

The major argument of this work is that in order for a text planner to be able to compose a message that is expressible in language, the text planner must be aware of what linguistic resources are available to it and make its decisions accordingly. This is accomplished in the architecture presented here by providing the text planner with a representation language in which to plan the utterance that embodies these resources and the constraints on their composition. In developing that representation language, we must first answer two kinds of questions: (1) what are the resources of language and what are their abstract properties? And (2) which of those properties are essential to a text planner trying to compose an utterance from an application program? I do not attempt to answer these questions in this chapter (I leave that to Chapters 4 and 5) but rather present the work that motivated the solution which included both analysis of actual texts and experiences building a text planner that works from real application programs.

This bi-directional approach to natural language generation, working both from real language data and from existing application programs, is essential at this stage in generation research. On the one hand, today's application programs are not sophisticated enough to motivate the wide variety of complex constructions that are used by people, especially in technical written prose. On the other hand, simply working with language data does not provide concrete situations to work from, so questions about the relationship between the language and the information cannot be addressed.

The first part of this chapter presents the data analysis of revised texts: manuscripts written by competent writers and edited by professional editors. I found that analysis of revised text was a particularly good way of exploring variation in language: different ways of saying the same thing. First, it is a naturally occurring phenomena, so real data is available. This avoid the pitfalls inherent in making up examples and thus in a sense engineering both the problem and the solution (cf. Danlos). Second, revised texts provide multiple versions of a portion of the text (the original and the revised) in a context where both the original goals of the writer and the surrounding text remains the same. I look in particular at what level of generality is the most powerful in describing the changes and show how the Text Structure representation captures this level of generality. In what follows, I also look at the generation process itself and at how the architecture presented here, including the Text Structure representation, provides an account of why revision is necessary to produce written quality text.

In the second part of this chapter, I focus on the constraints imposed from the other side of the generation process: the input. Using one of the early applications of the SPOKESMAN system, a military tactical planning program, I look at what level of abstraction allows the text planner to compose the utterance without having also to contend with the complexities of syntactic detail.

In both of these very different approaches to the problem, linguistic analysis and text planning, three characteristics stand out as important in the abstract representation of linguistic resources: constituent structure, functional relations between constituents (e.g. matrix and adjunct elements) and the semantic type that the constituent expresses (e.g. event or entity). The goal of this chapter is both to motivate these terms and define them practically.

3.1. Analysis of revisions

Analysis of naturally occurring data is important in understanding a process one is trying to model. In the work presented here, I use the analysis of revised text to aid in developing an architecture for Natural Language Generation. Careful analysis of revisions can not only provide a descriptive account of well-written text but can also provide a framework in which to develop an explanatory account of the generation and revision processes themselves. Analysis can help determine what decisions were made originally and how those decisions were changed to improve the text. Work in generation to date has focused primarily on simply producing grammatical sentences with the appropriate content. This work allows us to look closer at a much subtler kind of decision making: that which improves the style and readability of the text. I have limited the data to texts written by competent writers and edited by professional editors in order to filter, on the one hand, errors, and on the other, changes to content.

The analysis presented here contributes to our understanding of natural language generation in three ways:

The first phase of the analysis, described in §3.1.1, was simply to itemize the changes and look at how they functioned to improve the text. The goal of the next phase was to look for "classes" of revisions which have the same general description for both the original and revised versions. Identifying classes allows you to develop criteria for representational levels and decisions within the generator so that both the original and revised texts may be generated (i.e. are within the competence of the generator) and to develop strategies for recognizing and revising new instances of the class when they are found in subsequent texts. In §3.1.2, I address issues in generalizing over instances from the data, and in §3.1.3, I sketch a level of representation which attempts to capture those generalizations. The final phase, described in §3.1.4, is to look at the implications of the analysis for the architecture of a generation system.

3.1.1 *Description of the data*

The first phase of the work was to simply collect samples of revised texts and look at the kinds of changes that were made. In the data I have analysed so far, there were approximately 500 instances of revisions. Nearly all the text samples were technical papers revised by a professional editor who was not the author. Since the original authors were all competent writers, there were few actual "errors" (such as grammatical or spelling mistakes) and since a goal of the editors was to improve the style without altering the original meaning of the text, there was minimal change to the content.[22] Therefore, this sample allowed me to focus on changes made to improve the style of the text. More than half the instances were from one particular document.[23]

3.1.1.1 *The kinds of revisions that were made* In this section, I present a survey of the most common kinds of revisions I found. I have grouped them for descriptive purposes; the categories are not meant to be exclusive nor is the order reflective of the frequency of each kind.[24] There were sixteen kinds of revisions in the data I examined. Each is listed below in a section set off by the name of the revision in bold followed by a description of what happens in that kind of revision and some illustrative examples taken from my data set.

Ellipsis: This category contains deletions of an identical word (or pro-form of the word) in a corresponding syntactic position in a conjoined phrase. In the following example, the subjects of conjoined clauses are elided in the revised version.

1. A: Definitions are made more systematic and explicit, they introduce a new functional element, and incidentally they also reflect more expertise in text analysis.

   B: Definitions are made more systematic and explicit, introduce a new functional element, and incidentally reflect more expertise in text analysis.

Deletion of function words: These revisions involved the deletion of closed class words (e.g. prepositions, determiners) with little or no other alteration to the structure. Most common were those of the form shown in 2 below; others, such as 3, involved some rearrangement of the phrase.

2. A: Each of the fields specifies...

   B: Each field specifies...

3. A: The size of the units is arbitrary,...

   B: The unit size is arbitrary,...

[22] I am not claiming that the original and revised text have the exact same meaning–one can argue that any change to the text affects the meaning, however subtly–only that the change is minimal in this type of editing.

[23] This document was a draft of Bill Mann and Sandra Thompson's paper "Rhetorical Structure Theory: A Theory of Text Organization". The draft was edited by a professional editor, Tom Strini, and then rechecked by both Mann and Thompson, who rejected any changes that altered the intended meaning of the text.

[24] The overlap of instances and variation in the data made it impossible to partition the instances of changes into categories; therefore I did not do any quantitative analyses, such as frequency counts.

Deletion of connective words: While these might be grouped with deletion of function words (above), I felt there were sufficient numbers of them to warrant a separate category. In most cases, the connective was replaced with a semicolon; in others there was a change to two separate sentences. As shown in 4 and 5, the connective which was deleted usually conveyed a stronger relation than was actually present, and the parallel structure of the two connected clauses sufficed to bind them.

4. A: The term writer refers to the writer of the text being described; similarly *reader* refers to the intended readers(s) of the text...

   B: The term writer refers to the writer of the text being described; *reader* refers to the intended readers(s) of the text...

5. A: The Enablement provides information designed to increase the reader's ability to perform the action, while Motivation provides information designed to increase the reader's desire to perform the action.

   B: The Enablement provides information designed to increase the reader's ability to perform the action; Motivation provides information designed to increase the reader's desire to perform the action.

Pronominalization: While there were few cases of a full noun phrase changed to a pronoun (e.g. "the text" --> "it"), there were several of the form shown below in which a head noun was deleted and the quantifier stood as an indefinite pronoun.

6. A: The relations Enablement and Motivation form a subgroup since they both involve evoking a reader action...

   B: The relations Enablement and Motivation form a subgroup since both evoke a reader action...

Change in part of speech: In this type, a change in the part of speech of a lexical item both changes what element is the head of the phrase and also allows some functions words to be deleted. The changes cross many different parts of speech; while the most common change was from noun to verb (as in 7 and 8), there were also changes from adjective to adverb (as in 9), from verb to noun (as in 10), and from adjective to verb (as in 11).

7. A: Hoey thus makes a distinction between ....

   B: Hoey thus distinguishes between ....

8. A: People are frequently in strong agreement ....

   B: People often strongly agree ....

9. A: This section defines the terminology of RST in a way that is independent of the particular languages and text types to which it has been applied.

   B: This section defines the terminology of RST independently of the particular languages and text types to which it has been applied.

10. A: None of these people necessarily agrees with the way we have interpreted their advice.
    B: None of these people necessarily agrees with our interpretation of their advice.

11. A: The goals are different from ....
    B: The goals differ from ....

Elimination of semantic redundancy: This was one of the most common types of change (it is also one dwelled on in most writing textbooks). In many of these examples, some lexical item semantically entails the information expressed in another part of the phrase, thus licensing its deletion. In example 12, "developing" is a process, so to say explicitly "the process of" is redundant; in example 13, the definition of "audience" is "who the writer is writing for", so it also does not need to be explicitly stated; and in example 14, it is clear that the number refers to the total.

12. A: We have been in the process of developing RST...
    B: We have been developing RST...

13. A: *reader* refers to the intended readers(s) of the text, the audience for whom the writer is writing.
    B: *reader* refers to the intended readers(s) of the text, the audience.

14. A: The connected BARRNet campuses currently have about 5,000 active IP hosts in total.
    B: The connected BARRNet campuses currently have about 5,000 active IP hosts.

Elimination of contextual redundancy: Redundancies also occur when information which is available in the context is made unnecessarily explicit in the text, as in the example 15, where it is clear that the announcement is being used as an example, and in example 16, where it is clear that the sentence refers to the text in the example shown above.

15. A: **Elaboration** is nicely illustrated by this example, an announcement in the newsletter *Language Sciences*.
    B: This announcement from the newsletter *Language Sciences* nicely illustrates **Elaboration**.

16. A: So, for example, we note that it is the conference, rather than Sweden, that is the element elaborated in the text above.
    B: So, for example, we note that the conference, rather than Sweden, is the element elaborated.

Raising a subordinate clause to matrix position: Most of these changes involved the elimination of a semantically weak matrix, such as the existential "there", as in example 17, and the background information in 18. In many of these examples the weak matrix was a hedge, such as "seem" or "appear", as in 19.

17. A: There are no doubt other relations which might be reasonable constructs...
    B: Other relations might be reasonable constructs...

18. A: In our analyses, we have worked with units that are essentially clauses,...
    B: In our analyses, units are essentially clauses,...

19. A: The text appears to contain a number of non-sequiturs, ...
    B: The text contains a number of non-sequiturs, ...

Movement of an adjunct phrase: There were several examples where an adjunct which syntactically could fit in a variety of places was moved. In example 20, the phrase "for the whole text" is a distraction in its original position and is moved to the end of the sentence. In 21, a separate sentence is moved into an adjunct position in a noun phrase.

20. A: the analyst is effectively providing an account for the whole text of a plausible reason the writer might have had for including each part.
    B: the analyst effectively provides a plausible reason the writer might have had for including each part of the whole text.

21. A: A very few texts can be analyzed only if the adjacency constraint is relaxed. These are typically advertisements in which a title line plays a role in the body of the text.
    B: A very few texts, typically advertisements in which a title line plays a role in the body of the text, can be analyzed only if the adjacency constraint is relaxed.

Changes to structural relations: These changes not only involve movement of phrases, but also changes in the relations expressed (or implied) between them. In example 22, there are changes to both the order of the phrases and which is subordinate, which results in a subtle change in causality. In 23, the structural relations are changed simply by changing the connective words rather than actually moving the phrases. The first clause changes from the matrix to a subordinate clause, the second becomes the matrix, and the third, which was originally in a coordinate relation to the first, now becomes subordinate to the second. In 24, a relative clause becomes the matrix clause and the matrix becomes a relative clause.

22. A: The purpose of this paper is to make Rhetorical Structure Theory (RST) more examinable and usable by making it more explicit.
    B: The purpose of this paper is to make Rhetorical Structure Theory (RST) more explicit and thus more usable and open to examination.

23. A: It is still based on judgments, necessarily, but since it provides a checklist of affirmations it makes it easy to identify the claims underlying a particular analysis.

 B: Though still based on judgments, necessarily, it provides a checklist of affirmations and thus makes it easy to identify the claims underlying a particular analysis.

24. A: The types of relations Martin considers are similar to those we suggest...

 B: Martin considers types of relations similar to those we suggest...

Passive to active: Nearly all writing textbooks contain a section on "making your writing more active" which includes both choice of active verbs and use of the active voice. There were many instances in the data of passive voice changed to active (note there were no changes from active to passive). The four strategies employed are listed below:

INTRODUCTION OF AN AGENT. These examples were passives which had no agent expressed. It is interesting to note that the only agent ever introduced was "we". When the implied agent was the reader or the analyst, for example, instead of the writers, some other strategy was used.

25. A: Unit 1 is taken as nuclear.

 B: We take Unit 1 as nuclear.

CHANGING THE VERB. In these examples, the passive was avoided by choosing a different verb whose required arguments were already present. (Again, the agent was not expressed in the original.)

26. A: An example of the Evidence relation can be seen in this extract from a letter to the editor of BYTE magazine.

 B: This extract from a letter to the editor of BYTE magazine has an example of the Evidence relation.

METATHESIS. In these cases, the verb and the arguments remained the same, but the relations between them changed so that one of the arguments could act as an agent. Most of them seemed conventional in technical writing style ("examples illustrate", "analysis notes information") rather than metaphorical.

27. A: The structure is shown in Figure 2.

 B: Figure 2 shows the structure.

SIMPLE PASSIVE TO ACTIVE WITH THE "BY" PHRASE. This final strategy is the one we most often associate with the change from active to passive, but interestingly, it was the least used. For example, in one sample document there were only two instances of the "by" phrase in the fourteen passives changed.

28. A: **Elaboration** is nicely illustrated by this example, an announcement in the newsletter *Language Sciences*.

    B: This announcement from the newsletter *Language Sciences* nicely illustrates **Elaboration**.

Choosing a more precise lexical item: Changes of this type and the next, which adds information to the text, were fewest. This is not surprising, since making the text more specific would require more content changes: remember this is a technical paper being revised by an editor, not one of the authors. (Note in 30 this also shortens the text.)

29. A: ..., the paper examines several claims and findings of RST: <lists three>

    B: ..., the paper examines three claims and findings of RST: <lists three>

30. A: knowledge of the context in which the text was put forth,

    B: knowledge of the context in which it was written,

31. A: The starting point for analyzing a text is to divide it into units.

    B: The first step analyzing a text is dividing it into units.

Making something inferable explicit: These changes seem in direct contrast with many of those discussed above in that they make the text less concise by adding redundancy. In example 32, both the context and the capitalization of "Antithesis" identify it as a relation, yet the editor decided to strengthen the point by making it explicit. In 33, "agreement" is available from the previous sentence, but there is a great deal of intervening text, so simply saying "this" is potentially ambiguous.

32. A: ... the definition of Antithesis.

    B: ... the definition of the Antithesis relation.

33. A: This includes responsibility for providing...

    B: This agreement includes responsibility for providing...

Changing a function word: While these changes did seem to improve the text, it is very difficult to explain why. For example, in two cases "may" was changed to "might", as shown in 34. There may (might?) be some rule governing which to use, but I don't recall ever being taught it. In three cases, a preposition was changed, as in 35. Prepositions are well known to be slippery: they are a bane to non-native speakers. It is difficult to determine why one might choose the wrong one initially or how to evaluate that another is better.

34. A: For some texts, more than one analysis may be appropriate;

    B: For some texts, more than one analysis might be appropriate;

35. A: ... the first two paragraphs from a notice in a UCLA personnel newsletter.

B: ...the first two paragraphs of a notice in a UCLA personnel newsletter.

3.1.1.2 *Possible functions of revision* The sixteen categories of revisions described in the previous section all function to improve the text in some way (at least this was the goal of the editor who made the changes). Looking at the data from this perspective, we can describe it in terms of the different types of improvements made, which we will call *revision goals*. The following are the four revision goals I identified in the data:

- Making the text more concise: This set constituted over half the total revisions. The changes were for the most part local and many involved only deletions, without any companion additions or reorderings. Types of revisions in this category include use of ellipsis (mainly subject reduction), pronominalization, deletion of function words ("size of the units" --> "unit size"), elimination of semantic redundancy ("grouped together" --> "grouped"), and change in part of speech ("for the comprehension of the element" --> "comprehending the element").
- MAKING THE TEXT MORE EXPLICIT: Changes of this kind were the fewest, but this is not surprising, since making the text more specific would require more content changes and this data is revised by an editor rather than the author. There were three major types: choosing a more precise lexical item ("several claims" --> "three claims"), making something which is inferable explicit ("This gives rise to..." --> "This view gives rise to ..."), and restoring elided subjects. Note that making the text more explicit is often in direct conflict with making it more concise.
- CHANGING THE EMPHASIS: This set includes those changes in which whole phrases of the text were moved or the structural relations between phrases in the text were changed. Examples include movement of an adjunct phrase and movement of a subordinate clause into main clause position (and vice versa).
- MAKING THE TEXT MORE ACTIVE: This type is one often harped on in writing textbooks. Examples include changing from passive to active voice and eliminating hedge verbs, such as "seem" or "appear".

One might consider using these goals to guide a revision of a text, as writing instructors do. However, in order to do that one must be able to connect the rather high-level terms of the revision goals (e.g. conciseness, activeness) with the linguistic resources that accomplish them. As I argue in the preface to this work, there is no adequate technical vocabulary available that easily and generally describes the kinds of revisions that I found in the data.[25]

[25] There are other researchers who use such high-level terms in their work; for example DiMarco & Hirst (1988) define style in terms such as "abstract" and "concrete" and Hovy (1987) uses a vocabulary of rhetorical and pragmatic goals in his generator PAULINE, such as

Consider , for example, conciseness, which was one of the most interesting categories, as well as the one with the most instances. Virtually all writing textbooks agree that conciseness is a good thing—and that you must be careful not to to go far:

> *Vigorous writing is concise. A sentence should contain no extra words, a paragraph no extra sentences....This requires not that the writer make all his sentences short, or that he avoid all detail and treat his subjects only in outline, but that every word tell. (Strunk & White, p.23)*

> *Almost all writing suffers from wordiness—the tendency to use more words than necessary. When useless words weigh down your prose, the meaning is often lost, confused, hidden.... Beware, however, ... you don't want your prose to become so thin or brief that your meaning disappears completely. Therefore, cut out only the* unessential *words. (Wyrick, p.60)*

While all agree on the message, none tell you how to decide which words are necessary and which are superfluous. The best they do is provide some examples, such as these from Wyrick (p.61). Revisions such as these were quite common in the text I analysed.

Wordy: She made her decision after giving consideration to his report.
Concise: She decided after considering his report.

Wordy: Each candidate should be evaluated on an individual basis.
Concise: Each candidate should be evaluated individually.

The differences between the "wordy" and "concise" versions do not fall neatly into some single category in the traditional categories of decisions in generation, such as lexical choice, choice of syntactic structure, or organization of the information. They are more easily described in terms of which element is functioning as the head of the phrase, and whether that element is semantically strong (e.g. a content word) or semantically weak (e.g. a function word). Before we can make use of the revision goals in a generation system, we must first develop a vocabulary for describing the changes. In the next section I look more closely at general ways of describing these kinds of decisions.

3.1.2 *Goals for the analysis: generality*

Our overall goal is to use the study of revisions to drive the development of a theory of natural language generation. We therefore want to move from a descriptive analysis (as in the last section) to an explanatory analysis. One important issue in such a move is finding what level of generality in which to describe the data will best improve the explanatory power. Generality can be achieved in two ways:

level of formality ("highfalutin" vs. "colloquial") and force (forceful, neutral, or quiet). While both of these efforts are interesting in that they help us understand in general "style" and "pragmatics", neither fully integrates their vocabulary with the individual linguistics resources that accomplish these high-level goals.

- Within a single example: In a particular pair of original-revised texts the simplest description of the change will be the most general; therefore, if we can postulate a single high-level difference which will cause the surface differences to fall out necessarily, it will be more explanatory than simply addressing the surface differences independently.
- Across a body of data: A description that covers the most examples will be the most general and explanatory and will require us to postulate the least number of generation and revision strategies.

The next two subsections look at particular examples of these two dimensions of generality.

3.1.2.1 *Levels of decision making within one example* A change from one surface form to another can be described with respect to many different points in the generation process.[26] Here we look at how one example can be described at three different levels and what a revision component would have to change if it operated at one rather than another of the levels.

Consider the example (repeated below) in which the phrase *each of the fields* is made more concise by being changed to *each field.* At the lowest level of description, there are three surface changes: the deletion of two function words ("of" and "the") and a morphological change in the head ("field") from plural to singular. A pattern matcher would be all that was necessary to coordinate these changes at the surface level; however, that approach would require a great many independent specialists to handle the different cases (for example, to avoid changing "all of the fields" to "all field").

2. A: Each of the fields specifies...

   B: Each field specifies...

At a more general level, there are two decision points that directly lead to the surface changes: the change in the determiner (roughly whether the determiner is "the" or "a") and in the number of the head. At this more abstract level of description, we need not specify the "of", as it is uniquely determined by these two factors: its deletion may be seen as a side effect of the other decisions. While a "revision specialist" at this level would still have to be particular to each quantifier (to avoid making the mistake on phrases quantified by "all", for example), this would be a more general place to change the determiner policy and the number than at the level of the surface form, since information on the number of the quantifier is also necessary for subject–verb agreement.

At a still more general level, these changes can be motivated by a single decision: the perspective chosen to express "field": is it seen as a definite set, "the fields", or as an indefinite element of the set, "a field" (the indefinite determiner is superceded by the quantifier in the example)? A single change at this level would account for multiple differences at lower levels. However, if a

26 The description here is intended to be theory neutral, that is, not subscribing to any particular architecture for the generation process. I use "highest" to mean the level closest to the application program and "lowest" to mean closest to the final text.

revision specialist were making the change, it would need to know the relation between the perspective and the resulting degree of conciseness of the text. It must also evaluate whether the change will change the intended meaning of the text: the original choice may have been for a particular emphasis, for example to contrast one subset with another ("which of the photographs on the righthand side...").

Another example of a single perspective choice that covers a number of surface differences is the decision/decide type of variation (discussed in more detail below). While out of context this change is simply a change in the part of speech, there are many accompanying grammatical changes that must go on within a context. For example, a noun phrase must express number and have a determiner, and a verb phrase must express tense and include obligatory arguments. All of these surface distinctions can be captured by the difference between using an *event* perspective or an *object* perspective. We look more closely at this difference in Chapter Four.

3.1.2.2 *Generalities across the data* The second way of achieving generality is choosing a description that covers the most examples.[27] Such a description allows you to posit fewer strategies for generation and revision overall. For example, it is clear that the following examples can be treated uniformly:

1. make a decision ---> decide
2. make a distinction --> distinguish

They can be described as deleting the verb "make", changing the direct object from a noun to a verb, and making it the matrix verb in the clause. This level of description is analogous to the surface level categorized above and would require strategies associated with individual lexical items, such as *make.*

A slightly greater level of generality lets you include examples like (3) and (4) in the same group. Rather than describing the change in terms of a single lexical item, "make", we can describe it in terms of a class of lexical items, i.e. weak verbs, including "give" and "be".

3. give a validation of x --> validate x
4. is a description of x --> describes x

In these examples, the weak verb is deleted and the verb form of its argument moves to matrix verb position. Note that when the noun has an argument, marked by "of" in (3) and (4), the argument remains and becomes the direct object of the verb.

The weak verbs in the above examples are idiomatic to the lexical item (decision, distinction, validation) and carry little or no information. The content is carried in the object to the weak verb; in the revised versions, the object moves to the matrix verb position, with an accompanying change in the part of

27 While the advantage of general descriptions in developing an explanatory analysis is clear, it is also important not to become too general. The *reductio ad absurdum* that covers all the data is simply that "something changed". However, this does nothing to help us understand the differences or design generation, evaluation, or revision strategies. The appropriate level of generality must help explain phenomena as well as describe them.

speech. Weak verbs may also be hedges, where the weak verb places the object in a more distant perspective with respect to the reader. These are often in the passive, as in (5), creating a distance from the author as well:

5. are seen to emanate --> emanate
6. the text appears to contain --> the text contains

Note that in these examples, the argument which moves is already a clause, so our general description of this class need not specify the change in the part of the speech, only that the element moved must be a verb to move into matrix verb position.

An even greater level of generality would allow us to extend our description to other phrase types, including examples of arguments (and adjuncts) becoming the head of phrases such as NPs and adverbial phrases, as in the following:

7. the sort of relation --> the relation,
8. a way that is independent --> independently

The change can now be described as a weak element in head position being displaced by a strong element that was previously in an argument or adjunct position. While the examples differ in the type of phrase being modified and the particulars of the modification (e.g. whether the part of speech changed in the new head), they are all examples of a change in how an element functions in a phrase. This general description allows us to look at one kind of choice in multiple situations.

3.1.3 *Analysis of the data using Text Structure*

Analyses such as those above can guide us in determining the intermediate structures and decision points necessary to generate both the original and the revised texts. There are three kinds of information that must be represented in order to capture the generalizations described in the previous section:

1. constituency: many of the examples involved the movement of entire constituents with little or no internal change to the constituent;
2. functional relations (e.g head, argument, matrix, adjunct);
3. semantic type of the constituent (e.g. event, individual) which reflects the perspective through which the information is being viewed.

In this section we look at how this information is represented using the Text Structure notation. As we see in Figure 3.1, which represents the changes in example 7 (repeated below), the Text Structure notation is particularly useful in capturing these three kinds of information: each node represents a constituent of the utterance, the label in bold signifies the functional relation of the node to its parent, and the second label is a lexical item followed by its semantic type.

Since our focus in this chapter is to look at examples of revisions, I will only briefly describe the notation itself; the details are described in Chapters 4 and 5. There are two kinds of subtrees in the Text Structure: a *composite*, in which one of the children is the MATRIX and the other children are ADJUNCTS, and a *kernel*, in which the children are ARGUMENTS of their parent, which is the HEAD. In the diagram, the label in bold signifies the functional relation of the node to its parent; the labels for the roots are either HEAD, signifying a kernel, or COMPOSITE. The second label is the *contents* of the node. In the text planner, the contents is a first class object representing the information expressed by the constituent; in the diagrams here, it is a lexical item followed by its semantic type. Italics are used to abbreviate constituents which are peripheral to the point being illustrated.

7. A: Hoey thus makes a distinction between ....
   B: Hoey thus distinguishes between ....

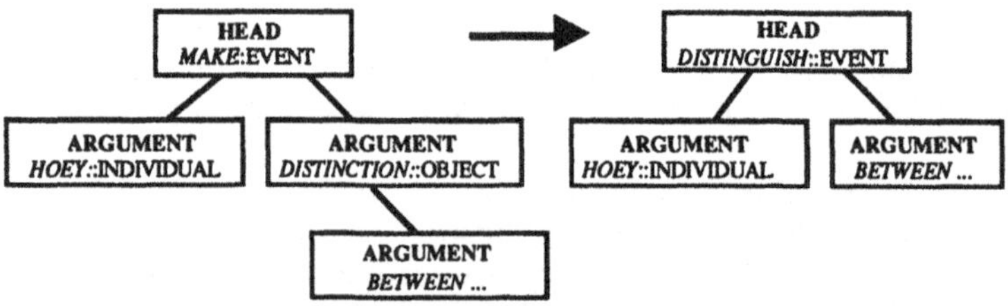

Figure 3.1 Text Structure for "make a distinction" vs. "distinguishes"

3.1.3.1 *Constituency* Fundamental to most of the revisions in the data is the ability to manipulate entire constituents. A constituent may be as small as a word or as large as a paragraph (though few examples in the data I analysed manipulated constituents larger than a sentence). In the following example, an adjunct that originally appeared as a separate sentence is moved to a position as an adjunct to an object and is realized in the text as a restrictive relative clause.

21. A: A very few texts can be analyzed only if the adjacency constraint is relaxed. These are typically advertisements in which a title line plays a role in the body of the text.
    B: A very few texts, typically advertisements in which a title line plays a role in the body of the text, can be analyzed only if the adjacency constraint is relaxed.

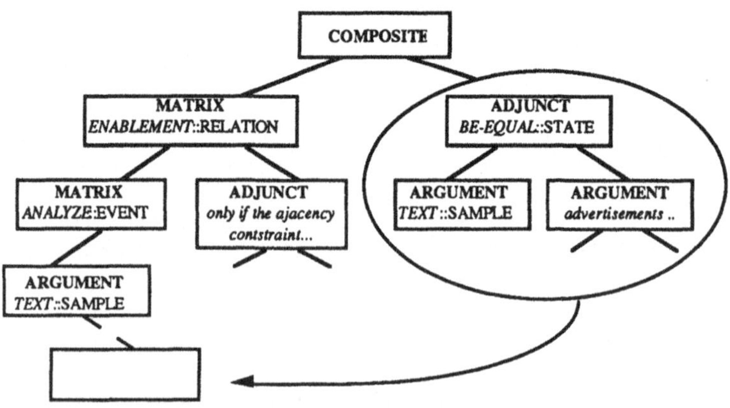

Figure 3.2 Text Structure for moved constituent

As shown in this example, one of the primary features of the Text Structure representation is that it transcends the traditional division between structure above the level of the sentence (what is often called "discourse" or "rhetorical" structure) and structure below the level of the sentence (usually described only in syntactic terms).

3.1.3.2 *Structural relations* In our generalized description of the changes described in §3.1.1, what structural role a constituent had in the utterance played a key part. In the example shown below, the second argument of the initial tree becomes the head of the revised tree. Note that the movement does not change the subconstituents of the element that moved.

19. A: The text appears to contain a number of non-sequiturs, ...

B: The text contains a number of non-sequiturs, ...

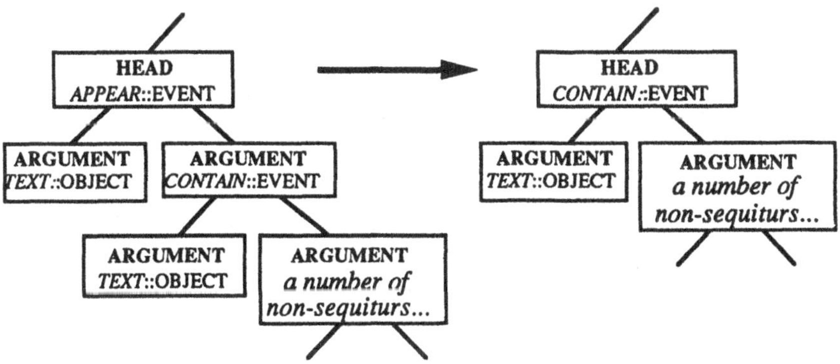

Figure 3.3 Text Structure for "appears to contain" vs. "contains"

3.1.3.3 *Semantic categories* The Text Structure representation also captures the conceptual information and perspectives expressed by a particular combination of linguistic resources, where a "linguistic resource" is more than simply a word, but also syntactic structures, closed class lexical items, inflectional morphology and the like. For example, a single word in an utterance is a combination of the lexeme itself, its part of speech, and grammatical features such as number. The lexeme carries most of the content. Part of speech can signal perspective, for example the verb *decide* focuses on the process whereas the noun *decision* focuses on the result. (Grimshaw (1988) presents a more complex discussion of this distinction and its implications). Grammatical features, such as number, also in some sense reflect perspective. The combination of grammatical resources in a phrase can signal perspective on an object, such as indefinite entity (*a dog*), definite object (*the dog*), and multiple instances (*dogs*) (Talmy 1987). This kind of information is captured in a semantic type.

In addition to expressing content and perspective, linguistic resources differ in their options for combining with other resources. For example, you can both *decide quickly* or *make a quick decision*, but the result perspective is forced when you need access to the result, as in *make an important decision* (cf. **decide importantly*).[28] The text structure captures this constraint through the semantic types at each node. In the first structure, the RESULT is available and thus can be modified by a PROPERTY (in this case "important"), whereas in the second structure only the EVENT is available, which cannot be modified by a property; therefore the revision in this case is not allowed. It would only be possible if there was manner adverb for "important" available as a linguistic resource.

A: Michael made an important decision.

B: *Michael decided importantly.

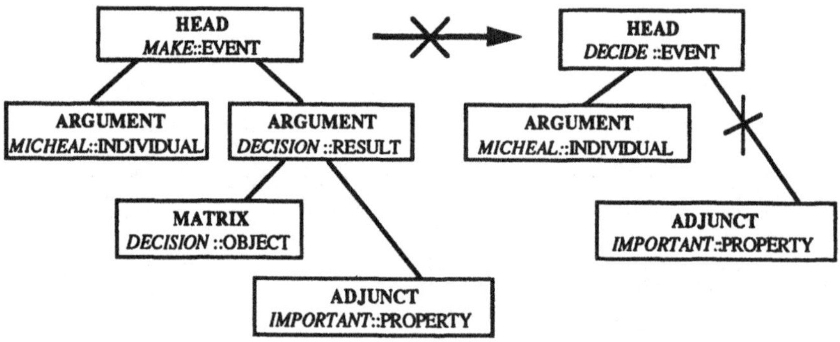

Figure 3.4 Text Structure for "make a decision" vs. "decide"

3.1.4 *A theoretical framework*

A descriptive analysis such as that presented in the previous section outlines the range of phenomena under consideration independent of any particular theoretical framework for the process itself. In order to make use of the analysis in the design of a generation system, we must provide such a theoretical framework, one which would allow us to explain the data in terms of the generation process. In this section, I present the considerations which contributed to the theoretical framework adopted in this work.

First, let's review the processes we are trying to explain. We can summarize them in terms of three questions:

- How was the original text produced?
- What changes were made to produce the revised text?
- How could the need for the changes be noticed?

Our overall goal is to span the distance between the data itself and the answer to these three questions. I begin by proposing a framework based on an efficiency

28 Following the general convention in linguistics, I use a "*" to mark ungrammatical sentences and a "?" to mark questionable ones.

model of generation and then consider the question of why revision is necessary in this framework to produce written quality text.

3.1.4.1 *An efficiency model of generation* Consider the following examples of revisions which function to make the text more concise:

1. in a way that is independent --> independently
2. the way that we interpreted their advice --> our interpretation of their advice

These phrases both fall into the class described in §3.1.2.2: they began with a semantically weak head which was modified with the semantically important information. The change makes the semantically important information in the modifying phrase into the head of the whole phrase, with a corresponding change in perspective.

The existence of the two versions, original and revised, presents an interesting problem of how decisions are made during initial generation. In the first example, we can assume that *independently* is a word the author knew when he wrote the original text. Why didn't he use it? Why didn't he make the optimization that would produce the revised text in the original generation pass?

This apparent variance in ability on the part of the speaker can be explained by taking into account the relative familiarity of the situation the speaker is in. In McDonald, Meteer, & Pustejovsky (1987), we argue on the grounds of efficiency that there is a direct link between the familiarity of the situation and the ease of generation. When the speaker is in a familiar situation (an extreme case is answering the phone), fewer decisions need to be made about what to include in the message and how to express it. We can think of "familiar" situations as reified objects with an established mapping to the linguistic resources for expressing them. New ideas and contexts ("unfamiliar" situations) can be expressed by composing familiar ones (as in descriptions of objects we don't have names for). However, in expressing these composite objects we will have to use general strategies, as we will not have any already established way of expressing them.

There are two other important aspects of this efficiency model: decisions are made locally (and not necessarily simultaneously), and they are made indelibly (there is no backtracking—generation is not search; see McDonald 1984). A result of these design criteria is that a message (or message element) built compositionally in multiple steps may be functionally equivalent to some "familiar" object, but the speaker cannot necessarily know that in advance and therefore cannot take advantage of the familiar object's established mapping to linguistic resources.

3.1.4.2 *Why revision: tension between goals* Now let's look at our earlier example in terms of this framework. The larger context in which the example appeared was as follows:

> *This section defines RST* ***in a way that is independent [independently]*** *of the particular languages and text types to which it has been applied.*

If the speaker had already chosen "independent" to modify the event (*defining RST*), then an established mapping would have produced the adverb form "independently". However, suppose the speaker first decides to modify the manner of the action, but has not yet decided on the particulars of the modification. He can choose a compositional construction which provides a weak head that simply contributes "manner" (*in a way*) and then later add modifications to the head. Notice in the examples below that this construction allows many options for expressing information that cannot be expressed simply as an adverb in English:

in a way that is dependent on the particular language...
in a way that emphasizes...
in a particular way ...

This makes the construction more appropriate when the particulars have not yet been chosen because almost no options have been cut off. One can continue talking, just saying "in a way", without immediately establishing the particulars and still feel relatively confident that any choice will be acceptable.

Figures 3.5 and 3.6 show this incremental production using the Text Structure representation. Figure 3.5 shows the progression of Text Structures used in generating the original version (9.a), and Figure 3.6 shows the progression for the revised version (9.b), where the lexeme "independent" is now given the type "manner" rather than the type "property" which it had in the original. Again, the object types Event, Property and Manner capture constraints on the composition of the elements. They may be thought of as "conceptual constituents" in Jackendoff's terms (Jackendoff 1983), and they map to syntactic constituents in later stages of the processing. By using abstract linguistic terms such as these to represent the message built by the text planner, we can ensure that the message will be expressible, that is, that there will be linguistic resources available that the parts of the message can map into.

As this example shows, the initial formulation of this model of generation appears to have the potential to help account for the variance in writing ability on the part of an individual writer. Expressing complex notions requires choosing between a number of linguistic resources which will compose into an utterance. Furthermore, written text has greater demands on its form than spoken text since the audience is not present to interact with the speaker when the text is unclear or ambiguous. The need for revision stems from the tension between such multiple goals in the generation process: tension between making choices that make the text clear (e.g. making as much explicit as possible), that make the text concise (e.g. leaving as much implicit as possible to reduce the number of words), and that leave open the most degrees of freedom (e.g. the most possibilities for composing more information into the utterance). This tension may already be resolved in familiar situations, as discussed in the previous section. When the audience is known, the choice of what to make implicit and what to leave explicit can be made with greater assurance; when the extent of what is to be communicated is known, there is less of a need to leave open more degrees of freedom.

9. A: This section defines the terminology of RST in a way that is independent of the particular languages and text types to which it has been applied.
   B: This section defines the terminology of RST independently of the particular languages and text types to which it has been applied.

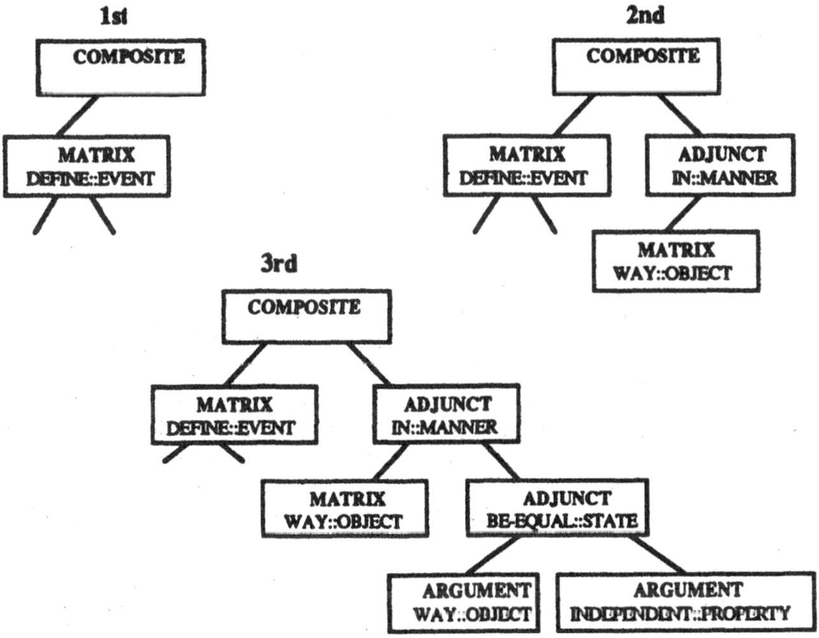

Figure 3.5 Composing Text Structure "in a way that is independent"

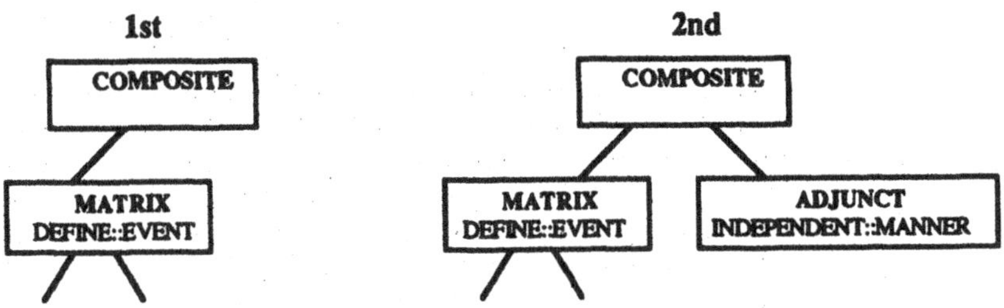

Figure 3.6 Composing Text Structure: "independently"

3.1.5 *Conclusion*

Revisions of text provide a window into human language production[29] in much the same way as speech errors do. Garrett (1975) used speech errors to posit levels of processing, roughly semantic, syntactic, and phonetic. Similarly, classification of changes during revision suggest initial generation strategies as well as revision strategies. For example, our paradigmatic case of replacing a weak verb and direct object with a strong verb (*make a decision --> decide*) reflects both the revision strategy "make the text concise" and initial generation strategies such as realizing a particular perspective (viewing *the decision* as an object in the original rather than as an event) or leaving the most options open (the nominalization is more open to modification: *make an important decision*). Formulating a vocabulary to describe these decision points and decision criteria will help to enable us to define both initial generation strategies and revision strategies.

The results of this work indicate the importance of text analysis in providing a descriptive account of well-written text (in contrast to a prescriptive account, as is found in most writing textbooks). Furthermore, generalizations of the data can guide us in determining the intermediate structures and decisions points necessary to generate variations of texts. Finally, the apparent need for writers to revise and the instances of revisions that I have analysed support an architecture for generation that favors efficiency and expressibility over initial optimality of expression. If that were not true, i.e. optimality were favored, then the "first draft" text in the data would not occur and revisions would not be necessary. This architecture accounts for variance of ability on the part of writers through the use of general generation strategies when realizing conceptual structures built compositionally. Improvements are made by evaluating the text and then regenerating it to produce more optimal text.

3.2 Motivations from applications

The previous section used the analysis of revised text to motivate the Text Structure representation from the perspective of language competence/expressiveness. In this section, I turn from the complexities of real texts to the complexities of real programs. I look at what early problems in designing a text planner for an application program motivated the design of a planning representation couched in abstract, rather than concrete (surface), linguistic terms.

3.2.1 *From application objects to language*

Application programs organize information in the way that most facilitates their reasoning about that information. Language, in turn, has many constraints on its structure. In some cases there is a fairly direct mapping between the

[29] Following the practice of psycholinguists, I use the term "production" to distinguish what people do from what machines do.

elements of an application program and the elements of an utterance. More often, however, this mapping is very complex. In this section we show examples of these complexities taken from one of our generation applications and then in §3.2.2 show how the Text Structure representation abstracts away from the complexities while still retaining the constraints on how elements can be composed into an utterance, thereby simplifying what a text planner needs to know, yet ensuring that what it plans will be expressible in language.

The following examples are from the AirLand Battle Management ("ALBM") project (Hirschberg 1987).[30] The ALBM system comprises several expert systems designed to aid in tactical mission planning at the Corps and Division levels. The role of the text generator in ALBM is to produce the Operations Orders ("OPORD"), which is a highly structured military document containing the complete specification of the mission. We concentrated on sections expressing the various tasks each military unit was assigned in order to accomplish the mission.

We look at particular examples of complexities in the mapping of a TASK OBJECT, which is the program's underlying representation of a task, to its expression in English. The TASK OBJECT defines the who, what, why, when, and where of a military activity. The notion of a task recurs throughout mission planning and execution and is therefore central to many components of the ALBM system.

3.2.1.1 *The structure of Task Objects* We begin the discussion by laying out the structure of the TASK OBJECTS and what information is contained in them and then look at the simplest example of mapping between these objects and text. TASK OBJECTs are implemented in ALBM as KEE[31] frames with slots for the information that make them up: the who (agent), what (action), what.object (object of the action), why, when, and where of the task. The structures in Figure 3.7 show the underlying representation for a typical although rather simple task, which would be expressed as *The 10th Corps defeats the 8th CAA* (or in the command form as *Defeat the 8th CAA.*). Note that the information that appears in this utterance is not in the task frame directly but rather in other KEE objects, such as the ACTIONS and OBJECTS frames shown below the first frame. This allows the slots to carry more complex information than a single value.

[30] Work on ALBM was sponsored by the Defense Advanced Research Projects Agency, the US Army Ballistic Research Laboratory, and the US Army Center Communications and performed under contract to Lockheed Missile and Space Company, Inc., Austin Division, under contract DAA1587-C-0006. For a more detailed description of text generation in ALBM, see Meteer, 1989b.

[31] KEE™ is a frame representation language developed by Intellicorp.

```
(MISSION.TASK.OBJECTS107
 ((WHAT #[Unit: ACTIONS108 FC.3])
  (WHAT.OBJECT #[Unit: OBJECTS109 FC.3])
  (WHERE ())
  (WHY ())
  (WHEN ())
  (WHO #[Unit: UNITS.FRIENDLY113 FC.3])))

(ACTIONS108
 ((ACTION #[Unit: DEFEAT |FC_OPERATIONS|])))

(UNITS.FRIENDLY113
 ((VALUE #[Unit: 10TH.CORPS |FRIENDLY_INSTANCES|])))

(OBJECTS109
 ((VALUE #[Unit: 8.CAA |THREAT_INSTANCES|])))
```

Figure 3.7 Underlying KEE Objects for "Defeat the 8th CAA"

The WHO, WHAT, and (depending on the action) WHAT.OBJECT slots are required in order to express a task. This is both a pragmatic constraint (in order for there to be a task, someone needs to be doing something) and a linguistic constraint (in order to express the task as a sentence, it must have a main clause: minimally a verb and its arguments). The other slots contribute adjuncts that express supporting information which is not required for the grammaticality of the expression, for instance the location in the WHERE slot. For the TASK OBJECT in Figure 3.7, *The 10th Corps defeats the 8th CAA*, the mapping from slot values to words in the sentence is rather direct, as shown in Figure 3.8.

Who:	#[Unit: 10TH.CORPS]	==>	<subject>	10th Corps
What:	#[Unit: DEFEAT]	==>	<verb>	defeat
What.object:	#[Unit: 8.CAA]	==>	<direct object>	8th CAA.

Figure 3.8 Correspondence between slot values and words

The WHAT slot directly contributes the verb of the sentence (*defeat*), the WHO slot the subject (*The 10th Corps*), and the WHAT.OBJECT slot the direct object (*the 8th CAA*), collectively making up the MATRIX clause for the sentence.

3.2.1.2 *Complex mappings* If all of the mappings from task objects to their expression were as direct as in the above example, then complex generation techniques would not be necessary. Parameterized templates could be used to map each part of the representation to a particular part of the sentence.[32] However, when the information being represented is as complex as in a system like ALBM, there is seldom such a direct correspondence. Furthermore, as the amount of information being conveyed and the variety of relations to be

[32] This scheme, called *direct replacement*, is one of the earliest approaches to text generation and is still used today in many "closed world" applications where the number of possible situations that can exist in the application program is predictable and relatively small.

expressed increases, so does the grammatical complexity of the text produced. We will now go through a series of examples illustrating this complexity.

In our first example, the action object, #[Unit: DEFEAT |FC_OPERATIONS|], had a corresponding English verb, *defeat*. However, not all of the actions that appear as the value of the WHAT slot have a verb associated with them. For example, the action shown in Figure 3.9, #[Unit: COVERING.FORCE |FC_OPERATIONS|], needs a verb added to it before it can be expressed: "*conduct* covering force operations" or "*establish* a covering force". Note that the ACTIONS object in Figure 3.9, and the others in subsequent examples, is a part of an instance of MISSION.TASK.OBJECTS, where it fills the WHAT slot, similar to the one in Figure 3.7.

```
(MISSION.TASK.OBJECTS85
 ((WHAT #[Unit: ACTIONS78 FC.3])
 (WHAT.OBJECT (#[Unit: OBJECTS87 FC.3])
 (WHERE #[Unit: LOCATIONS88 FC.3])
 (WHY ())
 (WHEN ())
 (WHO #[Unit: UNITS.FRIENDLY91 FC.3])))

(ACTIONS78
 ((ACTION #[Unit: COVERING.FORCE |FC_OPERATIONS|])))

(OBJECTS87
 ((CARDINALITY (ALL))
 (ECHELON (FIRST))
 (SIZE (#[Unit: THREAT.DIVISION TASK]))))
```

Figure 3.9 Underlying KEE Object for "Conduct covering force operations ..."

Some action objects will have an even more complex expression in language, as in the example in Figure 3.10, where the action requires two verbs: "*Force* the lead divisions to *deploy*". Here the WHO slot contributes the agent of the *force* action, while the WHAT.OBJECT slot (#[Unit: OBJECTS87 FC.3], *the lead divisions*) is not the object of the forcing but rather the agent of the second action, *deploy*. Since the entire FORCE.DEPLOYMENT task is an adjunct (it is the purpose of the COVERING.FORCE task in the second example), it is expressed as an infinitival clause (which introduces the "to" and blocks the expression of tense) and the syntactic rules allow the agent of the "force" action to be deleted in the description: "Conduct covering force operations to force the lead divisions to deploy."

```
(ACTIONS86
 ((ACTION #[Unit: FORCE.DEPLOYMENT |FC_OPERATIONS|])))
```

Figure 3.10 Underlying KEE Object for "force the lead divisions to deploy"

3.2.1.3 *Composite actions* In the examples we have looked at so far, the value of the WHAT slot has been a single action from the military activity hierarchy. In general, however, the action can be a composition of a type plus an action, as shown in the examples in Figure 3.11. In both of these tasks the main action is simply #[Unit: MILITARY.OPERATIONS |FC_OPERATIONS|]. In the first the type is DEFENSIVE, and the composition of the action and type is expressed as a single verb ("defend"). In the second, the type is OFFENSIVE, and while its structure is analogous to the DEFENSIVE case, the expression is quite different, since the analogous verb in English ("offend") has a very different meaning than the one intended here. In this case, the action is expressed with a helping verb ("*conduct* military operations") and the type contributes a modifier ("offensive"). These two examples point out that, as is often the case, analogous structures in the representation are not always expressed analogously in language.

```
(ACTIONS100
 ((ACTION #[Unit: MILITARY.OPERATIONS |FC_OPERATIONS|])
 (TYPE #[Unit: DEFENSIVE |FC_OPERATIONS|])))

(ACTIONS117
 ((ACTION #[Unit: MILITARY.OPERATIONS |FC_OPERATIONS|])
 (TYPE #[Unit: OFFENSIVE |FC_OPERATIONS|])))
```

Figure 3.11 Underlying KEE Objects for "defend ..." and "conduct offensive operations..."

Figure 3.12, which is expressed as *Prepare to conduct offensive operations*, also exemplifies a further complication of the mapping from actions to verbs. In this task, the WHEN value is a schedule object of type PREPARE, which, rather than contributing an adjunct, contributes the main verb, "prepare". This creates a new main clause which takes as an argument the clause that expresses the task action.

```
(MISSION.TASK.OBJECTS116
 ((WHAT #[Unit: ACTIONS117 FC.3])
 (WHAT.OBJECT ())
 (WHERE #[Unit: LOCATIONS119 FC.3])
 (WHY #[Unit: PURPOSES121 FC.3])
 (WHEN #[Unit: SCHEDULES120 FC.3])
 (WHO #[Unit: UNITS.FRIENDLY122 FC.3])))

(ACTIONS117
 ((ACTION #[Unit: MILITARY.OPERATIONS |FC_OPERATIONS|])
 (TYPE #[Unit: OFFENSIVE |FC_OPERATIONS|])))

(SCHEDULES120
 ((TYPE PREPARE)))
```

Figure 3.12 Underlying KEE Objects for "Prepare to conduct offensive operations."

In this section we have seen four kinds of complexities in the mappings from the application program's representation of actions to their surface expressions in language: (1) an action which has no verb associated with it in English (e.g. *covering force*); (2) an action which requires two verbs (e.g. *force to deploy*), (3) analogous actions which are expressed differently (e.g. to *defend* but not to *offend*, rather to *conduct offensive operations*) and (4) an action contributing a complement and other information contributing the main verb (e.g. *prepare to conduct offensive operations* where PREPARE is information from the WHEN slot and the action is an OPERATION of type OFFENSIVE).

3.2.2 *Text Structure as an intermediate level*

The examples thus far have shown that the possible surface expression of task actions varies widely; similar variation can be found in the expression of many other slots. However, this apparent disparity between the underlying representation and the way it is expressed in language is in fact not as large as it may seem initially. There are a great many consistencies both on the input side (in the structure of the application program) and on the output side (in the structure of the text produced). On the input side, the Task Objects always have the same slots and the slots have a predictable range of types for their values. On the output side, there are many structural regularities in the expression of a task. These consistencies can be taken advantage of to simplify the work of a text planner through the use of a suitably designed intermediate representation. For instance, all of the examples were expressed as a single sentence composed of a required portion (the MATRIX of the sentence) and optional ones (the ADJUNCTS). The matrix was always an EVENT composed of the action and its ARGUMENTS. We capture these kinds of structural regularities in the Text Structure.

In this section we illustrate the parts of the Text Structure using our earlier example, *The 10th Corps defeats the 8th CAA*. We then look at how the Text Structure abstracts away from linguistic details using the example, *The 10th Corps conducts covering force operations to force the lead divisions to deploy.*

3.2.2.1 *Constituent structure* The Text Structure is a tree capturing the *constituent* structure of the utterance. Figure 3.13 shows the Text Structure for "The 10th Corps defeats the 8th CAA." Each node (rectangular box) represents a constituent in the utterance and contains information about that constituent, for example the relation between the constituent and its parent (the labels in bold) and the information expressed by the constituent, called the CONTENTS of the node (indicated by the lower labels). The CONTENTS may be an object directly from the application program (such as the TASK.OBJECT in the top node) or an object built by the text planner (such as the EVENT object in the matrix node below TOP).

The generator builds the Text Structure for the utterance from the application program objects. Once represented in terms of Text Structure, the utterance can easily be mapped to the linguistic surface structure, where more detailed syntactic decisions are made, such as subject-verb agreement and the actual placement of the arguments and adjuncts.

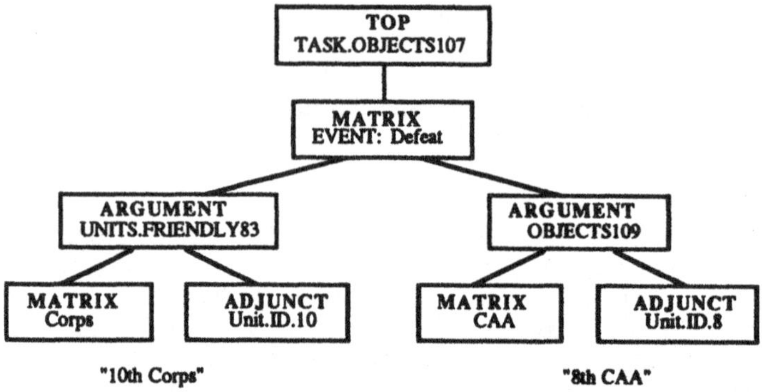

Figure 3.13 Text Structure for "The 10th Corps defeats the 8th CAA."

3.2.2.2 *Abstracting away from syntactic detail* The Text Structure in Figure 3.14 exemplifies some of the ways the Text Structure representation abstracts away from linguistic details. An event (head) and its arguments form a semantic unit regardless of its grammatical function in the sentence. In this example there are three event/argument structures, each with a different grammatical function: the *conduct* event is a main clause, the *force* event is an adjunct to the main clause, and the *deploy* event is an argument to the *force* event. At the syntactic level, the three verbs in this sentence have very differently properties, varying on whether tense is expressed and whether the subject is explicit or implicit: *The 10th Corps* ***conducts*** *covering force operations <10th Corps>* ***to force*** *the lead divisions* ***to deploy***.

The text structure captures the uniformities in structures like these without having to deal simultaneously with the syntactic repercussions of the grammatical details. For example, a main clause in English is required to express tense, whereas certain kinds of adjunct clauses (such as the one in this example) do not:[33] they use the infinitival or "to" form of the verb (e.g. "to force"). A clause in argument position may or may not express tense depending on the verb it is an argument of (e.g. "Bill forced Tom *to go*" vs. "Bill knew that Tom *left*"). The Text Structure abstracts away from these details and treats all event-argument structures the same way because the differences have no impact on the decisions a text planner must make. The surface decisions needed to make the expression grammatical will be made at a later stage of the processing.

[33] The temporal information needed to express tense must also be available in the application program. How that information is represented and what defaults to use when it is not is beyond the scope of this work.

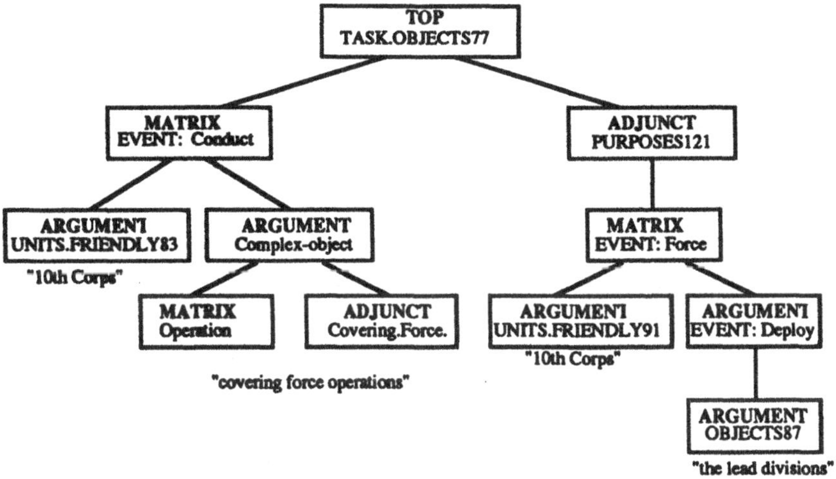

Figure 3.14 Text Structure for "The 10th Corps conducts covering force operations to force the lead divisions to deploy."

Another example of how the Text Structure abstracts away from linguistic detail is the matrix-adjunct structure. This structure is simply a constituent that is made up of one main subconstituent and zero or more subconstituents elaborating the main one. This kind of structure appears at all levels of text, from a paragraph with a topic sentence, to a main clause with subordinate clauses, to a head noun modified by adjectives. The matrix-adjunct structure appears three times in the Text Structure shown in Figure 3.14: (1) the main clause (EVENT: conduct) modified by the purpose object (PURPOSES121); (2) the purpose clause itself (EVENT: force), which has no adjuncts; and (3) the argument "covering force operation", which is composed of the matrix (Operation) and the adjunct (Covering.Force). (The other arguments, which are not expanded in the figure, are composed of a matrix and adjuncts as well.)

While the structure of the information is the same in all of these cases, the details of their linguistic realization are quite different. For example, the syntactic form of the subconstituents may differ: in (1) the matrix and adjunct are both clauses whereas in (2) they are nouns. The final order of the adjunct with respect to the matrix may also differ. If the adjunct is an adjective it is required to precede the head noun, whereas a purpose clause, such as in (3), usually follows the main clause. Again, this is a case of details that are not germane to the text planner's task and can properly be left to later processes.

3.3. Summary

In Chapters One and Two, I argued for the necessity of an abstract linguistic representation in text planning to ensure that the utterance being composed will be expressible in language. In this chapter, I have shown motivations for the

Text Structure representation from two different perspectives: the analysis of revisions of written text and the composition of a message in a text planner. In the data analysis, Text Structure allowed different kinds of revisions to be described generally; for example, the constituency and structural relations represented in the Text Structure led to a uniform description for changes in weak head constructions (*make a decision* --> *decide*; *the sort of relations* --> *the relations*) even when their surface forms were quite different. In text planning, the Text Structure simplified the mapping from application program objects to their expression by abstracting away from the surface syntactic details of the language. In the next chapter, I describe the details of Text Structure representation.

4 The Text Structure

Generation is a decision-making process in which the generator must choose from the linguistic resources of the language those resources that will express the message to be communicated. I have argued in the previous chapters that an intermediate level of representation is needed within the text planner with which to compose the utterance and that this representation should be in abstract linguistic terms. Making the vocabulary in which the text planner makes its decisions be an abstraction over the concrete resources of the language simplifies the decision making in the composition process, since the text planner need not deal with the particular grammatical details of the language. Furthermore, since the abstract vocabulary captures all and only those combinations of resources that occur in the language and since its terms constrain the composition with other terms, the representation serves to ensure (1) that the decisions that the text planner makes when composing the utterance will not have to be retracted, that is that the utterance the text planner composes will be *expressible* in language and (2) that the choices available to it reflect the distinctions that can be made in the concrete resources, that is that it allows the text planner to take advantage of the *expressiveness* of the language.

Before defining the representation I have designed to meet these criteria, the Text Structure, I return to the two questions posed earlier: (1) what are the resources that the language provides and what are their abstract properties? And (2) which of those properties are essential to a text planner trying to compose an utterance from an application program? In answering these questions, I first look in detail at a single example, showing what the concrete resources are and how we can abstract over them. Then, in §4.2, I describe the linguistic motivations of Text Structure and its three main characteristics: constituency, structural relations between constituents, and categorization of constituents in terms of semantic categories. Finally, in §4.3, I define the Text Structure and describe its implementation in the Spokesman generation system. In particular, I look at how the considerations of a text planner working in the context of an application program affect what needs to be represented. In Chapter Five, I describe how Spokesman's text planner uses the Text Structure in composing the utterance.

4.1 Linguistic resources

In this section, I address the question of what the linguistic resources are and what abstractions we can and should make over them. I begin by looking at the *concrete* resources, that is those that actually appear in a stream of text. I then look at what various complexes of these resources express taken as a group. I show how by abstracting over these complexes of concrete resources we can provide the text planner with a vocabulary of abstract resources that constrains the possibilities to only those that appear in the language. In §4.2, I look more generally at how work in linguistics can help develop a more complete vocabulary of abstractions.

4.1.1 *What are the resources of language?*

The linguistic resources are all the syntactic structures, words, and grammatical features available to the speaker of the language. The most obvious resource is the words. However, words are not necessarily single "meaning units", nor do they all contribute the same kinds of information. Words may be composed of a root and one or more grammatical affix, such as the plural marker "-s" or the past tense marker "-ed". Also, some words contribute content information, whereas others contribute only relational information, such as the preposition "of".

Words and the grammatical markings are not the only concrete resources. There is also of course the syntactic phrase structure. While this structure is not visible in written text, it is available from the intonation in spoken text, and numerous psychological studies have shown that it is real in the minds of the speaker and hearer (Pierrehumbert 1980; Fodor, Bever, & Garret 1974). The phrase structure indicates the constituency (what words are grouped together) and the relations between the constituents which in English is mainly expressed by the order of the constituents, although it is sometimes explicitly marked with an affix or preposition.

We can divide linguistic resources into two general classes:

The lexical resources: these are what are often called the *open class* words (the nouns, verbs, and adjectives), and they carry most of the content. They are by far greatest in number and new items are easily added, such as names of invented articles ("computer", "dishwasher") or slang items ("groovy").

The grammatical resources: these include the *closed class* words, grammatical markings, and phrase structure. Closed class words (prepositions, articles such as "a" and "the", and other function words) form a smaller and far more stable set than the open class words. Also included are grammatical markings, such as number and tense, and the form of the word—its part of speech—which may or may not be explicitly marked with a suffix, such as "-ly" or "-tion"; like closed class words, there are a relatively small number of these grammatical markings and new ones enter a language only rarely. The phrase structure itself is also a resource. The syntactic structures that make up phrase structure are like the other grammatical resources in that there is a stable set and they express only certain kinds of relational information. They are different in that since it is harder to point to them in the text, their labels tend to be more theory dependent.

Talmy points out that there is a difference in the kinds of information these two types of resources convey and that the kinds of notions that are expressed by grammatical resources are the same across languages:

> *The grammatical elements of a sentence determine the majority of the structure of the Cognitive Representation, while the lexical elements together contribute the majority of its content.*[34]

Talmy's extensive cross-language research resulted in a set of categories for the notions expressed grammatically in language. In §4.2 I look at these categories in more detail.

4.1.2 *The concrete resources of language*

The concrete resources are those that actually appear in the word stream, as we described above. Abstract resources are aggregations of concrete resources with some parameters bound and others left open. In what follows we ground the notion of concrete resources by looking closely at one fairly simple sentence. Our goal will be to look at how we can project back from these concrete resources to a vocabulary of abstract resources. We will use the following sentence as our example.

Karen likes watching movies.

This sentence has the following lexical resources:

Karen: is a proper name referring to a unique person;

like: is a verb expressing a state of enjoying an activity or being fond of an object;

watch: is a verb expressing the process of observing something;

movie: is a motion picture show.

In addition, it has the following explicit grammatical resources:

-s: the simple present tense marker on the verb "like";

-ing: the gerund marker on the verb "watch", emphasizing the process aspect of the action.

-s: the plural marker on the noun movie.

Elements that are not there also express information. The fact that there is no determiner ("a" or "the") with "movies" indicates that it is not a particular set of movies being referred to (as in "the movies") but a general sample of movies. Note that it is not just the lack of the determiner that provides this information, but the whole constituent the particular noun is in and the fact that it is plural. If the noun phrase were singular, then there would have to be a determiner before "movie" (*"Karen likes watching movie"). With other nouns in the head position, the lack of a determiner can mean other things. For example, there is also no determiner in the first noun phrase in the sentence ("Karen"); however, in this case, since the head is a proper noun, it does refer to a unique individual.

[34] Talmy, 1987, p.1

If a determiner is used with a proper noun, it has a more general meaning of "an entity with that name" (as in "All the Karens I had ever met had dark hair and then I met a Karen with red hair").

We will term this kind of composition, where the same resource means different things in different contexts, "non-linear" composition; in contrast to "linear" composition, where each element contributes an identifiable part of the whole and what it contributes is not context dependent. The identification of which grammatical resources non-linearly co-occur and grouping those sets as a single abstract resource is a powerful method of constraining the text planner to keep its choices only to those that are expressible in language, as we shall see in the next section where we develop abstraction resources for the sets of concrete resources that appear in the constituents described above.

As we discussed earlier, the phase structure is also a concrete resource, which expresses how the constituents group together and certain kinds of relations between them. In our example, the phrase structure of the utterance (shown in Figure 4.1), tells us that "movies" are what is watched, that "watching movies" is what is liked, and that "Karen" is that one that likes watching movies.

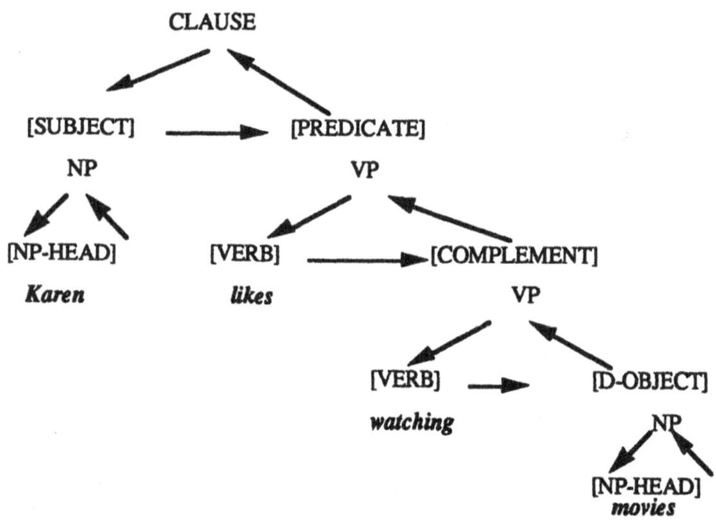

Figure 4.1 Syntactic resources[35]

[35] The notation in the diagram is the notation used in the linguistic component, Mumble-86. While it is slightly unconventional in that it explicitly represents the path that will be followed in traversing the structure, it is in other respects fairly standard in its terminology. I use it here since it is the notation I am most familiar with and because it lends a concreteness and reality to the diagrams since this is the structure the linguistic component will actually build when generating this sentence.

4.1.3 *Abstractions over concrete resources*

Allowing a generation system to select the concrete resources directly, as did virtually all of the systems described in Chapter Seven, makes available many more degrees of freedom than the language actually permits. As we saw in the previous section, some combinations of concrete resources occur in language, while others do not. Furthermore, we saw that the combination of the lexical resource in the head of a constituent and the grammatical resources in the constituent as a whole can combine non-linearly, so that the choice of the lexical and grammatical resources cannot be made independently of each other.

In this section, we look at how we can abstract over combinations of concrete resources by treating a particular set as a whole and naming it, rather than treating the resources as a set of independent features that happen to have appeared together. The vocabulary of abstractions we derive then becomes the terms in which the text planner makes its decisions. It is incapable of selecting a set of resources that is not expressible because it is not allowed to choose them independently.

For example, the two noun phrase constituents in our example ("Karen" and "movies") express two different perspectives on the entities they refer to. "Karen" is expressed with the perspective NAMED-INDIVIDUAL and "movies" is expressed as a "SAMPLE-OF-A-KIND".[36] We can think of these perspectives as **semantic categories**: "semantic" because they represent something about the meaning of a constituent, not just its form, e.g. "Karen" is referring to a person as a unique individual with a name, in contrast to referring to her as an anonymous individual (e.g. "a woman"). A concrete surface constituent can then be abstractly represented in the text structure for the purposes of the text planner as the combination of a lexical item and a semantic category.

The set of available semantic categories corresponds to what is expressible in the language. By restricting the text planner from selecting concrete resources directly and independently and by requiring it to work with such intermediate abstractions, the generator is prevented from choosing a set of features that cannot be realized. Figure 4.2 shows the "abstract" resources for the two noun phrases of our example. The upward arrows begin at the surface constituent being abstracted over and point to the boxes showing abstract resources: the lexical item in italics and semantic category following it. We will return to how to develop a complete set of semantic categories in the next section.

[36] "Sample" intended to mean "indefinite set"; the choice of names for categories is meant to be evocative of what they mean, while staying away from terms that have special meanings in other theories. Within Text Structure, these terms only need to be consistent. The names themselves do no work, except to help the observer understand the system.

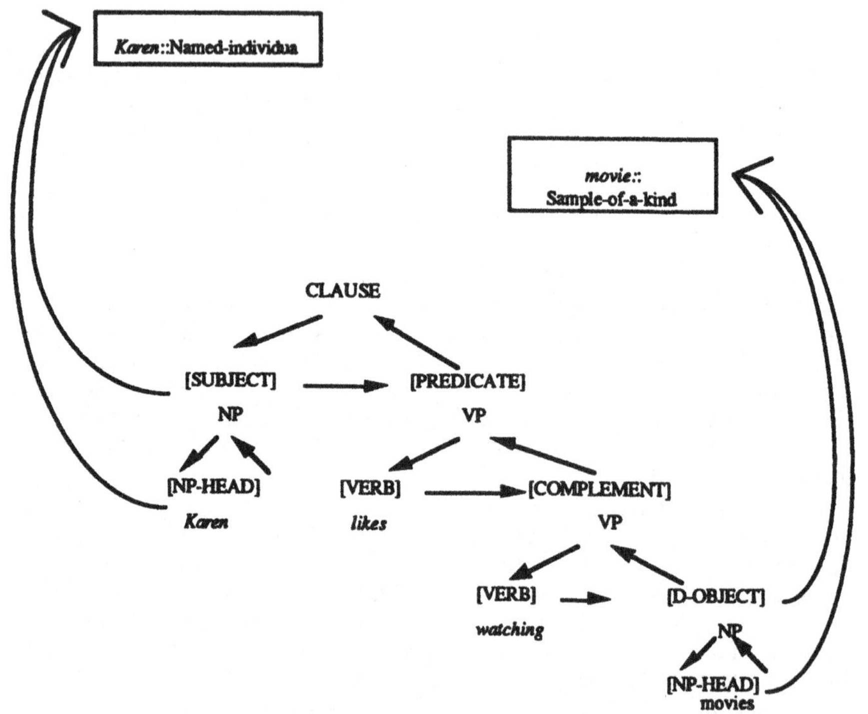

Figure 4.2 Abstractions over concrete resources

We can create the same kinds of abstractions for the other constituents of our sentence, as shown in Figure 4.3. In addition to abstracting over combinations of concrete resources by only representing the semantic type of a constituent, we can also represent the structural (syntactic) relations between the constituents. In Figure 4.3 the concrete relations of subject, direct object, etc. are represented abstractly as arguments and marked with a semantic relation.[37] (We look at other other structural relations, such as matrix and adjunct, in the next section.)

[37] The semantic relations shown here, "agent" and "patient", are capturing internally consistent relations. They are not attempting to carry the kind of weight and meaning as, say, the terms in theta-theory.

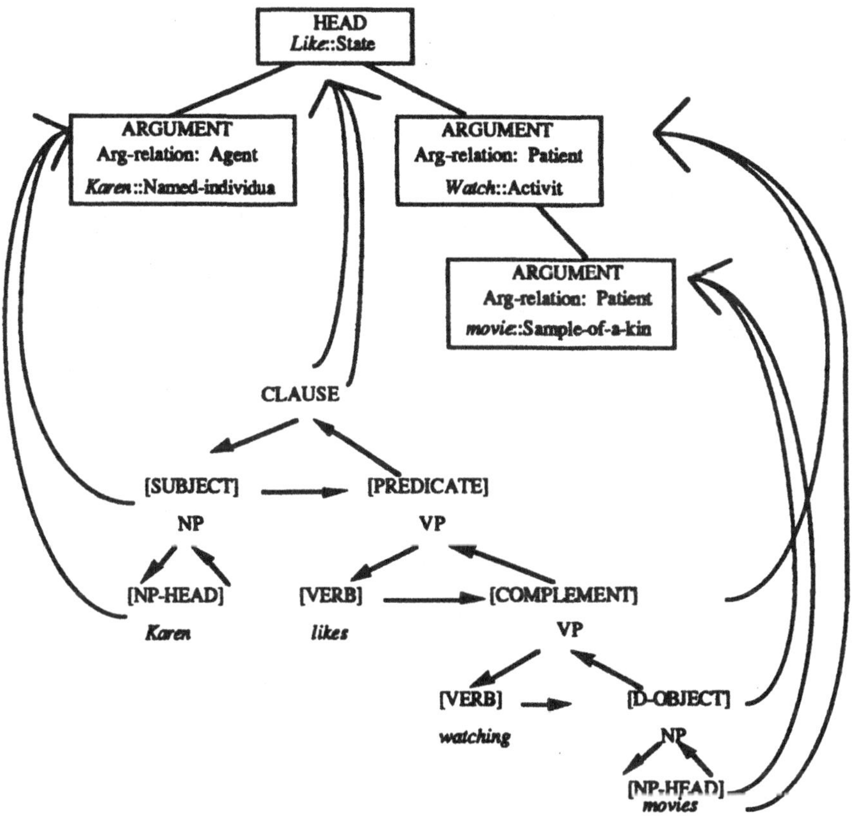

Figure 4.3 Abstractions over concrete resources

In this example, we have identified three kinds of information that are essential to an abstract representation of the concrete resources language provides:

- the constituency,
- the semantic category of the constituent, and
- the structural relations among the constituents.

In the next section we look in more detail at these kinds of abstract information, and in §4.3 I show how they can be used for text planning.

4.2 Determining the vocabulary of Text Structure

The use of an intermediate level of representation in a text planner to constrain decision making is in principle independent of the actual vocabulary of abstractions used in the representation. The vocabulary in the Text Structure representation will continue to evolve as we understand more about the representation of knowledge and about language itself. What I show in this section is the methodology I used to determine the particular vocabulary of abstractions used in the Text Structure in Spokesman which I will describe in §4.3.

The set of semantic categories available as resources to a text planner is an abstraction over the concrete resources in a language. In determining these categories and other abstract resources, we must remember their purpose: they are to constrain the text planner to do only what is *expressible*; that is the set of abstractions should include all and only what is realizable in the language. Furthermore, it should provide the text planner with the distinctions that allow it to take advantage of the *expressiveness* of the language.

Not every conceivable abstract notion is appropriate for Text Structure. In order for the vocabulary to be useful in ensuring expressibility, it must directly project on to the actual resources of language. Terms such as "forceful" or "hasty", which are used by researchers such as Hovy and DiMarco to control affect and stylistics in text, may be useful as criteria for making decisions, but since they do not project reliably on to actual resources, they cannot provide constraints and thus would only obscure the abstractions. Also not included are semantic terms which attempt to represent lexical meanings, such as those used in Lexical Conceptual Structure (Hale & Keyser 1987). Their terms are more like descriptions than categories, for instance "develop linear separation in material integrity" and "come forcefully into contact with". There appears to be in unbounded number of terms and no way to limit their proliferation.

The development of the full vocabulary of particular abstract resources to be used in the text structure is an ongoing process. I have identified three kinds of abstractions that are needed: semantic categories, constituency, and structural relations among constituents. The motivation for determining the abstractions comes from analysis of the language itself and what is expressible. A great deal of work has already been done in linguistics that can contribute to defining the vocabulary of abstractions.

In §4.2.1, I look at the work of four linguists in particular who have influenced my development of the current set of semantic categories in Text Structure: Jackendoff, Talmy, Pustejovsky, and Grimshaw. While their work is very different in character, all explore regularities in language using a more semantic than syntactic vocabulary. Using the work of these linguists, I show how we can determine abstractions over the concrete resources that are useful to a text planner. In §4.2.2, I look at constituency both above and below the level of the sentence and show the utility of a single set of abstractions for both of these levels, which are usually treated as completely independent.

4.2.1 *Semantic categories*

While most linguists work in either an entirely syntactic vocabulary or an entirely semantic vocabulary, some are relating the two vocabularies. Most notably, Jackendoff (1983) posits a set of conceptual categories that are held to project on to the syntactic categories of language. He makes the following claim about the relationship between language structure and meaning:

> *Each contentful major syntactic constituent of a sentence maps into a conceptual constituent in the meaning of the sentence.*[38]

Included in his vocabulary of conceptual categories are Thing, Path, Action, Event, and Place.

However, while Jackendoff's categories are useful in that they span the entire language (since they are projections from the syntactic categories), they are not fine enough to capture the constraints necessary to ensure expressibility or the distinctions necessary to ensure expressiveness. For example, two of the semantic categories in the example in §4.1, NAMED-INDIVIDUAL and SAMPLE-OF-A-KIND, are subsumed by the same category in Jackendoff's set, OBJECT. Similarly, his category EVENT has finer distinctions available in the actual resources: a finite verb (one which expresses tense) with its arguments expresses what I call an EVENT (*Peter decided to go to the beach*), whereas a nonfinite verb can express a generic ACTIVITY (*to decide to go to the beach*). Nominalizations make the event or activity into an OBJECT and different forms of nominalizations can pick out different aspects of the event, such as the PROCESS (*Deciding to go to the beach took Peter all morning*) or the RESULT (*The decision to go to the beach caused controversy*).

In using these finer semantic categories in the planning vocabulary for generation, we are making a stronger claim than Jackendoff's, namely that the categories define what combinations of surface resources are possible. For example, an ACTIVITY cannot have a tense marker, since by definition it is not grounded in time. The categories also serve to *constrain* how constituents are *composed*. For example, if we choose the EVENT perspective (e.g. *Peter decided to go to the beach*), we can add an adjunct of type MANNER to it (*Peter **quickly** decided to go to the beach*) but we cannot add an adjunct of type PROPERTY (**Peter **importantly** decided to go to the beach*).[39] However, if we choose an OBJECT perspective (*Peter made **a decision***), the PROPERTY adjunct can be added (*Peter made an **important** decision*). The work of lexical semanticists such as Talmy can contribute to determining what these abstract categories should be.

4.2.1.1 *Semantic features for grammatically expressed notions* Talmy, using a more analytic approach to semantic categorization than Jackendoff and taking into account a wide variety of different languages, determined a set of categories for the notions expressed grammatically across languages. From these categories he defined a multidimensional matrix of features, shown in Figure 4.4. The following are some of the features Talmy defines (1987):

[38] Jackendoff, 1983, p. 76.

[39] Following the general convention in linguistics, we use a "*" to mark ungrammatical sentences, and a "?" to mark questionable ones.

Dimension has values *time* and *space*. These allow us to distinguish *matter* from *action*, or, in Jackendoff's terms, *objects* from *events*. The distinction is clearest in the nominalizations of certain verbs: "to pit a cherry" is an action, whereas "a pit" is matter. The distinction also extends to other verbs and noun forms, such as "to call" vs. "to make a call" or "to decide" vs. "to make a decision".

Plexity has values *uniplex* and *multiplex*. This feature is conceptually the equivalent of number; however, the use of this term avoids confusion with the grammatical notion of number where a conceptually singular item may be marked plural in the language ("trousers") and vice versa ("furniture").

Boundedness has values *bounded* and *unbounded*. This feature is capturing whether something is continuous or individuated as an entity. It is similar to the traditional linguistic notion of "mass" and "count" for nouns but also applies to verbs: "Milk" is unbounded and a mass noun ("I want some milk"), whereas "cookie" is bounded and a count noun ("I want a cookie"); "walk" is unbounded, whereas "sit" is bounded.

Figure 4.4 below shows how these and other features form a system which establishes what combinations of features are expressible in language.

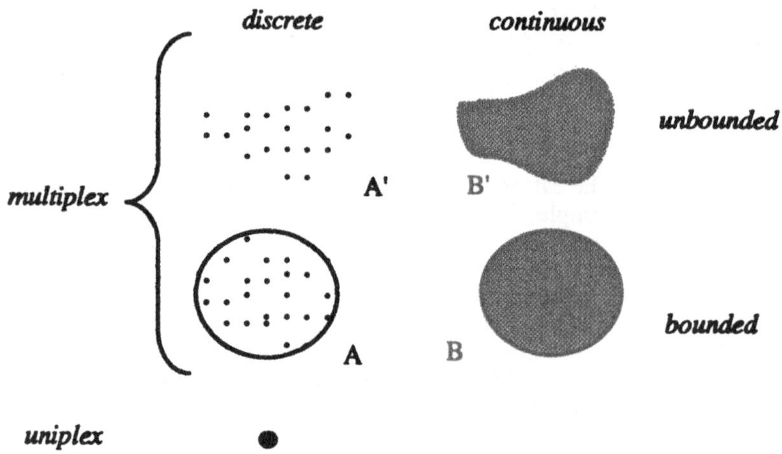

+ the distinction between *matter* and *action*, which crosscuts all of the above

Figure 4.4 Talmy's multidimensional system of categories for grammatically specified notions in language[40]

According to Talmy, lexical items have an intrinsic set of features values. By adding grammatical features to a phrase headed by the lexical item, those features can be changed. For example, the lexical item *dog* is UNIPLEX/

40 Talmy, 1987, p. 16.

DISCRETE/ MATTER. Note there is no word that is UNIPLEX/ CONTINUOUS and that all items with the feature uniplex are also bounded, by definition. This system of features avoids incoherent notions such as a single entity that has no bounds. By adding the plural morpheme to dog (*dogs*), it becomes MULTIPLEX/ DISCRETE/ MATTER. In a noun phrase with a determiner, we can add a feature for boundedness: *the dogs* is bounded, whereas *dogs* is unbounded, indicating an indeterminate set of dogs. Other lexical items have different intrinsic features. *Furniture* for example is intrinsically multiplex/matter. In order to make it uniplex, we have to use a partitive construction (a *piece of furniture*) which picks out a single element.

4.2.1.2 *Semantic categories for objects* The semantic categories in Text Structure reflect what combinations of grammatical features can be expressed in a constituent. Particular combinations reflect particular perspectives that may be taken on the same entity. Consider the following sentences:

(1) *I talked to **Peter**.*

(2) *I talked to **the guy Susan hired**.*

(3) *I talked to **a guy Susan hired**.*

All three can be descriptions of the same event; however, whether a proper name (with no determiner) or a definite noun phrase (with *the*) or an indefinite noun phrase (with *a*) is used depends on how the speaker chooses to characterize the situation to the hearer. The determining factor in this case is likely to be whether the speaker believed that the hearer knew the person (Peter) by name (as in 1), knew only of the existence of the person by being aware of the hiring event (as in 2), or didn't know either (as in 3). These distinctions are captured in a set of semantic categories: NAMED-OBJECT, UNIQUE-OBJECT, INSTANCE-OF-KIND.

Another semantic feature that is expressed grammatically is whether the object is singular or plural, uniplex and multiplex in Talmy's terms. Two categories in the set distinguish multiple objects from individual objects: SAMPLE-OF-A-KIND (***People** Susan has hired often stay with the company*.), DEFINITE-SET (***The people** Susan hired went to personnel on Wednesday*.).

By creating semantic categories that incorporate "objectness" along with definiteness and number, the choice among these perspectives becomes a single choice, rather than a succession of choices each of which binds a different feature, and thereby eliminates an opportunity for choosing an inexpressible combination of features. It also lets the choice be stated independently of how it will eventually be realized, providing greater flexibility. For example, when referring to items from a truckload of chairs, tables, couches, etc. with the perspective SAMPLE-OF-A-KIND, we can use the inherently plural lexical item *furniture,* which would need no overt morphological marking. If we wanted to single out an item without committing to the particular one, as in INSTANCE-OF-KIND, a partitive construction would be necessary: *a piece of furniture.* The use of semantic categories allows the perspective to be chosen without consideration for the grammatical details of its actual expression, simplifying the text planner's task.

4.2.1.3 *Semantic categories for events* So far, I have focused mainly on the set of semantic categories the text planner uses as the abstract resources for referring to objects. The same methodology can be used for determining a useful set of categories for expressing actions. While Talmy's categories apply to actions as well as matter and they are useful to some degree in teasing out the distinctions needed by the text planner, I have found the work of linguists whose work focuses on events and argument structures more useful. I describe the work of two such researchers here, Pustejovsky and Grimshaw, and how their work has influenced my development of semantic categories.

Pustejovsky's work is probably best described as computational lexical semantics, focusing on developing representations of word meaning and on the descriptive adequacy and computational tractability of such representations. His work on Event Semantic Structure, which captures the underlying structure of verbs, is most relevant here, although his work on Qualia Structure, which represents the "essential attributes of an object as defined by a lexical item", has long-range implications for other aspects of the system, such as lexical choice (see Chapter Eight). One of the primary components of Event Structure is the *event type*, which can be either state, process, or transition. Lexical items have a primitive event type and, since the notion of event type is recursively defined in the syntax, phrases and sentences have an event type as well. This is similar to what can happen with Talmy's features, where the grammatical context can change the intrinsic feature set of the lexical item. The following examples show how a single lexical item in different syntactic contexts can express different event types:[41]

(1) The door is closed. (state)
(2) The door is closing. (process)
(3) John closed the door. (transition)

This three-way distinction is finer grained than Jackendoff's EVENT category and both captures the effects of non-linear composition of resources and provides constraints on the composition of these types with other resources. For example, if a STATE is occurring presently, it is expressed with the simple present tense in English ("Karen *likes* ice cream"), whereas if is a PROCESS, the present time is expressed with the present progressive ("Karen *is watching* a movie"). A PROCESS can be composed with a durative adverbial adjunct, whereas a TRANSITION cannot ("Karen watched TV for an hour"; *"Peter solved the problem for an hour"). Similarly, a TRANSITION can be composed with a frame adverbial, whereas a PROCESS cannot ("Peter solved the problem in an hour"; *"Karen watched TV in an hour"). These "idiosyncrasies" can be captured systematically and transparently in the abstract vocabulary provided to the text planner.

41 Pustejovsky, 1991, p.417.

Grimshaw's analysis of nominals (1988) can help define conceptual object types which convey particular perspectives on events. Each object type will establish some resources and leave others as parameters to be specified. The object types can also restrict what other types they can (or must) compose with. Consider the following phrases which reflect three different perspectives on *decide*: event, process-object, and result-object:[42]

(a) Peter decided to go
(b) Peter's decision to go
(c) *Peter's decisions to go
(d) [Peter made] a decision
(e) [Peter made] the important decisions
(f) ?[Peter made] an important decision to go

(a) is an event: it requires arguments; it can be specified for tense; it cannot be specified for number[43] or determiner (it is inherently singular and definite). (b) is a process-object: it requires arguments and cannot be specified for tense. Although it is a nominal, it also is inherently singular and definite, (cf. c). (d) and (e) are result nominals. They are parameterized for number and definiteness and can also take modifiers, which are not as natural for process nominals, as shown by (f).[44]

Figure 4.5 shows a hierarchy of the semantic categories that captures the distinctions described in the above work.

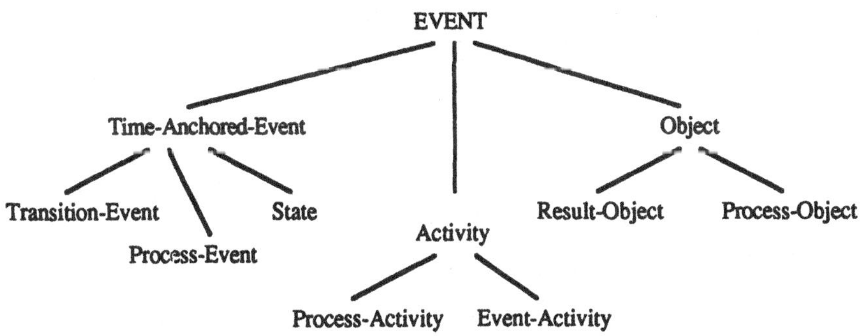

Figure 4.5 Partial hierarchy of semantic categories

Let me repeat that what is important here is not whether this current set of semantic categories is the final one (claiming that would be tantamount to saying

42 Following the general convention in linguistics, I use a "*" to mark ungrammatical sentences and a "?" to mark questionable ones.

43 Rather it cannot be specified grammatically for number; plurality can be expressed lexically: *Peter kept deciding, Peter decided three times.*

44 Grimshaw claims process nominals do not take modifiers and result nominals do not take arguments; however, that strict an analysis seems problematic with sentences such as *Peter's final decision not to go made his mother happy.*

the whole field of linguistics is "complete") but rather to establish a methodology for arriving at the set.

Having looked at the development of the set of semantic categories that can be expressed by a constituent, we now return to the constituent structure itself and look at what abstractions are available there.

4.2.2 *Constituent structure*

So far, we have focused on the semantic category expressed by a constituent. We now turn to the constituent structure of an utterance as a whole and the structural relations between constituents. That language is sequential, that is one word follows another, is an inescapable fact of how we speak, hear, read, and write language. But in addition to being sequential, the elements of a text are hierarchically organized into constituents. This fact of language has been shown to be psychologically real (Fodor, Bever, & Garret 1974). The study of constituent structure within the bounds of the sentence has been a core part of linguistic theory throughout traditional, structural, and modern linguistics. Francis, in this quote from a 1958 text, describes constituency in structuralist terms:

> *Every [syntactic] structure may be divided into its* ***immediate constituents****,...., which may in turn be divided and subdivided until the* ***ultimate constituents*** *(in grammar, the words) are reached.*[45]

Structuralists diagramed their sentences with boxes that looked like "those famous 'Chinese boxes' that fit one within the other".

Constituency has also been adduced in nearly all work done on texts above the level of the sentence, for example in the work of Kintsch (1985), in Polanyi's Linguistic Discourse Structure (Polanyi 1986, Polanyi & Scha 1984), in the "linguistic structure" of Grosz & Sidner's model (Grosz & Sidner 1986), and in Rhetorical Structure Theory (Mann & Thompson 1987). Work in this area is usually termed "discourse structure" or "text structure" (which contrasts with my usage of the term, as discussed in §2.1.3.4) and the minimal units are generally clause-sized or larger.

Few researchers have attempted to look at constituency below the level of the sentence and above that level together. An exception is Longacre, who assumes that:

> *Discourse has grammatical structure and this structure is partially expressed in the hierarchical breakdown of discourses into constituent embedded discourses and paragraphs and in the breakdown of paragraphs into constituent embedded paragraphs and sentences—not to speak of further hierarchical parcelling out into clauses, phrases, and word structures.*[46]

[45] Francis, 1958, p. 293.
[46] Longacre, 1979, p.115.

A text planner needs to be capable of planning entire paragraphs of text. By making the constituent structure uniform above and below the level of the sentence, the text planner can use the same mechanisms for adding a paragraph to a text as an adjective to a noun phrase. A node in Text Structure can dominate a constituent of any size, from a word to a paragraph, to an entire text, capturing the uniformity of constituency at all of these levels.

Also uniform are the structural relations among constituents. Structural relations capture how a parent and its children are related, and, more importantly, where additional nodes can be added to the Text Structure. The structural relations form two basic subtree types in Text Structure, kernels and composites, as shown in Figure 4.5.

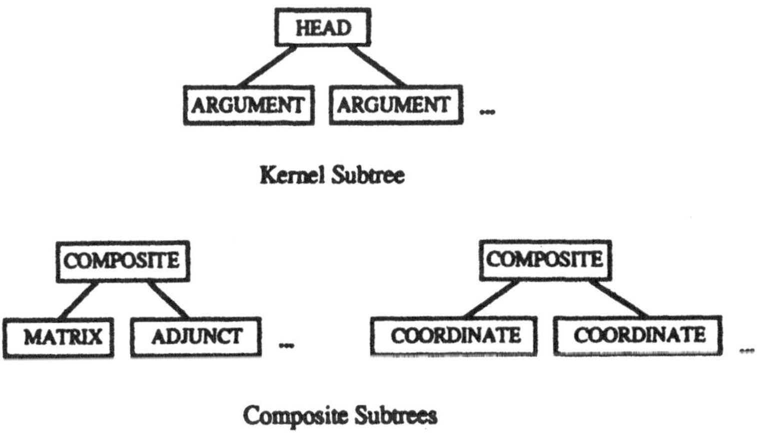

Figure 4.6 Subtree types

A **kernel** has a head at the root and arguments as children, and is essentially a predicate/argument structure, such as a relation expressed by a verb or a subordinate conjunction. A kernel is atomic, that is, it can only be extended top down in a single action of the text planner and its head (or head and a subset of the arguments) cannot be modified independently of the whole. A **composite** subtree can be built incrementally, that is new child nodes can be added after the initial expansion of the node.[47] There are two types of composite subtrees: the first has one special child, the matrix, and zero or more adjunct children; the second has two or more equal elements. This is similar to the distinction in systemic linguistics between parataxis and hypotaxis:

> *Parataxis is the linking of equal status. Both the initiating and continuing elements are free, in the sense that each could stand as a functioning whole. Hypotaxis is the binding of elements of unequal*

[47] Expansion must keep within the limits of top down, left to right constraints of the tree traversal, of course, which we describe in Chapter Five.

status. The dominant element is free, but the dependent element is not.[48]

These two kinds of structures are also distinguished from what Halliday calls a "multivariate" structure, "a configuration of different functional relationships, like theme-rheme, actor-process-beneficiary-goal.", which is similar to my kernel subtree type.

Another similarity between Halliday's paratactic/hypotactic distinction and my two types of composite subtrees is that the structures are independent of the size of the units being composed:

Parataxis and hypotaxis are general relations which are not restricted to the rank of the clause. They define complexes at any rank: clause complex, group or phrase complex, word complex.[49]

This is not necessarily adhered to by all those who use Halliday's theory in their work; Matthiessen & Thompson (1987) working in the RST framework, argue that clause combinings (both hypotactic and paratactic) should be treated with discourse relations (above the level of the sentence), but that other kinds of modification, such as adverbials and modifiers of noun phrases, should be treated differently. While they present strong arguments of why relations between clauses are similar to relations between sentences and paragraphs, they do not explain why they separate these from clause internal relations.

4.3. The Text Structure representation

In the previous section, we have described the Text Structure from a linguistic perspective, looking at what theoretical vocabulary can be used at Text Structure to abstract effectively over concrete linguistic resources and thus insure the selection of expressible combinations of resources. In this section, we describe Text Structure from the complementary perspective of a text planner. The central difference in viewing Text Structure from this perspective is that its role in organizing the process of composing the utterance comes to the forefront. In the discussion in §4.2, I focused on the capacity of Text Structure for constraining decision making and capturing distinctions; in this section, I focus on its actual use in the derivation of an utterance.

I first provide a definition of Text Structure[50] and then describe its representation in Spokesman's Text Planner. I look at what information is contained in a Text Structure node, then at what kinds of objects can fill the contents field of a node, and finally at the structural relations in a tree of nodes

[48] Halliday, 1985, p.198.

[49] Ibid.

[50] Note that I do not attempt a formal definition. I agree with the text linguist Beaugrande that "Formalism should not be undertaken too early. Unwieldy constructs borrowed from mathematics and logic are out of place in domains where the basic concepts are still highly

and what kinds of subtrees can be formed. In Chapter Five, we will look at how Spokesman constructs the Text Structure and uses it in its decision making.

4.3.1 *Definition of Text Structure*

Text Structure is a tree in which each node represents a constituent in the utterance being planned. Each node is a tuple containing the following:

- the information being expressed. This is called the "contents" of the node. It is either an application program object or a *Text Structure Object* with a semantic category and (when applicable) a lexical item, depending on the moment in the derivation;
- the structural relations to its parent and to its children;
- a backpointer to the object in the application program that the constituent expresses. (This need not be a single object in the application, but could be some part of an object or a composite of objects.)

4.3.2 *Text Structure nodes*

Text Structure nodes carry a great deal of information in them about the constituents they dominate, such as the information the constituent expresses and the semantic category of its expression. Nodes also are the bookkeepers of the text planner, recording information about the state of the traversal of the tree (e.g. whether a node is *new*, already *expanded*, or *completed*) and information about what objects have been referenced.

A node is a record structure with twelve slots, each of which is described below, including its possible values and role in the system. The first two represent the tree structure itself:

PARENT: the node which is the parent of this node (the root has no parent);

CHILDREN: a list of nodes that are the children (immediate constituents) of this node;

The next two slots contain the structural relations of the node:

STRUCTURAL RELATION TO PARENT: the function the node is playing in the tree with respect to its parents and siblings. The relations include *matrix, adjunct, argument, coordinate.*

STRUCTURAL RELATION TO CHILDREN: the function the node is playing in the tree with respect to its children. The relations include *head* and *composite*. The head relation indicates that it and its children (arguments) are an impenetrable subtree. Composites, which have one matrix child and zero or more adjunct children, are open to the addition of more adjuncts.

The next two are the links to the information the constituent expresses:

approximative. Such constructs give a false sense of security of having explained what has in fact only been rewritten in a formal language." (Beaugrande, 1981, p.4)

CONTENTS: a single object which represents the information that the constituent expresses. It may either be an object directly from the underlying applications program or it may be a *Text Structure object*, in which case it will both compose information from other sources and define a particular perspective on that information. Text Structure objects are typed by semantic category (e.g. *event, state, unique-individual, named-individual, anonymous-individual*, etc.). They are discussed in more detail in §4.3.3;

BACKPOINTER: points to the object in the application program that the constituent expresses. Retaining the backpointer independently of the contents assures that if a single entity is referred to by two different perspectives (with two different semantic categories) the text planner can know that they are in fact the same object for subsequent reference purposes.

The remaining slots are used by the control structure. I include them here for completeness; they are discussed in more detail in Chapter Five.

CONTROL-STATUS: one of *new, expanded, completed, expressed*. This value is altered by the two passes as the tree is built and traversed;

ANNOTATIONS: keep track of information about the constituent which is not already captured in the contents object, such as notations of tense, modality, or number. Annotations can be passed from parent to child in some cases, particularly in coordinate structures;

RESTRICTIONS: keep information about the semantic type restrictions on the contents of the node, for example whether the contents must be an *object* or a *proposition*. This also has consequences for what nodes may be added as children to this node;

ENTITIES-REFERENCED: a list of the application and Text Structure objects that are directly referenced at this node. (To get all the entities referenced within this constituent, you need to take both this field and *entities-referenced-below.)* This information is also stored in a table (reference-table) for easy access when determining whether a reference is new or a subsequent reference—given an object, the table returns the nodes that directly reference that object;

ENTITIES-REFERENCED-BELOW: a list of application and Text Structure objects that are referenced by the nodes below this one in the tree. This list is calculated as the traversal walks back up the tree in the first pass;

WEIGHT: the number of nodes beneath this node in the tree; it is calculated when a node is returned to so the value is either nil (node is not complete) or the exact (and unchanging) number of nodes beneath that one.[51]

[51] Weight is not currently used; it is intended to provide information to heuristics for extending the text structure.

4.3.3 *The contents of Text Structure nodes*

The contents field of a Text Structure node contains an object representing the information expressed by that constituent. Since object types are used to define mappings (links between object types and routines for processing objects of that type), the contents field is restricted to being a single, first-class typed object, rather than an expression or a list. The object may come directly from the application program or be a composite of application program objects (referred to as a "domain object") representing application program information, or it may be a Text Structure object, which aggregates information and commits it to a linguistically motivated semantic type.

In a strong sense, it is these objects that drive the processing of the text planner, as the mappings from their types determine what actions are to be taken when a node is being processed. As part of the actions, the contents of a node may change, beginning as an application program object and then being replaced by a Text Structure object carrying the same information but now also committing to a semantic type, such as EVENT or OBJECT. In this section we discuss each of these possibilities in more detail.

4.3.3.1 *Application program objects* In our data driven approach, the application program provides the content of the utterance. Thus instances of application program objects are part of the description of the utterance at the early stages of processing (i.e. they appear in the Text Structure early in the derivation of the utterance). These objects are processed by the text planner using predefined *mappings* from their types to the routines that know how to process instances of those type.

The fact that application program objects are allowed to populate the Text Structure poses interesting issues for the integration of the generation system and the application program. First, application objects must be of known types. For instance, there is no way to infer the meaning of a slot name in an application frame so as to decide how its value relates to the whole or to decide how that information should be used; this information must be expressly supplied. Second, how the types are organized within the application program will have consequences for the generator: the number of mappings decreases drastically if the types are hierarchically organized, since the mappings can often be associated with nodes further up the type hierarchy rather than needing a separate mapping for each type. Third, since the object types of the application program are used directly, no separate domain model is needed to drive the generator.

4.3.3.2 *Domain objects* It is often the case that the application program doesn't have a single object expressing a particular complex of information, yet for efficiency there is a requirement in my system that the text structure be populated with single, first-class objects, since such objects have a type that can be used unambiguously in the mappings to processing routines. When the application cannot supply a first-class object, a *domain object* is defined within the text planner as compensation. These objects are compensating for lacks in the application program. Some are general, that is, applicable to nearly all underlying programs, such as the object type TRIPLE, which is an instance of a frame-slot-value combination. It is important to be able to manipulate this kind of information as a unit; however, application programs rarely implement it as a first-class object, hence our compensation by making it a domain object. Figure 4.7 shows a portion of an application program object in the Main Street program, an instance of type person, and a domain object TRIPLE representing the relation between the person and her location.

```
#<PERSON KAREN
   CONCEPT-NAME: PERSON
   NAME: KAREN
   LOCATION: #<HOME MACK-AND-KARENS>
   JOB: NIL
        SKILLS: (#<MANAGING> #<COOKING>)
   ...>

#<TRIPLE
   OBJECT: #<PERSON KAREN>
   ROLE: LOCATION
   VALUE: #<HOME MACK-AND-KARENS>>
```

Figure 4.7 Application program object and domain object TRIPLE

Other object types are strictly topic specific and relate to the ways particular aggregations of information are conventionally expressed. For example, in military command and control applications, such as Semi-Automated Forces, orders to subordinate units are expressed in a five-paragraph format, where each paragraph has a specific function. We consequently define an "OPORD" domain object which has five fields to aggregate the information contained in each of the paragraphs of operations orders.

Another function of domain objects is to provide more informative objects where the application program simply has a primitive data structure, such as a string or number, which cannot be understood outside of its context. For example, if a vehicle object has a slot named "speed" whose value is an integer and another slot named "fuel-capacity" whose value is also an integer, there must be a way to determine that the measure for speed is in terms of miles per hour and that fuel capacity is in terms of gallons. We create an object of type SPEED and an object of type FUEL-CAPACITY, each with a value slot for the value and use instances of these objects instead of simply the integers.

4.3.3.3 *Text Structure objects* While objects from an application program are essential to drive the content of the utterance, their granularity is rarely isomorphic to what is required by the constituency of natural language, nor do they necessarily carry all of the information a constituent requires (such as tense, number, gender). To compensate, the text planner uses the Text Structure Objects (TSOs) which reflect the semantic categories readily expressed in language and the granularity of constituents in language. In

Sections 4.1 and 4.2, I discussed how we can develop the set of semantic categories by both abstraction over the concrete resources and by using the work of linguists who describe syntactic regularities in semantic terms. In this section, I describe the semantic categories that are used in Spokesman's set of TSOs. I also look at other kinds of TSOs that are used to control the derivation process and direct the selection of concrete resources once the Text Structure has been completed.

It is important to remember that Text Structure Objects reflect the semantic type of the *expression* of the information in an object, not necessarily some intrinsic type of the object itself. An object from the application program may map directly to a single Text Structure Object, to several different Text Structure Objects; or the Text Structure Object may not be derived from a single application object but rather be a composition of elements from various application objects. We discuss in Chapter Five how the text planner chooses between types when there are alternatives and how it composes types from elements of the application program.

We first list the set of Text Structure object types that reflect semantic categories currently used by the system and a description of each.

EVENT: This type represents a kernel event consisting of the action and its arguments; an event object has an event slot for the action and slots for each possible argument type. Those that are filled will become its children when the object is expanded. We are using the thematic relations agent, patient, source, goal, location, and theme as the set of possible argument types. This is meant to be a generic set as we have not yet looked closely at what will be needed overall. (Currently the system uses EVENT for both transition and process events.)

STATE: A state object has a state-relation slot and slots for theme and rheme. The theme argument is "what is being talked about" and the rheme argument is "what is being said about it".[52]

ACTIVITY: This type represents a non-temporally anchored, agentless event. It has a slot for the action and the same set of arguments as event (minus the agent slot).

OBJECTS: There are several kinds of OBJECTS, each binding some of the parameters expressible in a surface noun phrase.

INSTANCE-OF-KIND: singular, indefinite;

UNIQUE-OBJECT: singular, definite;

SAMPLE-OF-A-KIND: plural, indefinite;

DEFINITE-SET: plural, definite;

NAMED-OBJECT: singular, no determiner, proper name.

SUBORDINATE-RELATION: has a relation and an object related.

[52] Note this is a different use of theme than the "theme" that is a possible argument in an event argument, although their definitions in linguistic theory are very closely related.

COORDINATE-RELATION: has a relation (e.g. conjunction) and a list of objects related.

In addition to capturing semantic types, some Text Structure objects serve to direct the processing, as we will see in more detail in Chapter Five.

ARGUMENT-RELATION: The arguments of objects such as event and state are placed in argument-relation objects with a slot for the particular relation (such as theme, agent, etc.) and a slot for the object related. In an argument relation, the relation directs the mapping from the Text Structure to the linguistic specification, but does not itself appear in the utterance.

LEX: indicates this is a leaf of the text structure and that its contribution to the utterance will be a lexical item.

COMPLEX-EVENT: a composite object consisting of a matrix event and its adjuncts.

COMPLEX-STATE: a composite object consisting of a matrix state and its adjuncts.

COMPLEX-MODIFIER: a composite object consisting of a matrix modifier and its adjuncts.

4.3.4 *The Text Structure tree*

We have looked at the information contained in the individual nodes of the tree, and in particular at the types of objects that can fill the CONTENTS slot of the node. We now return to the tree itself and look at how it captures the *constituency* of the utterance.

Text Structure nodes are related in two ways: (1) by standard tree relations (parent, child); (2) by a set of structural relations: matrix, adjunct, head, argument, coordinate. As I described in §4.2.2, these relations form two basic kinds of subtrees.[53] In the first, which we term a KERNEL tree, the root is the head element and governs the relations of children to it. In the second, a COMPOSITE tree, the root just serves to gather the children into a constituent. In one type of composite tree, one of the children is special (the matrix) and the others are related to it (as adjuncts); the root serves to dominate the matrix and adjuncts, but is not itself a relation. The second composite tree type is a COORDINATE tree, where the head is a relation such as "conjunction" or "disjunction" and all the children relate to it equally.

The main distinction between the kernel and composite subtrees is that kernels are atomic and cannot be extended once they are expanded. In contrast, composites can be extended incrementally. New children can be added to composites at any time (within the bounds defined by the tree traversal algorithm, which we will describe in detail in Chapter Five).

In any internal subtree in the Text Structure, each node has two relations, one with respect to its parent and siblings and another with respect to its

[53] Subtrees here refer to only a node and its immediate children; we are not presently addressing definitions for multilevel subtrees.

children. For example, a node that is the matrix of a composite could also be the root of a kernel, and thus be a head with respect to its children.

4.3.4.1 *Resource trees* As part of the resource knowledge used by the text planner, we define *resource trees*, which are reified instances of the tree types. For example, Figure 4.8 shows the definition for a COMPLEX-EVENT-TREE, which restricts the matrix to being a Text Structure Object of type STATE or EVENT and restricts the adjuncts to being of type MANNER or LOCATION. It also specifies a constructor function which builds the subtree.

```
(define-composite-tree complex-event-tree (matrix &rest adjuncts)
  :constructor-function build-complex-event-tree
  :matrix-restrictions (state event)
  :adjunct-restrictions (manner location))
```

Figure 4.8 Resource-tree definition

Resource trees provide a library of basic elements that the text planner can select. A resource tree for the text planner can either be a kernel subtree, a composite subtree, or a combination of basic trees; however, they must be minimal in the sense that there are no internal recursive nodes. We return to subtree types and their role in the text planner in Chapter Five, where we describe how the text planner uses resource trees in the construction of the Text Structure.

5 The Architecture of Spokesman

In the previous chapter, I described the theoretical motivations behind the Text Structure representation and defined its implementation in the Spokesman Generation system. As we saw, these two perspectives on the same representation led to different considerations in the actual details. In particular, the actual implementation must organize the process of composing the utterance in addition to providing the constraints and capturing the possibilities necessary for ensuring expressibility and expressiveness.

In this chapter, I look at the role of Text Structure in Spokesman: how Spokesman constructs the Text Structure and how it then uses it to construct the linguistic specification that is input to the linguistic realization component. Spokesman provides an instance of how a text planner can use the Text Structure. The actual choice and construction mechanisms in Spokesman are independent of the theory of the terms and expressions that make up the Text Structure and the necessity of this level of representation for text planning.

The examples in this chapter are from two of the military domains Spokesman has generated text for. I begin with examples from the AirLand Battle Management project (ALBM), which, along with being the first application Spokesman was integrated with, also has the simplest examples: the objects in ALBM are so predictable that there was no need for elaborate choice mechanisms, and the target text was specified by military training documents, so there was little choice in how they could be expressed. The goal in using these examples is to walk through the basic construction mechanisms without the complication of the choice mechanisms. For later examples, I use the Semi-Automated Forces domain, which produces similar texts as ALBM (Operations Orders for military units), but has more opportunity for variety since the underlying objects are themselves more complex and varied that those in ALBM. In Chapter Six, I walk through a detailed example of all the mechanisms described in this chapter using the Main Street simulation for examples.

5.1 Overview of Spokesman

In this first section, I preview the overall architecture of the system as it was described in Chapter One. While the system is conceptually divided into two components, a text planner and a linguistic realization component, its more salient architectural feature is its division into multiple levels of representation, each increasingly less abstract and more linguistic, from the application program objects to the final text. The components and levels are shown in Figure 5.1.

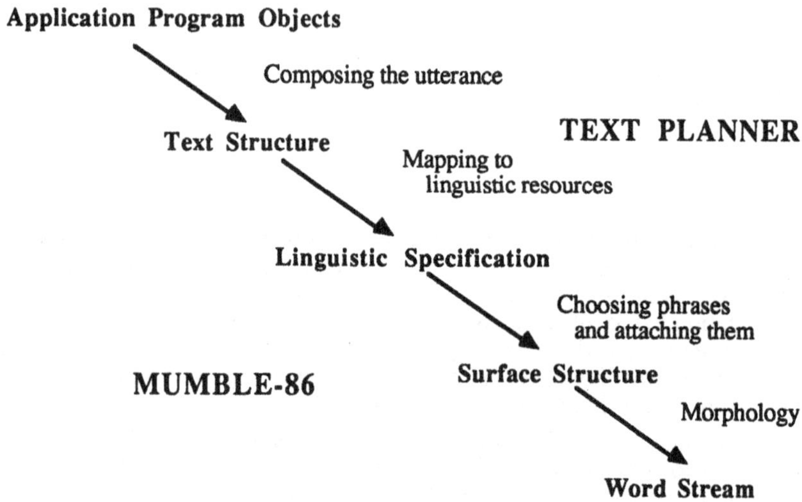

Figure 5.1 Levels of representation in Spokesman

Multiple levels of representation contribute to the use of *progressive refinement*, wherein the text planner begins by building an abstract representation of the utterance, and then fills in details conservatively, as it passes through the levels. The careful choice of an abstract representation in which to plan is an essential part of progressive refinement, since the terms in which the planning is done must serve to constrain the decisions so that no choice is made that will ultimately lead to the failure of the plan. The Text Structure constrains the actions taken by the planner to ensure that it will not have to backtrack and that the utterance being planned will be *expressible* in the target language, that is that there will be linguistic resources available to realize the elements of the plan and their composition will be in accordance with the rules of composition in the language.

A key factor in making the system efficient is its use of *message directed control*, that is the representation of the utterance at each of the levels controls the processing. Text Structure controls processing in two ways:

- The order of the actions taken is controlled by the *tree structure*: it is constructed top down and left to right, and it is traversed top down to produce the linguistic specification.
- What actions are taken at each node of the tree are governed by the *mapping* from the object in the contents of that node to the routines or choice sets for processing it.

In the rest of this chapter, I look in detail at the processes and objects used by the text planner both to construct the Text Structure and from it to produce the linguistic specification which is input to the linguistic realization component.

5.2. Building the Text Structure

In this section, we look more closely at the processes that construct the Text Structure. The main construction operation is increasing the depth and breadth of the tree by adding more nodes. In addition, the Text Structure construction processes may affect the CONTENTS of the nodes, e.g. by replacing application program objects with Text Structure objects of particular semantic categories. The processes also choose or build objects for the CONTENTS of subnodes being added. The routines may annotate the nodes with information that may be needed deeper in the tree or later when building the linguistic specification for that constituent, and they may place restrictions on the nodes to guide later expansions and extensions.

We first provide an overview of the two construction processes that add nodes to the tree, *expanding* and *extending*, and the resource objects used by these processes. Next, we look at an example of how these resources are used. Finally, we look at some of the finer-grained choices made by the Text Structure construction processes. The control structure itself is described in detail in §5.4.

5.2.1 *Expanding and extending Text Structure nodes*

The Text Structure tree is constructed using one of two operations:

- EXPANDING: This is a *top down* construction process. When a node is being visited for the first time (see §5.4: control), the CONTENTS of the node is mapped to a routine that divides it into subconstituents, builds nodes for those subconstituents, and adds the new nodes as children to the current node. (All arguments are introduced as a result of expansions.)
- EXTENDING: This operation grows the tree from *left to right*. After the node has been expanded, new children may be added at the rightward edge. (Linearization of subnodes in the Text Structure need not correlate with linearization in the final text.) Extensions always occur at composite nodes and the children are added as adjuncts. The Text Structure tree may be extended either immediately after expanding a node or as the traversal returns back up the tree. Once a node is "completed" (i.e. it is below and to the left of the point of traversal), it cannot be extended further. (See the discussion of control in §5.4 for a more complete description.)

These two operations are equivalent to the operations of a Tree Adjoining Grammar (TAG, Joshi 1985). Minimally, a TAG comprises a library of elementary trees (which are minimal in the sense that there are no internal recursive nodes) which can be composed using one of two basic operations: substitution and adjunction. Text Structure is a TAG in that the resource trees (see §4.3.4.1), which are selected by the text planner, are minimal and the two operations for composing Text Structure, expansion and extension, are equivalent to the TAG operations of substitution and adjunction.

The advantages of a TAG for generation at the syntactic level are argued by Joshi (1987) and exemplified in McDonald & Meteer (1990). Similar advantages exist for TAGs at the text planning, including incremental generation and defining an appropriate domain of locality. As pointed out by Joshi in a recent talk,[54] it would be surprising if the structure of discourse were significantly less complex than the structure of syntax. He argued that a grammar for discourse should have the power of a tree adjoining grammar, and not just the power of a context free grammar which is the case for most discourse grammars, which only have substitution operations, such as RST.

There is another advantage of using a tree adjoining grammar at the text planning level when the linguistic realization component is also as TAG (as in the case of Spokesman, which uses Mumble-86 as the linguistic component). There is a natural correspondence between the derivation of the structures at the planning level with the derivation of the surface realization, since both use the same mechanisms for composition. Furthermore, the elementary trees of the Text Structure which have realizations as phrases at the syntactic level are lexically headed and are typed with a semantic category that maps to a syntactic phrase type (e.g. event --> clause; object --> noun phrase). The combination of lexeme and semantic category defines a mapping between the structures at the text planning level and the tree families at the syntactic level which assures that the realization accurately reflects the underlying semantic structure. Shieber and Schabes (1990) defining a similar mapping between logical forms and the elementary trees which they call "Synchronous TAGs". However, that mapping is stipulated, whereas the mapping in Text Structure is derived from the linguistic abstractions in the text planner.

5.2.1.1 *Expanding Text Structure nodes* Expanding the Text Structure is a top-down process that adds children to the leaf nodes of the tree. Expansion is directed by a mapping associated with the object in the contents of the leaf currently being processed. A *mapping* is a fixed link between an object and the possible actions that can be carried out. In general, the mapping is defined for an object *type*, rather than for individual objects and is used by all objects of that type. Mappings have parameters that are evaluated when they are used.

When there is only one possible action, the mapping is to a *template*, which defines a sequence of actions to be taken when the mapping is instantiated. When multiple actions are possible, the mapping is to a class of alternatives, called a *realization class*; each alternative in the class is characterized by the situation in which it can be used.

In the examples discussed in Section 3.2 (e.g. "The 10th Corps defends forward in sector"), the task descriptions were generated from Task Objects which all have the same set of slots: who, what, why, when, and where (in contrast, for example, to the SAF application, where the set of slots is dependent on the type of task). This uniformity allows us to use a template to expand the

54 "Tree Adjoining Grammars for Natural Language Generation" at the Soviet Workshop on Text Generation, Borjomi, Georgia, former USSR, September 23-27, 1991.

text structure. Figure 5.2 shows the mapping and text structure template for the Task Objects.

```
(define-mapping (k:unit 'K::MISSION.TASK.OBJECTS)55
  :class-to-text-structure-table
   (:template-name expand-task-object
    :arguments ( (get.value current-task-object 'k::what)
                 (get.value current-task-object 'K::where)
                 (get.value current-task-object 'K::when)
                 (get.value current-task-object 'K::why)))

(define-text-structure-template EXPAND-TASK-OBJECT (what where when why)
 (let ((main-event (instantiate-task-action-mapping what)))
    (create-a-subnode :root current-node
                      :contents main-event
                      :relation 'matrix)
    (if when (instantiate-text-structure-mapping when))
    (if where (create-a-subnode :root current-node
                                :contents where
                                :relation 'adjunct))
    (if why (create-a-subnode   :root current-node
                                :contents why
                                :relation 'adjunct))
    (put-children-on-agenda (children current-node))))
```

Figure 5.2 Mapping and template for TASK OBJECTS[56]

The DEFINE-MAPPING form sets up the mapping from the KEE unit MISSION.TASK.OBJECTS (a type in the KEE knowledge base used for this application) to a template. The arguments, which access the values of the unit's slots, are expressions that will be evaluated when the mapping is applied. (We discuss the mapping process and where else it is used in the text planner in §5.4.)

When using a template like this, some of the actions taken will differ depending on the value of the slot; for example, different event objects will be built depending on the value of the WHAT slot: the value DEFEND builds an intransitive event (e.g. "The 10th Corps defends in Area Alpha"), the value COVERING.FORCE builds a transitive event with the verb "conduct" (e.g. "The 10th Corps conducts covering force operations"). In order to handle this variation, the EXPAND-TASK-OBJECT template creates an EVENT object by instantiating another, embedded mapping for the value of the WHAT parameter (the TASK-ACTION-MAPPING) which combines the WHAT and the WHO into an EVENT object (look at the first line of the EXPAND-TASK-OBJECT template). An example of this mapping, as used by instances of the KEE type DEFEND to the INTRANSITIVE-EVENT template, is shown in Figure 5.3. Since the agent is always composed with the action, the WHO parameter is accessed as part of the

55 The prefix "k:" indicates that this is a symbol or function bound in the application program.

56 This code has been slightly modified to improve readability.

task-action-mapping. The EVENT object returned by the embedded mapping is placed in the matrix subnode by the template. When the WHERE and WHY slots have values, these objects are simply placed in adjunct subnodes without change; they will be transformed into Text Structure objects and expanded when the tree traversal process reaches them (see discussion of control in §5.4.)

```
(define-task-action-mapping (k:unit 'K::DEFEND)
  :template-name INTRANSITIVE-EVENT
  :arguments (  current-action
                (get.value current-task-object 'K::WHO)))

(define-text-structure-template INTRANSITIVE-EVENT (event agent)
   (build-event-object event agent))
```

Figure 5.3 Mapping and template for DEFEAT Action

Figure 5.4 shows the TASK OBJECT from the application program and the expansion of the Text Structure that occurs when the example template is executed for it. This particular task object will be realized as "The 10th Corps defends forward in sector to force the lead divisions to deploy". The Text Structure began as simply the node marked TOP with MISSION.TASK.OBJECTS99 as its contents. When the mapping for objects of type MISSION.TASK.OBJECTS (in Figure 5.2) was called, the what, where, when, and why parameters were bound to the value of those slots in that instance of the task object (i.e. the instance MISSION.TASK.OBJECTS99). Then the template EXPAND-TASK-OBJECT was executed, adding the three subnodes to the tree.

```
(MISSION.TASK.OBJECTS99
 ((WHAT (#[Unit: ACTIONS100 FC.3]))
  (WHAT.OBJECT ())
  (WHERE (#[Unit: LOCATIONS102 FC.3]))
  (WHY (#[Unit: PURPOSES82 FC.3]))
  (WHEN ())
  (WHO (#[Unit: UNITS.FRIENDLY105 FC.3]))
  ))
```

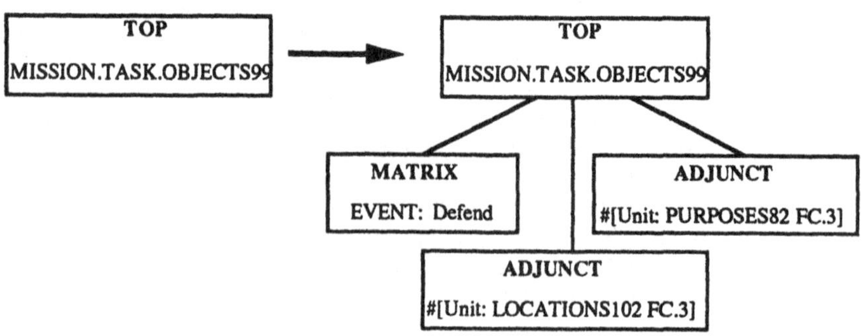

Figure 5.4 Application object and expanded Text Structure

5.2.1.2 *Choosing among alternative expansions* In the previous example, there were no alternatives in how the Text Structure could be expanded—the work was done by templates and the templates were implemented as open code, which means that there were no explicit principles constraining what actions have have been taken. When working with static and predictable application programs, these techniques are sufficient (see McDonald & Meteer 1988). However, as applications become more complex and as more variety in the text is required, the decision-making processes of the text planner need to be more sophisticated.

In this section, I describe the resource objects used to extend the Text Structure in this more complex situation: resource trees and realization classes. In §5.2, I show an example of how realization classes are used to make choices.

To define better the possible ways the Text Structure can be extended, we use *resource trees*: predefined Text Structure subtrees that are instantiated as needed (see discussion in §4.3). These resource trees are gathered into *realization classes*, which define the choices available to the text planner for any given case. Realization classes play the same role as templates, but they provide greater versatility and discipline. Realization classes are used in cases such as a DEFEND action in the application program which could be realized either as an event ("The 23rd Tank Battalion defended Objective Alpha") or as an object ("The 23rd Tank Battalion's defense of Objective Alpha"). Since these alternatives are common to many kinds of actions, their structure can be predefined (as was shown in §4.3) and then collected into a realization class to facilitate the text planner choosing between them, depending on the context. Part of developing the Text Structure representation has been developing a grammar of resource trees, analogous to the elementary trees of a Tree Adjoining Grammar (Joshi 1987). The set of trees in a TAG define the possible phrases in the language and the points in them where additional phrases may be added. Analogously, the set of resource trees defines the allowable Text Structure subtrees and the ways they can be extended.

This notion of classes of alternatives is used throughout the text planner and linguistic realization component. For example, *argument structure classes* group the alternative surface argument structures of individual verbs and are drawn on in the mapping from text structure to a linguistic specification (see §5.3.4). *Tree families*[57] in the linguistic realization component group syntactic phrases (elementary trees in the TAG grammar) to be used in the mapping from the linguistic specification to the surface structure. In all cases, each alternative in a class consists of some structure that will be instantiated if that alternative is chosen, plus a set of characteristics that differentiates that alternative from the others in the class. When the class is executed, the characteristics are compared

[57] The use of the term "tree families" for the classes of alternatives in Mumble is relatively recent (since the 1987 documentation, in which they were called "realization classes") and reflects their similarity to the constructions of the same name in TAG theory. (See Schabes *et al.* 1988.)

to the context provided by the representational level at which the choice is made (i.e. Text Structure for realization classes and surface structure for tree families). If more than one choice (alternative) in a class is acceptable, then a simple mechanism, such as taking the first choice or the most specific choice, is used to select one of them.

A realization class has two sets of alternatives, *expression choices* and *elaboration choices*.[58] When a realization class is used, the first thing that happens is one of the expression choices (i.e. a resource tree) is chosen and instantiated to expand the Text Structure tree at its present point. This top-down action determines the constituents of the node being expanded. Next, each of the elaboration choices is evaluated to determine which are *salient*, that is whether the information in them is interesting in this context. From this subset, those that are also legal (that is, their resulting semantic type is consistent with the current context) are added into the text structure at this time; the other salient but incompatible choices are put on a global list from which they may be added to the Text Structure later on if possible. We discuss saliency and legality in more detail in §5.2.2.

```
(define-realization-class MARCH (who)
 :EXPRESSION
 ((:result-type proposition
   :body        (complex-event-tree  :matrix (:event self :agent who)
                                     :adjuncts () ))
  (:result-type object
   :body        (complex-object-tree :type uniplex-discrete-individual
                                     :matrix ((build-lex-leaf self))
                                     adjuncts () ))
 :ELABORATION
 ((ROUTE
   :result-object  (triple self 'route (get-slot-value 'route))
   :result-type    path
   :salience       interesting-route)
  (FORMATION
   :result-object  (triple self 'formation (get-slot-value 'formation))
   :result-type    manner
   :salience       interesting-formation)))
```

Figure 5.5 Realization class[59]

Figure 5.5 shows a realization class. It has two expression choices: the first will result in an EVENT perspective (e.g. *the 23rd TB marches*) and the second in an OBJECT perspective (*a march* or *the march*, depending on the context). There are also two elaboration choices: one adds the route of the march (*along route alpha from ES7088 to ES7018*) and another adds the formation information (*in line formation*).

[58] In more recent applications (such as Main Street), these two sets of alternatives have been given separate classes (realization classes and expression classes) rather than being two parts of one resource object. This is a notational change, trying to make the purpose of the objects clearer, and does not reflect any theoretical difference.

[59] SELF is a special variable bound to the object that is mapped to this realization class.

An expression choice establishes the structure that will be built if the choice is taken, along with its arguments (all in the :BODY field). In the first choice in Figure 5.5, the body is the resource tree COMPLEX-EVENT-TREE, with keyword arguments for the matrix and adjuncts. Figure 5.6 shows the definition of this tree.

```
(define-composite-tree COMPLEX-EVENT-TREE (matrix &rest adjuncts)
  :constructor-function BUILD-COMPLEX-EVENT-TREE
  :matrix-restrictions (STATE EVENT)
  :adjunct-restrictions (MANNER LOCATION TIME))
```

Figure 5.6 Resource tree

As I have said, an expression choice also includes the characteristics for distinguishing among choices. The characteristics of each choice are compared with the current situation (the context provided by the Text Structure built so far) and the one that fits is chosen. Expression choices use two kinds of characteristics: a RESULT-TYPE and a general TEST function. The RESULT-TYPE indicates the semantic category of the new contents object if this choice is picked (semantic categories are described in Chapter Four). If there are restrictions on the current node, the selection process checks that the RESULT-TYPE is consistent with them. (If there are no restrictions, any type is considered legal.) Next, if there is a TEST field (there are none in example 5.4), the function in that field is evaluated to see if it is satisfied in the current context. (Again, the lack of a test is interpreted as positive, rather than negative.) If there is more than one legal choice, the first one is chosen.[60]

Other characteristics for distinguishing among choices are being experimented with, such as ILLOCUTION and FACET. ILLOCUTION would distinguish among speech acts, such as "describe" or "refer", "question", "contrast", or other discourse functions of the expression. FACET would pick out the aspect (subpart) of the contents object this choice will express. We are still exploring the vocabulary for these and other fields.

5.2.1.3 *Extending the Text Structure using elaboration choices* Elaboration choices specify the different aspects of an object that may be added to the utterance. Each choice gives the resulting structure and the characteristics for making the choice. In considering whether to take an elaboration choice, the result-object field of the choice must be evaluated to produce the object which would become the contents of the node to be added if this choice is taken. In the current applications, the result is generally a frame-slot-value triple or a conjunction of such triples;[61] however, the result could in principle be any first-class object. Once this new object has been made available, the choice's characteristics are checked to see if it is important enough in the present context to be included and if it can legally to be added to the Text Structure.

[60] This could be improved by adding the notion of "most specific", as is done in tree families.

[61] Note that as I discussed in Chapter Four, §4.3.3, triple objects are Text Structure object compensating for the lack of comparable first-class objects in the application program.

In order to determine whether the information the object conveys is important enough to be included given this context, the expression in the choice's SALIENCE-FUNCTION field is evaluated. Salience functions can be very particular and are usually domain dependent. The salience function DEFAULT-INCLUSION-CHECK simply ensures that the result-object is well defined (i.e. its parts are not nil). Other salience functions in the current version of Spokesman are INSTANCE-ONLY, which checks that the object is an instance, rather than a class, and GENERIC-DESCRIPTION-ONLY, which checks the opposite. Two other fields are also included in the design, but not used in the two military domains: RELATION, which specifies how the elaborating information is related to the whole, and SUBJECT-AREA, which is a list of subjects that are checked against the subjects-of-interest slots on dominating Text Structure nodes.

In order to determine whether an object may be added to the text structure at the current node, the selection process compares its RESULT-TYPE with the restrictions on the current node. The following correspondences indicate what combinations are legal:[62] (The type PROPOSITION covers semantic categories COMPLEX-EVENT and COMPLEX-STATE.)

result-type	restriction on current node
proposition	paragraph
manner	proposition
time	proposition
location	proposition or object
property	object

If the choice is both salient and legal, the object is added as an adjunct to the current Text Structure node. The relation of the adjunct is determined by the type of restriction on the current node. If the restriction is a proposition, it is added as a clausal adjunct, such as TIME, PATH, or LOCATION. If it is an object, it is added as a restrictive-modifier, such as PROPERTY.

If the choice is salient but not legal, it is added to a global list of optional-information-to-be-included. This list associates SELF (the object that was mapped to the class containing this choice) with the result object of the choice. In a subsequent pass up the tree, the choice will then be reconsidered at other points in the tree where SELF is mentioned to see if it is legal to be added there and added if it is.

Figure 5.7 shows another example of an elaboration choice:

```
(ROUTE-STARTPOINT
    :result-object (triple self 'dm.from[63] (point1-in-linear-objective self))
    :result-type   location
    :salience      default-inclusion-check)
```

Figure 5.7 Elaboration choice

[62] This list reflects what I have encountered in the current applications; it is by no means meant to be exhaustive.

[63] The "dm." prefix is a reminder that this is a symbol indicating the relation and not the word "from".

The first element in the choice is simply a label and is not used in the processing. The result-object field defines a frame-slot-value TRIPLE relating the application program object bound to SELF to the value of the expression (POINT1-IN-LINEAR-OBJECTIVE SELF) via the relation 'DM.FROM. (This triple has its own mapping to a realization class with its possibilities for expression.) The result-type of the choice is the semantic type LOCATION and the salience function is a default function that simply checks to see if there is in fact a value in the value slot of the triple.

5.2.2 *Using realization classes*

In this section, we go through a more detailed example of how the mechanisms described in the previous section extend and elaborate the Text Structure. I use the following utterance as an example: *A/1 TB withdraws along Route Gamma from ES70886 to ES701808 at 181548 May. The rear guard is 3/A/1 TB.* We begin at the point in the planning process where an application program object is the contents of a leaf text structure node, in this case the matrix of the task paragraph node, as shown in Figure 5.8.

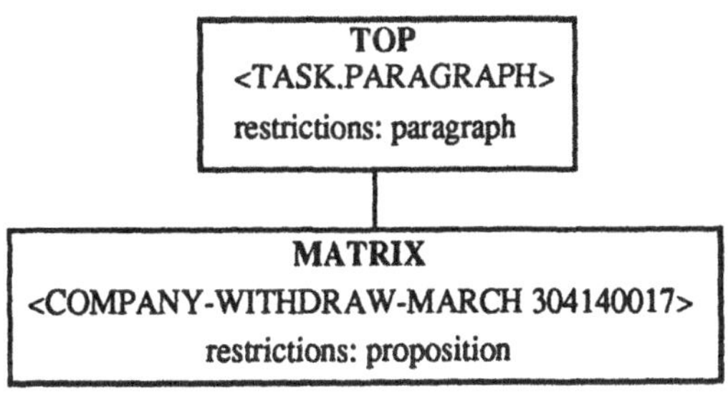

Figure 5.8 Text Structure in progress

In the ALBM example of the previous section, the application object was mapped to a *template* via its type; all task objects in ALBM were of the same type (MISSION.TASK.OBJECT) and all had the same set of slots (who, what, where, etc.). In this example, which is from the Semi-Automated Forces application (SAF), there are many types of tasks and the form a hierarchy in SAF's knowledge base. The set of slots is dependent on the type. The application object being expressed (shown in Figure 5.9) is mapped to a *realization class* (rather than a template) using the MAPPING for its type (also shown in Figure 5.9). The mapping takes the object to the section class WITHDRAW (Figure 5.10) and binds the parameter WHO of the class to #<WP-TANK-COMPANY WP-TANK-COMPANY-503 327027676>, ROUTE to #<COMPANY-RTE 304114775>, and the special variable SELF to the object #<COMPANY-WITHDRAW-MARCH 304140017>.

```
#<COMPANY-WITHDRAW-MARCH 304140017
    ((FORMATION NIL)
    (ROUTE . #<COMPANY-RTE 304114775>)
    (REAR-GUARD . PLATOON3)
    (START-TIME . 2820512907)
    (WHO . #<WP-TANK-COMPANY WP-TANK-COMPANY-503 327027676>))>

(DEFINE-MAPPING (concept 'COMPANY-WITHDRAW-MARCH)[64]
  class-to-realization-class-table
  (:realization-class WITHDRAW
  :arguments ((get-slot-value 'WHO) (get-slot-value 'ROUTE)))
...)
```

Figure 5.9 Instance of COMPANY-WITHDRAW-MARCH and mapping

The first step is to choose from the list of expression choices in the WITHDRAW realization class and expand the Text Structure accordingly. As in our earlier example, there are two expression choices in this class: one which results in a PROPOSITION and another which results in an OBJECT. These result types are matched with the type restrictions on the node being expanded to see if this choice can legally fill the node. Since the restriction on the current node is PROPOSITION, the first choice, which results in a proposition, is chosen.

The body of this choice builds an instance of the *resource tree* COMPLEX-EVENT-TREE with an EVENT as the matrix and a PATH relation as an adjunct. To instantiate this tree, its definition is consulted. Its constructor function does the following:

(1) replaces the object #<COMPANY-WITHDRAW-MARCH 304140017> in the current node with a COMPLEX-EVENT Text Structure Object;

(2) builds an EVENT object with one argument (the WHO as the agent) and puts it in a MATRIX subnode below the complex event;

(3) builds a RELATION object with the relation PATH and the related object, the TRIPLE (self 'route route), and puts it in an ADJUNCT subnode below the complex event.

The resulting Text Structure is shown in Figure 5.11.

[64] This form also sets up mappings to other tables which we do not show here. We return to this example and discuss the other mappings in sections 5.3 and 5.4.

```
(DEFINE-REALIZATION-CLASS WITHDRAW (who route)
 :EXPRESSION
 ((:result-type       proposition
   :body  (complex-event-tree
           :matrix (:event self  :agent who)
           :adjuncts ((  :relation path
                         :object (triple self 'route route))))
  (:result-type       object
   :body  (complex-object-tree  :type uniplex-discrete-individual
                                :matrix ((build-lex-leaf self))
                                :adjuncts  () )))
 :ELABORATION
 ((START-TIME
    :result-object    (triple self start-time
                       (make-military-time-from-simulation-time
                        (get-slot-value self 'start-time)))
    :salience         default-inclusion-check
    :result-type      time)
  (FORMATION
    :result-object    (triple self 'formation
                       (get-slot-value self 'formation))
    :result-type      manner
    :salience         interesting-formation)
  (REAR-GUARD
    :result-object    (triple self 'rear-guard
                      (get-slot-value self 'rear-guard))
    :result-type      proposition
    :salience         default-inclusion-check))
```

Figure 5.10 Mapping and realization class for WITHDRAW

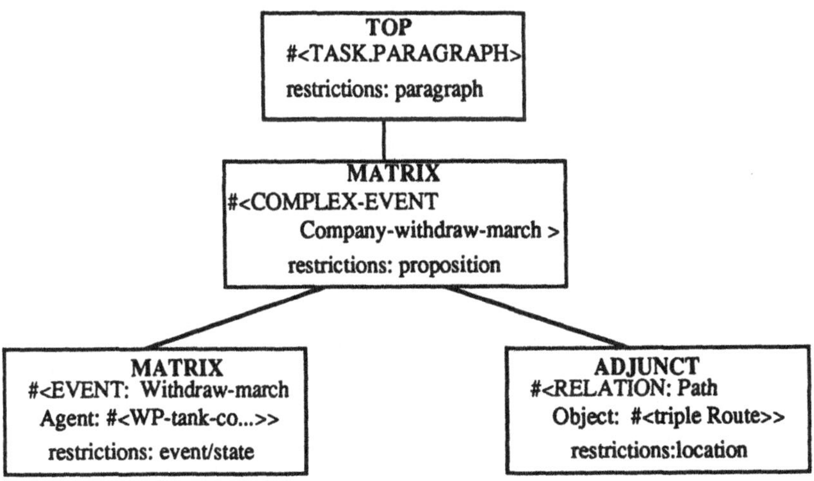

Figure 5.11 Text Structure after expansion

The next step is to choose among the elaboration choices of the realization class. There are three elaboration choices in this example: the start-time, formation, and rear-guard. The same actions will be taken for each: the text planner evaluates the result-object field in each choice, and builds a TRIPLE. It then checks the salience function to determine if the information expressed by the triple is interesting enough to be included. Finally, it checks the result type to determine whether the object can be added to the text structure at this point. As the current position in the text structure is still the matrix node with the PROPOSITION restriction, any choice which has a LOCATION, MANNER or TIME as a result type may be added as an adjunct. Let us look at each choice in turn:

- The START-TIME has a value, so it is considered interesting by the criteria of the default-inclusion-check, and results in a TIME type, which is compatible, so it is added in as an adjunct, as shown in Figure 5.12.
- The FORMATION does not have a value in this instance of the COMPANY-WITHDRAW-MARCH, so it is not considered salient and is thus not included.
- The REAR-GUARD has a value, but its result type is PROPOSITION, which cannot be added at this node. Therefore, the TRIPLE is placed on the list of *OPTIONAL-INFORMATION-TO-BE-INCLUDED* which will be checked later in the processing.

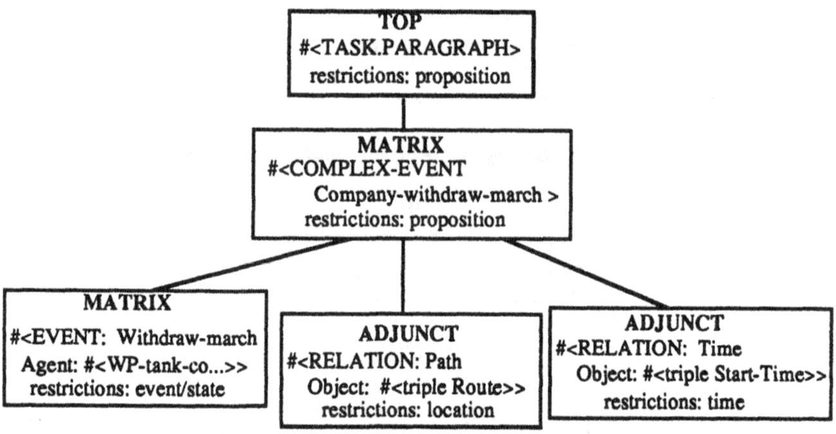

Figure 5.12 Text Structure with adjunct added

Later, when the control eventually returns up the tree to the Task Paragraph node (TOP), the rear-guard TRIPLE is added into the Text Structure since a proposition type may be added at that node. The final result is shown in Figure 5.13. (See §5.4 for a more complete discussion of the control loop.)

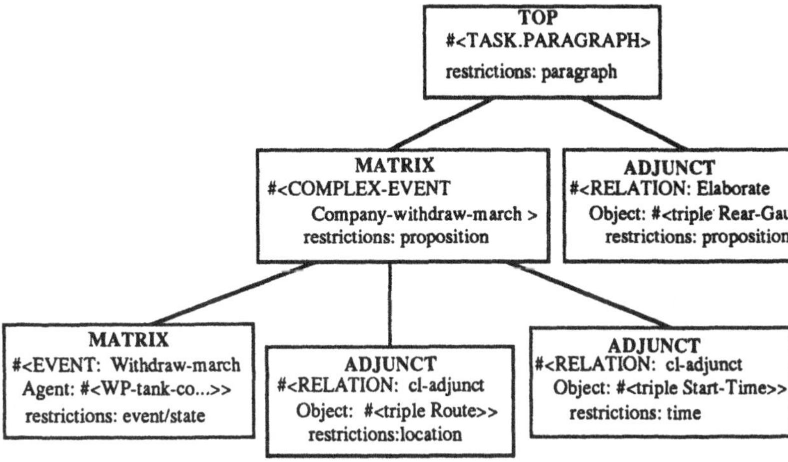

Figure 5.13 Text Structure after extension

5.2.3 *Making finer-grained choices*

As we saw in our previous examples, the Text Structure building procedures not only add nodes to the tree, they also create Text Structure objects and place them as the contents of nodes, often replacing the application object that was originally there. This commits the information in the node to be expressed as a particular semantic type, such as EVENT or OBJECT. In the case of the OBJECT type, a finer-grained choice needs to be made.[65] In §3.2, we listed the various subtypes of OBJECT and the different perspectives they express, for example a "unique object" (*the man*), a "definite set" (*the men*), an "instance of a kind" (*a man*). In this section we look at how the generator chooses among such alternatives.

We first look at the context in which this choice is made. Consider, for example, a subsequent utterance to our previous example. If after having said "A/1 TB withdraws along Route Gamma from ES70886 to ES701808 at 181548 May. The rear guard is 3/A/1 TB", the planner decides that the information that the march was completed is to be expressed, then it could be expressed as "The withdraw march was completed at 182015 May". Figure 5.14 shows the Text Structure in progress where the object #<COMPANY-WITHDRAW-MARCH 304140017> is now the argument to the matrix and has the restriction OBJECT.

[65] Finer choices will also need to be made for other types, such as EVENT, but given the needs of the military domains we have not yet addressed those types in as much detail as OBJECT.

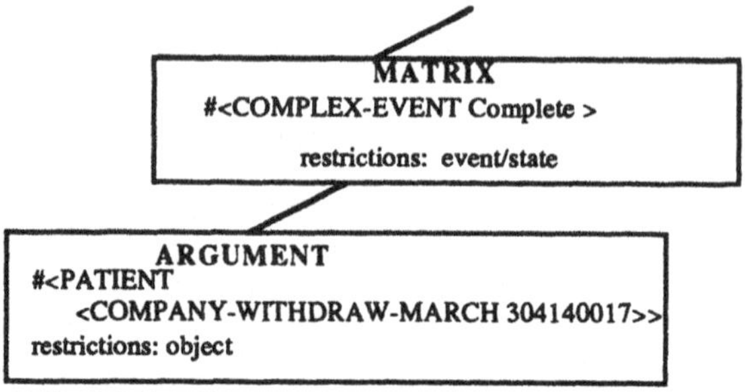

Figure 5.14 Partial Text Structure for "The withdraw march was completed..."

As in the previous example, the object <COMPANY-WITHDRAW-MARCH 304140017> uses the mapping for its type, COMPANY-WITHDRAW-MARCH, to the realization class WITHDRAW (shown in Figure 5.10). In this context, we will take a different choice from the realization class because the restrictions on the node are OBJECT, rather than PROPOSITION, as was the case in our earlier example. The second choice from the WITHDRAW realization class will be chosen (shown in Figure 5.15). This choice has as its body the resource tree COMPLEX-OBJECT-TREE.

```
(DEFINE-REALIZATION-CLASS WITHDRAW (who route)
 :EXPRESSION
 ((
    ... )
  (:result-type        object
   :body               (complex-object-tree
                            :type uniplex-discrete-individual
                            :matrix (build-lex-leaf self)
                            :adjuncts ()) ) )
...)
```

Figure 5.15 A realization choice

Like the COMPLEX-EVENT-TREE choice in our previous example, the COMPLEX-OBJECT-TREE choice has arguments MATRIX and ADJUNCTS. These arguments are handled in much the same way as those in the complex event tree choice shown earlier when the tree is constructed. This choice also has another argument, TYPE, which may be either one of the subtypes of complex object (INSTANCE-OF-A-KIND, UNIQUE-OBJECT, DEFINITE-SET, SAMPLE-OF-A-KIND, etc.) or, as in this case, it may be a class of alternatives, called a *perspective class*, which groups together several subtypes along with the characteristics that distinguish them. (Note that this is analogous to the use of templates when there is only one possibility and realization classes when there are multiple alternatives.)

A perspective class is used when there are still degrees of freedom left open, in particular what semantic category the constituent as a whole should be expressed as. In this example, the context restricts the choice to be expressed as an object, but the choice still remains whether it should be expressed as an instance-of-a-kind (*a withdraw march*) or a known-individual (*the withdraw march*) or, if more than one march is being referred to, as a sample (*withdraw marches*) or a definite set (*the withdraw marches*), etc.

The perspective class[66] that groups these choices is shown in Figure 5.16. To make the decision among the choices in the class, the information contained in the node and the context provided by the Text Structure tree must be taken into account. In this case, since the march is being referred back to and since there is only one march being referred to, the second choice, known-individual, is taken. In the next section, I look more closely at the perspective classes and the choice mechanism.

```
(DEFINE-PERSPECTIVE-CLASS uniplex-discrete-individual  (matrix)

  ((return-typed-complex-object 'instance-of-a-kind matrix)
     :context-features (introduce) )

  ((return-typed-complex-object 'known-individual matrix)
     :context-features (subsequent-reference) )

  ((return-typed-complex-object 'sample-of-a-kind matrix)
     :context-features (introduce)
     :operators ((multiplex)) )

  ((return-typed-complex-object 'definite-set matrix)
     :context-features (known)
     :operators ((multiplex)) ))
```

Figure 5.16 A perspective class

5.2.3.1 *Choosing from a perspective class* Perspective classes group subtypes of the same general semantic category (in the above case, the type OBJECT). Each subtype expresses some "perspective", which may be thought of as a particular set of semantic features that are expressed in language by a combination of grammatical features, such as the syntactic category of the constituent (e.g. noun phrase), its number (singular or plural), etc. In Chapter Four (§4.2), I described the motivations for the set of categories using the work of Talmy (1987). Talmy's extensive cross-linguistic analyses have yielded a vocabulary of the kinds of notions which are expressed grammatically in language, which he defines as a set of semantic categories, including matter/action, uniplex/multiplex, bounded/unbounded, and discrete/continuous. Phrases commit to certain combinations of values in these categories, as determined by their lexical head, morphological markings, and closed class

66 A perspective class can be seen as simply a specialization of a realization class. In more recent applications, I have experimented with eliminating the distinction; however, it is useful for the discussion here to retain it.

words.[67] For example "a dog" is matter, uniplex, bounded, discrete; "dogs" is matter, multiplex, bounded, discrete. "Furniture" is matter, multiplex, bounded, continuous. To make it uniplex, you must use a partitive construction: "A piece of furniture", which is matter, uniplex, bounded, continuous.

I have used these notions (along with the notion of definiteness) to define the possible subtypes of OBJECT. A perspective class groups these subtypes into classes. Each subtype in the class shares some features and differs in others. The features which vary are predictable by the context or by some information associated with the CONTENTS object. For example, the perspective class in Figure 5.16, UNIPLEX-DISCRETE-INDIVIDUAL, groups INSTANCE-OF-A-KIND and KNOWN-INDIVIDUAL. Both of these subtypes of OBJECT share the three features UNIPLEX, DISCRETE, and INDIVIDUAL, but they differ in definiteness. Which subtype to choose is dependent on whether this instance has already appeared in the text structure, that is if this is a *subsequent reference* to the instance.

If an instance of type *dog* were mapped to UNIPLEX-DISCRETE-INDIVIDUAL (Figure 5.16), the first choice would be taken if the entity were being introduced, that is the entity has not been referred to in the utterance so far ("a dog"); the second would be taken if this was a subsequent reference, that is the entity was being referred back to ("the dog"). ("Fido", a particular dog whose name is known, would be mapped to a different class.) The two other choices are available when a MULTIPLEX operator is applied. Operators look at information in the context to determine if one of the basic features of the class is different in this particular situation, for example if there are multiple entities of this type grouped. For example, the third choice would be made if there are multiple dogs being introduced and the fourth choice if those dogs are being referred back to.

Perspective classes can also provide options for other kinds of subsequent reference strategies. For example, some named objects are expressed by both their type and their name, in particular the "battlefield geometry objects" in the SAF application, such as *Objective Alpha* or *Avenue of Approach Frank*. When these objects are introduced, they need both the type and name to be identified; but in subsequent references, only the name is needed. The perspective class shown in Figure 5.17, UNIPLEX-DISCRETE-NAMED-TYPED-INDIVIDUAL, has multiple parameters, NAME and TYPE; the first choice builds a complex object with a matrix and adjunct and the second choice builds a named object with only a matrix.

As I discussed in Chapter Four, this use of predefined classes to govern the selection of abstract resources, and thus control what combinations of concrete resources can be selected, is central to ensuring expressibility.

[67] Open class words are those that carry content, such as nouns and verbs, whereas closed class words are function words such as prepositions and determiners. Talmy proposes a range between open and closed class words, rather than the usual dichotomy, and includes partitives (such as "*piece* of pie") and weak verbs (such as "*keep* dancing") as "more closed", since they express grammatical rather than content notions.

```
(define-perspective-class UNIPLEX-DISCRETE-NAMED-TYPED-INDIVIDUAL
                                        (name type)
 ((return-typed-complex-object          'named-object
    :matrix  type
    :adjuncts (restrictive-appositive . name))
    :context-features (introduce)
    :operators ())

 ((return-typed-complex-object          'named-object
    :matrix type )
    :context-features (subsequent-reference)
    :operators ())
...)
```

Figure 5.17 Perspective Class UNIPLEX-DISCRETE-NAMED-TYPED-INDIVIDUAL

5.3. Building the linguistic specification

Once the Text Structure (or a coherent portion of it) is built, it is mapped to the linguistic specification of the utterance, which is the input to the linguistic realization component, MUMBLE-86. (The representational levels in Spokesman are repeated below in Figure 5.18.) This *linguistic specification* completely specifies what is to be said and constrains how it is to be said. The text planner, in the Text Structure it has constructed, has determined the compositional structure of the utterance, the constituency, and the functional relations among the units. The possible realization of constituents is also highly constrained by the semantic types of the objects in the CONTENTS fields of the nodes. The mapping of the elements of the Text Structure to the linguistic specification uses the context provided by the Text Structure as a whole to constrain further realizations and resolve any remaining options in the choice of lexical heads. It also ensures that all of the information needed by the linguistic component is contained in the specification.

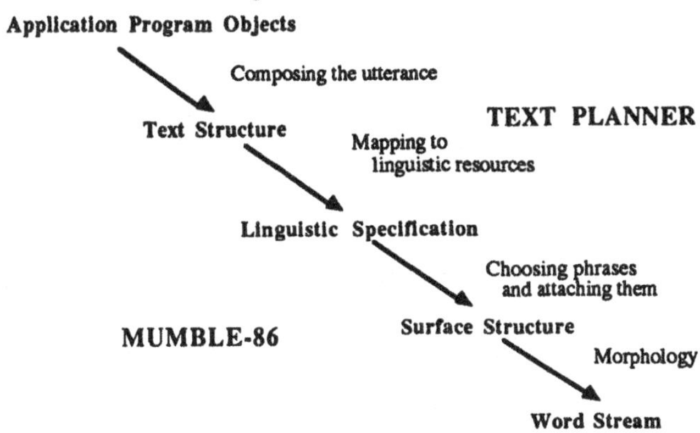

Figure 5.18 Levels of representation in Spokesman

The linguistic realization component, MUMBLE-86, handles linearization of words and phrases within each constituent and all of the syntactic decisions such as subject/verb agreement, the introduction of gaps ("the book that Susan bought <trace>"), and syntactically required pronominalization ("Peter bought himself a book"). Mumble's grammar is based on a Tree Adjoining Grammar (TAG) (Joshi 1985) which is defined in terms of elementary trees and rules for their composition. (See Meteer *et al.* 1987, for detailed documentation of Mumble-86.)

In this section, we look first at the specification language and its relationship to the Text Structure. We then look at the processes that build the specification from the Text Structure.

5.3.1 *The input specification language*

MUMBLE'S input specifications, like Text Structure, may be seen as expressions over a vocabulary of elementary terms and a syntax for their composition. In defining this language, our choice of terms and compositional operators was driven by what appears to be most useful at the linguistic level. The simplest expressions in the language, KERNEL SPECIFICATIONS, represent the choice of a class of phrases with a given lexical head and the specification of their arguments. This reflects our belief that one almost never chooses just to use a certain word, but, for example, rather to describe an action using a verb and a specific set of arguments (see also Kegl 1987). The result of realizing a kernel is a phrasal unit comparable to an elementary tree of a Tree Adjoining Grammar. (See Joshi, 1987, for a discussion of properties of a TAG which make it well suited to generation.) Formally, a kernel consists of a realization function and a list of arguments that are applied to it, where a realization function is typically a class of phrases, a "tree family", distinguished by the characteristics of the syntactic contexts in which they may appear. A tree family is similar in form to the realization classes and perspective classes described in §5.2. Executing the realization function consists of choosing among the phrases and instantiating the choice.

Larger, more complex utterances are formed by composing kernels: joining them syntactically according to the relationships among them. This process is analogous to adjunction in a TAG. In Mumble, these compositional expressions are called BUNDLES. They have three major parts:

(1) The HEAD is either a kernel or a bundle; it is realized first, as an "initial tree" into which other specifications are attached. Every bundle must have a head.

(2) FURTHER-SPECIFICATIONS have two parts, a specification (either a kernel or a bundle), and an attachment function, which constrains where the new tree may be adjoined to the surface structure already built; these correspond to the "auxiliary trees" of a TAG; a bundle may have any number of further specifications.

(3) ACCESSORIES contain information about language-specific syntactic details, such as tense and number. Each bundle type has a specific set of obligatory and optional accessories associated with it.

Note that bundles are not constrained as to the size of the text they produce: they may produce a single noun phrase or an entire paragraph. As with the Text Structure, the specification language focuses on the similarities found in constituent structure at all levels, rather than creating arbitrary distinctions between intra- and inter-sentential relations.

In addition to the head, accessories, and further specifications, bundles have a field for the UNDERLYING OBJECT and the BUNDLE TYPE. The underlying object is the object in the Text Structure from which the bundle was built. The bundle type determines the syntactic category of the phrase this bundle will produce. The bundle type is determined by the semantic type of the Text Structure object. For example, if the underlying object is an EVENT or a STATE, the bundle type will be a clause; if it is an INSTANCE-OF-A-KIND or a NAMED-OBJECT, then the bundle type will be a noun phrase. The bundle type also contains a driver function for processing the bundle and a list of the optional and obligatory accessories.

Figure 5.19 shows an example of a bundle specification for the noun phrase "Area of Responsibility Alpha". We look here at what the parts of the bundle contribute to the realization of the phrase and in the next section at the details of its relation to the Text Structure.

```
#<BUNDLE-SPECIFICATION GENERAL-NP
  UNDERLYING-OBJECT:  #<named-object>
  BUNDLE-TYPE:  #<BUNDLE-TYPE GENERAL-NP>
  HEAD:
   #<KERNEL-SPECIFICATION
     UNDERLYING-OBJECT:  #<lex Alpha>
     ARGUMENTS:  (#<WORD AREA> #<WORD RESPONSIBILITY>)
     REALIZATION-FUNCTION:#<SINGLE-CHOICE NP-COMMON-NOUN_OF-COMPLEMENT>>
  ACCESSORIES:
     ((#<NUMBER> . #<SINGULAR>)
      (#<PERSON> . #<THIRD>)
      (#<GENDER> . #< NEUTER>)
      (#<DETERMINER-POLICY> . #<NO-DETERMINER>)
      (#<PROPER-NAME>))
  FURTHER-SPECIFICATIONS:
     (#<FURTHER-SPECIFICATION
        ATTACHMENT-FUNCTION:
           #<SPLICING-ATTACHMENT-POINT RESTRICTIVE-APPOSITIVE>>
        SPECIFICATION:
           #<KERNEL-SPECIFICATION
               UNDERLYING-OBJECT:  #<lex>
               ARGUMENTS:  (#<WORD alpha>)
               REALIZATION-FUNCTION: #<SINGLE-CHOICE NP-COMMON-NOUN>>)>
```

Figure 5.19 Linguistic specification for "Area of Responsibility Alpha"

The *bundle type* in this example is GENERAL-NP, which commits the realization of this bundle to being a noun phrase. The *head* of the bundle is a KERNEL-SPECIFICATION. It has three parts:

- an *underlying-object*, which, analogous to bundles, points to the object from which the kernel was built;
- the *realization-function*, which indicates the particular phrase or class of phrases to be used from the resources of the linguistic realization component; note that in this case the realization choice is a SINGLE-CHOICE, indicating there is only one phrase possible; later we will see examples where the choice is a class of alternatives;
- the *arguments*, which in this case are words; in general, they may also be a specification, either a kernel or a bundle.

The *accessories* indicate the grammatical and functional features of the phrase. The determiner-policy (in this case NO-DETERMINER since it is a name) and number (e.g. SINGULAR) are used to mark the root of the noun phrase in the surface structure, which controls the determiner and morphology in the final stages of text production. The accessory PROPER-NAME is also a mark on the noun phrase root, controlling capitalization. THIRD-PERSON, SINGULAR, and NEUTER would control the choice of pronoun, if one were grammatically required. Some accessories are labels which guide the choice of realizations. For example, the accessory REDUCIBLE, which does not appear in this example, indicates the phrase is a subsequent reference and can be pronominalized if the syntactic context allows it.

There is one *further-specification* in this example. Further specifications have two parts: the *specification*, which is a bundle or a kernel specification that will build the phrase to be added into the phrase that was built by the head, and the *attachment function*, which indicates where the phrase should be added. Like realization functions, the attachment function can be a single point (as in this example) or a class of alternatives, such as a more general restrictive modifier that could be attached before a noun phrase if it is an adjective or after the noun phrase if it is a relative clause.

5.3.2 *The relationship between Text Structure and specifications*

There is a strong structural relation between the Text Structure and the structure of the specification language.[68] A composite subtree in the Text Structure, with a matrix and adjunct subnodes, creates a bundle: the matrix node contributes the head of the bundle and the adjuncts contribute the further specifications. A head-argument subtree contributes a kernel, where the head builds the realization function and the leaves build the arguments. A Text Structure leaf always contributes either a kernel or a lexical item.

The determination of the bundle type and the accessories of the bundle generally come from the semantic *type* of the object that is the contents of the Text Structure node, such as EVENT or UNIQUE-INDIVIDUAL. As we showed in

[68] This is not an accident: not only do they share designers, but the Text Planner was built specifically to work with Mumble-86.

Chapter Four, the perspective from which the object is expressed is captured in the Text Structure Object. The way that perspective is expressed in language is through the syntactic category of the phrase (e.g. noun phrase, clause) and the grammatical features of the phrase (e.g. number, tense). In the mapping from the Text Structure to the linguistic specification, this information is made explicit for the linguistic realization component to use.

Let's look at the relationship between the Text Structure and the linguistic specification in our earlier example, "Area of Responsibility Alpha." The specification shown above in Figure 5.19 was built from the Text Structure in Figure 5.20.

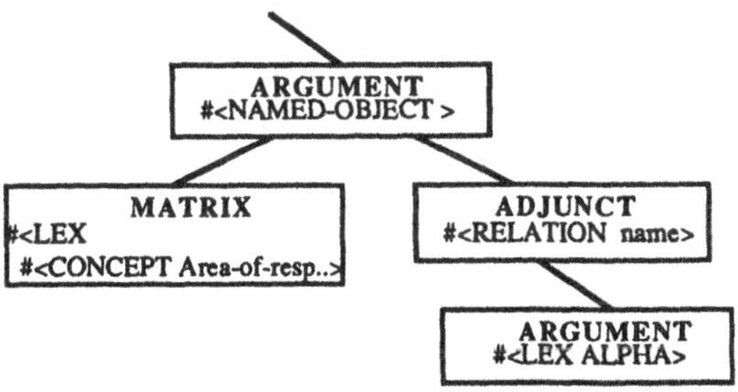

Figure 5.20 Text Structure for "Area of Responsibility Alpha"

The contents of the argument node at the root in this figure is a Text Structure object of type NAMED-OBJECT. The bundle of the corresponding specification and its accessories are built using a mapping from the type NAMED-OBJECT to the template EXPRESS-NAMED-OBJECT, shown in Figure 5.21. This template builds a GENERAL-NP bundle with the accessories needed for the expression of an entity from the named-object perspective. Note that it does not set the head or further accessories of the bundle. These are constructed by the children of this node.

```
(define-mapping 'NAMED-OBJECT
  :class-to-specification-table
    (:template-name EXPRESS-NAMED-OBJECT
     :arguments ()) )

(define-specification-template EXPRESS-NAMED-OBJECT ()
 (let ((bundle (general-np)))
   (singular bundle)
   (no-determiner bundle)
   (neuter-&-third-person bundle)
   (proper-name bundle)
   (when (eq (annotation self) 'reducible)
     (reducible bundle))
   bundle))
```

Figure 5.21 Mapping and template for NAMED-OBJECT

The root node in Figure 5.20 has two children: the MATRIX, whose contents is a LEX object, and an ADJUNCT, which contains a head RELATION object and an argument whose contents is a LEX object. In both instances, the LEX object contributes a kernel specification. Note however, as shown in Figure 5.22, it is the item in the object field of the LEX OBJECT field that actually does the work; the LEX object itself only directs what actual mapping should be used. (Note that a given object will often have a number of associated mappings because it can appear in different kinds of places in Text Structure with different functions accordingly.) The mapping for LEX uses the EXPRESS-LEX template. This template invokes a particular mapping from the lexical resource mapping table with the object field of the lex as the argument. It is this template returned by this "sub" mapping (not shown here) that will actually construct the kernel. (We discuss these "two-step" mappings in more detail in §5.4.)

```
(define-mapping 'LEX
  class-to-specification-table
    (:template-name  express-lex
     :arguments (object self)))

(define-specification-template express-lex (object)
  (instantiate-lexical-resource-mapping object))

(define-mapping  (concept 'area-of-responsibility)
  class-to-realization-class-table
    (:realization-class named-typed-individual
      :arguments ())
  object-to-lexical-resource-table
    (:template-name noun-part-arg
     :arguments ("area" "responsibility")))
```

Figure 5.22 Mapping and template for LEX

The adjunct node in Figure 5.20 builds the further specification of the bundle. The RELATION object, the contents of the adjunct, builds the attachment function and the ARGUMENT child of the relation builds the specification.

5.3.3 *Building specifications from Text Structure*

The process that builds the specification from the Text Structure is similar to that which builds the Text Structure itself (described in §5.2). Each node in the Text Structure contributes to the growing linguistic specification for the utterance.[69] As in the first pass, the tree structure itself determines the order of the actions, and the contents of the nodes determine what actions are taken. The Text Structure tree is traversed depth first, and at each node a mapping from the object in the contents field of the node to the specification building routines defines the possible actions.

69 This is not strictly true; however, since the exceptions are idiosyncratic, we will not address them here.

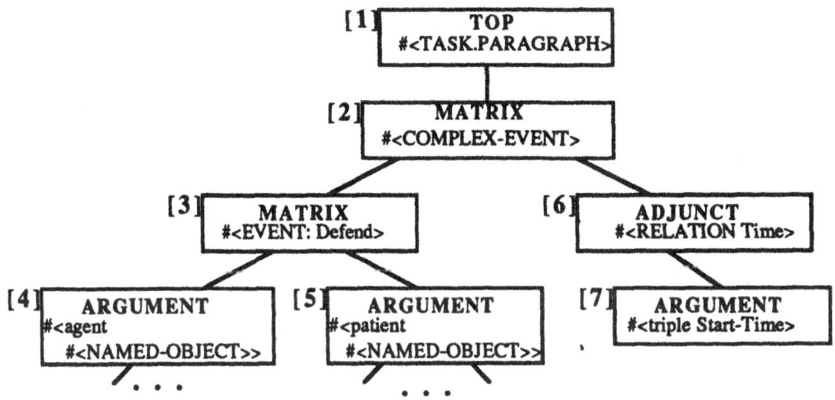


```
[1]#<BUNDLE-SPECIFICATION DISCOURSE-UNIT
[1]    UNDERLYING-OBJECT:#<Mission Def of COMPANY-DEFEND-AREA>
[1]    BUNDLE-TYPE: #<BUNDLE-TYPE DISCOURSE-UNIT>
       HEAD:
[2]      #<BUNDLE-SPECIFICATION GENERAL-CLAUSE
[2]          UNDERLYING-OBJECT: #<arg-rel>
[2]          BUNDLE-TYPE: #<BUNDLE-TYPE GENERAL-CLAUSE>
[3]          HEAD:#<KERNEL-SPECIFICATION
[3]                    UNDERLYING-OBJECT: #<Event>
                         ARGUMENTS:
[4]                      (#<BUNDLE-SPECIFICATION GENERAL-NP...>
[5]                      #<BUNDLE-SPECIFICATION GENERAL-NP...>)
[3]                    REALIZATION-FUNCTION:
                              #<CURRIED-REALIZATION-CLASS defend>>
[3]                    ACCESSORIES:
                              ((#<UNMARKED>) (#<TENSE-MODAL> . #< PRESENT>)))
           FURTHER-SPECIFICATIONS:
[6]          (#<FURTHER-SPECIFICATION
[6]                ATTACHMENT-FUNCTION:
                      #<ATTACHMENT-CLASS CLAUSAL-ADJUNCT>
                   SPECIFICATION:
[7]                 #<KERNEL-SPECIFICATION
                        UNDERLYING-OBJECT: #<triple start-time>
                        ARGUMENTS: (#<BUNDLE-SPECIFICATION GENERAL-NP ... >)
                        REALIZATION-FUNCTION:
                         #<CURRIED-REALIZATION-CLASS SPECIALIZATION-OF-PP+AT>)
    ACCESSORIES: NIL
    FURTHER-SPECIFICATIONS: NIL>>
```

Figure 5.23 Specification and Text Structure for "1/TB defends Objective Alpha at 14 1423 Apr".

The mapping of the contents object returns a specification, which is then added into the specification of the dominating node.[70] How it is added is determined by three factors: the relation of the current node node to its parent and siblings (head, argument, matrix, adjunct, coordinate), the type of the specification (a kernel or a bundle), and the type of the dominating specification.

Figure 5.23 shows a Text Structure tree and specification for "1/TB defends Objective Alpha at 14 1423 Apr." The numbers to the left of the nodes and to the left of the specifications indicate which portions of the tree built which portions of the specifications. (This is only meant as an indicator of the process; the complete details of this mapping are beyond the scope of this document.)

5.3.4 *Choosing from multiple alternatives*

As in the text structure mappings described in §5.2, when there is only one possible action, a template is instantiated, and when there are multiple actions possible, a class of alternatives is used. In all of the cases of mappings that we have looked at so far, only a single action was possible, so the mapping was to a template. In this section we look at an example of choosing from multiple alternatives in building the specification: choosing from an *argument structure class*. An argument structure class determines what realization function to choose from for an EVENT or STATE object by looking at what arguments have been made explicit in the text structure.

As we described earlier, a head-argument subtree in text structure builds a kernel specification, with the realization function contributed by the head and the arguments by the argument subnodes. An example of such a structure is the subtree with node [3] as its root in Figure 5.23.[71]

```
(define-mapping 'EVENT
  :class-to-text-structure-table
    (:template-name EVENT-STRUCTURE  :arguments ((event self)))
  :class-to-specification-table
    (:template-name  EVENT-KERNEL :arguments ((event self))))

(define-specification-template EVENT-KERNEL (event)
 (let ((r-fn (instantiate-realization-function-mapping  event)))
   (make-a-kernel r-fn)))
```

Figure 5.24 Mapping and template for EVENT

The mapping for the contents of this node, the EVENT object, is similar to that for LEX in that it is a "two-step" mapping: it uses a mapping from one of its

70 See previous note: the dominating specification is not always in the node directly dominating the current node; in the case where the direct parent is not contributing a specification, the process must walk up through parents to find the dominating specification.

71 Reminder: the labels on the nodes indicate the node's relation to its parent, so the MATRIX label is an indicator of how this node relates to its parent–not its role in the head-argument structure. The relation of a node to its children is not always explicitly shown in the diagram.

parts, the object in the EVENT field, to build the realization function. The mapping for EVENT is shown in Figure 5.24.

The realization function is the phrase or class of phrases that will be used by the linguistic realization component (LRC) to express this kernel. The alternative phrases in the LRC are grouped into "tree families" according to the lexical head of the phrase[72] and what arguments appear explicitly in the phrase. The argument structure class determines which tree family the syntactic component should use. The mapping for this example, from the COMPANY-DEFEND-AREA concept, is shown in Figure 5.25. The verb is bound to defend; however, there are still three possible classes of surface structures, depending on what arguments have been made explicit: the agent and the patient as in "Company A defended Area Alpha"; only the patient as in "Area Alpha was defended", or only the agent as in "Company A defended".[73] These alternatives are grouped into the argument structure class TRANSITIVE-ERGATIVE-EVENT (also shown in Figure 5.25). The characteristics of each choice, its available-argument list, look at the argument relations in the children of the node being processed to determine which arguments are available explicitly, i.e. are present as argument nodes in the Text Structure. As in the other classes of alternatives in the generator, if more than one choice which is acceptable, the first is chosen.

```
(define-mapping (concept 'COMPANY-DEFEND-AREA)
    class-to-realization-class-table
      (:realization-class company-defend-area :arguments ())
    object-to-realization-function-table
      (:argument-structure-class TRANSITIVE-ERGATIVE-EVENT)
       :arguments ((mumble::verb "defend" )))

(define-argument-structure-class TRANSITIVE-ERGATIVE-EVENT ()
    ((TRANSITIVE-VERB_TWO-EXPLICIT-ARGS )
      :available-arguments (agent patient))
    ((INTRANSITIVE-VERB_AGENT-EXPLICIT)
      :available-arguments (agent))
    ((TRANSITIVE-VERB_ONE-EXPLICIT-ARG)
      :available-arguments (patient)))
```

Figure 5.25 Mapping for COMPANY-DEFEND-AREA

5.4. Control of the Text Planner

In a message directed framework such as this one, the intermediate levels of representation drive the processing directly. Since the central representation in the text planner is a tree, its top-level control is a tree traversal, both for building

[72] Joshi's more recent work on lexically headed elementary trees for Tree Adjoining Grammars is in the same spirit as tree families, although they were developed independently.

[73] While the intransitive choice ("Company A defended") sounds a little odd in normal speech, it is quite common in military style, where what is being defended is often so obvious (such as your position) that it is never said.

the text structure and constructing the next level of representation (the linguistic specification of the message which is the input to the linguistic realization component). In this section, we take a close look at the top level of control in the text planner, from the first call to the generator to the call to the linguistic realization component, Mumble-86. We then provide more details on the mappings and how they are accessed from the control loop.

5.4.1 *Top-level control loop*

The most general top-level call to Spokesman is the function SAY-OBJECT, which takes a single object as its argument. This object may be from the application program or it may be an aggregation built specifically for the generator (see discussion of domain objects in Chapter Four, §4.3). It assumes that the type of the object passed to it is known to the text planner (that is, there is an established text structure mapping for it).

There are four major steps in the text planner:[74]

1. INITIALIZE-TEXT-PLANNER initializes global variables and tables;
2. TOP-LEVEL-TEXT-PLANNER builds the text structure;
3. TEXT-STRUCTURE-TO-SPECIFICATION traverses the text structure, building the input specification to MUMBLE-86;
4. SPECIFICATION-TO-TEXT calls MUMBLE-86 with the input specification, producing the text.

In the next sections we discuss each of these steps in more detail.

5.4.1.1 *Initialize the Text Planner* The first step is to initialize the variables and tables used at run time. The following global variables are initialized to nil:

- *AGENDA*: the stack used for controlling the tree traversal;
- ROOT: a pointer to the root of the text structure tree;
- CURRENT-TSN: a pointer to the node currently being processed (the top of the agenda); and
- *OPTIONAL-INFORMATION-TO-BE-INCLUDED*: a list of objects representing information that can optionally be added to the utterance. These come from the elaboration parts of the realization classes where an object is found to be salient but incompatible with the context at the time.

It also clears the REFERENCE-TABLE, which links objects to the nodes where they are expressed, and the table OBJECT-TO-REALIZATION-SPECIFICATION,

[74] These steps are executed sequentially in the SAF and ALBM versions; however, in the Main Street version, which produces multiple paragraphs, the steps are interleaved in a pipeline architecture, so that as paragraphs are planned, they are sent off to the linguistic component. We are also experimenting with finer-grained interleavings and parallel architectures, where the steps are conducted by separate processes, so that, for example, further extensions to the text structure can be made at the same time as the linguistic specification is being built for already planned portions of the utterance.

which keeps a link between objects and the input specifications that have been built to express them.

The next action is to build the top text structure node (the root). Its CONTENTS field is set to the object passed in (e.g. "object" in the top-level call to the "say-object" routine). The TS-RELATION field of this node is set to TOP and its PARENT to nil. The CONTROL-STATUS of the node is set to NEW and its CHILDREN field to nil. This node is then placed on the *AGENDA*.

5.4.1.2 *Pass 1: building the Text Structure* The second step of the text planner is building the Text Structure tree. Each node is visited twice, once going down the tree, when children are added to each node recursively, and once coming back up. The control loop uses the *AGENDA* and the control-status of the nodes to determine what actions to take. The control status of every node is initially NEW, is changed to EXPANDED when traversal goes down the tree, and then to COMPLETED as the traversal returns up. At the beginning of the loop, the variable CURRENT-TSN is set to the first item on the agenda.

When the traversal reaches a node whose control-status is NEW (the node is being visited for the first time), the node's control status is set to EXPANDED and the object that is in its contents slot is "instantiated". That is, the planner tries to find a text-structure mapping for the object in one of the appropriate tables (individual-to-text-structure-table or class-to-text-structure-table, see §5.4.2). If a mapping is found, then the corresponding routines are run; if none is found then that node is a leaf. As a result, child nodes may be created, added to the tree, and pushed on to the agenda (pushing the children assures that the traversal will continue depth first). Alternatively (or in addition) the CONTENTS object may be replaced in the text structure by another object built by the routine. Finally, there is a check for any children that may have been created for that node by earlier routines to ensure that all children are on the agenda.

When the control status is EXPANDED (the traversal is returning up the tree), the planner first checks the *OPTIONAL-INFORMATION-TO-BE-INCLUDED* list to see if there is any related information that might be added as a child of this node. If so, it adds the structures to the text structure and to the agenda. Note that in such a case, since more has been added below the current node, its control status does not change; it is not yet finished and may be visited again and again until there is nothing new that can be added (we discussed the conditions under which the text structure can be extended in §5.2). When there is nothing to be added, the control status is changed to COMPLETED and the final bookkeeping is done: the node's "weight" is calculated (how many nodes does this one dominate) and a list of the entities referenced by this constituent is compiled. Note that since this information is incrementally calculated as the traversal returns up the tree, it is a function of information contained in the children of the node; no complex traversal or look-ahead is needed.

When the control status is COMPLETED, the node is popped off the *AGENDA*. The structure of the tree remains because of the parent and child links in each node, and will be used in the next phase of the text planner—the building of the linguistic specification—which also conducts a traversal of the tree using an agenda. Note that now all the nodes will begin with control status COMPLETED.

5.4.1.3 *Pass 2: from Text Structure to specification* This phase traverses the text structure, producing the input specification for the linguistic realization component. Again, the traversal visits each node twice, once walking down the tree in the depth-first traversal and again on the way back up. This phase begins by putting the root on the agenda. CURRENT NODE is set to the first item of the agenda.

When the control status of the current node is COMPLETED (the initial situation, analogous to NEW in the previous phase), the specification mapping is instantiated. The routine that is run returns a specification which is added into the specification of its parent node, using the type of specification returned (kernel, bundle, further-specification), the TS-relation on the node (matrix, adjunct, argument, etc), and the type of the parent's specification. Finally, the node is marked EXPRESSED and its children are put on the agenda.

When the control status of the current node is EXPRESSED (going back up the tree), the TS-to-specification-final mapping for the current contents is checked (that is, if there is anything else that needs to be done to the specification) and when a mapping exists, the appropriate action is taken. Finally, the node is popped off the agenda.

5.4.1.4 *From specification to text* The final step of the text planner is to initialize the linguistic component, MUMBLE-86. The function *Mumble*, which is the top-level function for the component, is called with the linguistic specification built in the previous pass. (See Meteer *et al.*, 1987, for a complete description of the linguistic realization component.)

5.4.2 *Mappings*

The Text Structure tree controls the processing by determining when a particular node is considered. As this is an "object-oriented" system, what action is taken, however, is determined by what is in the contents field of the node. The contents field contains the information expressed by the constituent; it must either be an object from the application program (AP object) or a composite object built by the text structure (TS object). In either case, the object type has a predefined mapping to the action (or possible set of actions) to be taken (similar in spirit to "methods" from standard object-oriented programming languages, such as CLOS). Several different tables are used for the mappings, each accessed from a different context (for example, the two passes over the text structure access different tables). In this section, we describe the mappings and the forms used to set them up. We then look at the various places that may access the mappings.

5.4.2.1 *Table entries and templates* Mappings are predefined links between objects and the templates or other routines for expressing them. The object is usually a member of a class (type), so that all instances of that class use the same mapping; however, the mapping may be directly from an individual object if the way in which that instance of the class is expressed differs from other instances of that class. Mappings use a set of tables, which are accessed by both of the top-level passes of the text planner (both building the text structure and building the specification) and from within some of the templates. Figure 5.26 shows the special form that is used to set up the table entries. The text inside angle brackets describes the sorts of things that may appear at that position. The names in capital letters are typed substitution variables.

```
(define-mapping OBJECT-TYPE
  <table-name>
  :template-name TEMPLATE-NAME
  :arguments (<a list of expressions that match the template's
                                                   parameters>)

(define-text-structure-template TEMPLATE-NAME (<a list of parameters>)
  <code which is executed when the template is called>)
```

Figure 5.26 Mapping and template

The table entries consist of the name of a text planner resource (such as a template or a class of alternatives) and a set of arguments. In general, if there is only one possible action, the resource is a template containing code which is executed when the mapping is instantiated. If there are multiple alternative actions, they are grouped into a class and each choice in the class is annotated by the characteristics that determine when the choice should be made. When a mapping is instantiated, the object being operated on is bound to the special variable SELF, which can then be accessed freely in the code that performs the mapping, and then the parameters are evaluated.

The following are the contexts from which a mapping is accessed and the tables that are used in each context.

- *From the control loop of the first pass of the text planner* (when the text structure is being built): the object in the contents slot of the current node is used. It first looks up a mapping for the individual object in the INDIVIDUAL-TO-TEXT-STRUCTURE-TABLE. If it does not find one, it determines the class of the object and looks up a mapping for that class in the CLASS-TO-TEXT-STRUCTURE-TABLE. The mapping also sets up information about what entities are referenced in what constituents. It puts the current node in a table indexed by the object being mapped and adds the object to the list of entities referenced in the current node.
- *From the control loop of the second pass of the text planner* (when the specification is being built): the object in the contents slot of the current node is again used. As before, it first looks up a mapping for the individual object in the INDIVIDUAL-TO-SPECIFICATION-TABLE. If it does not find one, it finds that class of the object and looks up a mapping for the class in the CLASS-TO-SPECIFICATION-TABLE. As the second pass returns up the tree, the TS-TO-SPECIFICATION-FINAL-TABLE is accessed on the class or the individual as needed.

- Several specific tables are accessed *from within templates*. In these "two-step" mappings, one step takes to the template and the next uses the table specified within the template. They are used when the object type dictates the kind of action to take, but it is the value of one of the fields of the object that dictates the particular action. For example, in the first pass, the template for a TRIPLE object (i.e. a frame-slot-value combination) uses the mapping from the TRIPLE-TO-TEXT-STRUCTURE-TABLE for the particular object in the SLOT field of the TRIPLE to determine what action to take. Similarly, in the second pass, the mapping for a LEX object returns a template which in turn instantiates the mapping for the object in its LEX-OBJECT field taken from the OBJECT-TO-LEXICAL-RESOURCE-TABLE to construct the actual lexical item.

6 Text Structure in Action

In this chapter I look at the potential of Text Structure for solving hard problems in generation, including incremental text generation and portability. In the first section, I describe the incremental production of paragraph-length descriptions of the characters in the Main Street simulation program. I use a very simple selection algorithm for this task that gathers related and interesting information as the paragraph is being composed and realized. The approach emphasizes the need for keeping an explicit representation, the Text Structure, of what information has already been included and what opportunities are open for adding new information. In the second section, I look more closely at the interface between Spokesman and its applications and show how the modularity of Spokesman increases its portability.

6.1 Incremental text generation from the "Main Street" simulation

In the previous chapter, I described the mechanisms used by the text planner to construct the linguistic specification, the input to the linguistic realization component. In this section, I look at those mechanisms in a larger context: generating a multi-sentential utterance. The focus here is on how the Text Structure enables incremental text generation, i.e. interleaving the selection of the information and the composition of the utterance. In particular, I focus on how, as the Text Structure is constructed, the inclusion of one element can trigger the inclusion of other related information. The text planner uses the context provided by the Text Structure to constrain where this new information can be added. As I have discussed in detail in the previous two chapters, the Text Structure constrains such compositions in three ways:

- *how something can be expressed.* The text planner's options are restricted to Text Structure Objects and resource trees that define the expressible combinations of linguistic resources, and realization classes that group together alternative choices annotated by contextual restrictions on their use. The text planner does not have the opportunity to choose concrete linguistic resources directly and thus cannot select an inconsistent (i.e. inexpressible) set.
- *where nodes can be added to the Text Structure tree.* The structural relations among Text Structure nodes (e.g. matrix, adjunct, head, argument) provide a vocabulary that dictates what extensions are permitted. They dictate that only composite nodes may receive additional children after the node has been expanded, and that these children may

only be adjuncts. Kernel subtrees (a head dominating its arguments) may not receive additional children, reflecting the integrity of the predicate/argument structure. In addition, the control-status of Text Structure nodes (see §5.4) constrains the addition of new elements. It ensures that elements will only be added ahead of the point of speech.

- *what kind of information can be added at expansion points*. The semantic type of the object at a composite node constrains what semantic types can be added to the object as adjuncts. For example, an event composite can get location, manner, or time adjuncts, and an object can get location or property adjuncts.[75] A proposition (state or event) can also be added as an adjunct to an object if the object and an argument of the proposition are the same, ultimately producing a relative clause.

In this chapter, I walk through an example of the construction of an utterance. The example I use is part of a biography of a character in the Main Street simulation program. This domain is particularly suited to showing the Text Structure's capability to constrain composition for two reasons: first, Main Street records a great deal of information about its characters, places and other entities; second, this information changes as the simulation runs, so that what information is relevant will be different at different moments in the simulation and cannot be predicted in advance. These two factors make Main Street an extremely interesting environment in which to do generation research.

In §6.1.1, I describe Main Street in more detail; in §6.1.2, I describe the selection algorithm used to collect the information to be included in the biography; and in §6.1.3 I walk through an example of a portion of the biography in detail.

6.1.1 *Why is Main Street an interesting domain?*

Main Street (Abrett *et al.* 1989) is an object-oriented, event-driven simulation program which is designed to be a demonstration model of an economy. There is a set of eight characters who go through daily activities, such as eating, sleeping, going to work, reading books, going to movies, and watching TV. The characters are independent agents, as are the other entities in the program, such as the taxis, buses, etc. In this section, I will very briefly describe the kinds of information in Main Street and show some examples of the organizing structures. My goal here is not to explain how Main Street works, but rather to give a flavor of the quantity and complexity of the information it represents and manipulates.

There are two kinds of information in Main Street:

- *Information about the objects* which is represented in a frame-based knowledge representation called SFL ("Simple Frame Language", a

[75] There are some interesting future problems in type composition. For example, in the sentence "Peter wants a car until Thursday", the adjunct "until Thursday" is modifying an implicit state: "Peter wants *to have* a car until Thursday". Pustejovsky (1991) calls this phenomenon *type coercion*. I am currently exploring the phenomenon in Text Structure terms.

derivative of KL-One). Object types, called "concepts" are represented in a hierarchical knowledge base; they have "roles" which relate them to other concepts. The entities in the program are instances of these concepts. Figure 6.1 shows an instance of the concept "person" and Figure 6.2 shows a small portion of the hierarchical domain model. There are 641 concepts and 194 roles in the current version of Main Street.

- *Information about the actions*, which is represented in goal/procedure[76] networks in TARL ("Tactical Action Representation Language"). Goals have a set of achievement conditions and are each associated with an "achievement plan" (known as a GPP: "goal/procedure plan") that describes the alternative sets of subgoals and procedures that can lead to the satisfaction of that goal. Figure 6.3 shows an example of a goal procedure network for going to the movies. There are 50 goals and 82 procedures in the current version of Main Street.

One of the most interesting aspects of Main Street is the the way it integrates these two kinds of knowledge. Goals and procedures get their parameters from concepts in the domain hierarchy and instances of entities (people, stores, taxis, etc.) keep track of their current goals, completed goals, and current activities by keeping lists of instantiations of objects from the goals and procedures of the GPP networks.

Figure 6.1 shows an instance of a person, the character Abbie. The instance contains all the information about Abbie at a given moment in time, including what she is currently doing and what she plans to do. Many of the objects in the slots of this instance are themselves instances of concepts (indicated by "#<...>") and have other information associated with them that is not shown here. For example, the instances in the INTERESTS slot (in bold in the figure) not only keep information about what kinds of movies, TV, etc. the character likes, but also their previous experiences (such as what movies they have recently seen). We will look more closely at these objects in the walk through the example. Several of the slots have lists of objects as their values. I have abbreviated longer lists (with "...") in order to fit the instance on one page.

Figure 6.2 shows a portion of the concept hierarchy. The highlighted concept (OBJECT-WITH-LOCATION) dominates all the entity types that have a location slot (these types inherit the location slot from this concept). We can see from this that the concept PERSON is a specialization of MOBILE-OBJECT.

[76] A "goal" is something that succeeds or fails on the basis of conditions; a "procedure" completes or doesn't complete on the basis of the set of actions in the procedure.

```
#<PERSON ABBIE 313526034
 BELIEFS:                           ((CAR-LOCATION . 105))
 NAME:                              ABBIE
 CONCEPT-NAME:                      PERSON
 INVENTORY: (#<PERSONAL-INVENTORY-BY-AMOUNT-ITEM LIQUOR 313544004>
    #<PERSONAL-INVENTORY-BY-LIST-ITEM NEWSPAPERS 313544017>
    #<PERSONAL-INVENTORY-BY-LIST-ITEM BOOKS 313544032> ...)
 LAST-TIME-JOB-UPDATED:             0
 LAST-TIME-LOOKED-FOR-JOB:          NIL
 EMPLOYMENT-HISTORY:                NIL
 SKILLS:                            (#<MANAGING 313545576>)
 JOB:                               #<PLANT-MANAGER 313525223>
 GET-TO-WORK-INFO:                  #<GET-TO-WORK-MEMORY-CHUNK 321057612>
 CURRENT-GOALS:
    (#<READING-GOAL READ-MY-NEWSPAPER-GOAL ag:ABBIE s:ACTIVE 321745137>
    #<READING-GOAL BUY-AND-READ-NEWSPAPER-TODAY ag:ABBIE s:ACTIVE
        321745076>...)
 COMPLETED-GOALS:
    (#<PICKUP-ON-THE-WAY-GOAL PICKUP-ON-THE-WAY-GOAL ag:ABBIE s:SUCCEED
        321741006>
    #<GET-MEAL-GOAL EAT-BREAKFAST ag:ABBIE s:FAIL 321736057>
    #<GET-SOME-SLEEP-GOAL GET-SOME-SLEEP ag:ABBIE s:SUCCEED 321733457>
    ... )
 CURRENT-ACTIVITIES:
    (#<PRIMITIVE-WORK-AT WORK-AT ag:ABBIE s:IN-PROCESS 321736223>
    #<PERSON-WAITING-PROCEDURE WAIT-UNTIL-NEXT-MORNING ag:ABBIE s:TIMED-OUT
        321740032>
    #<READ-A-NEWSPAPER-PROCEDURE READ-MY-NEWSPAPER ag:ABBIE s:BLOCKED
        321750754> ...)
 ACTIVE?:                           T
 INTERESTS:
    (#<EATING-FOOD 313545604> #<READING 313545625> #<WATCHING-TV
        313545640> #<DRINKING 313545652> #<GOING-OUT-TO-BARS
        313545666> #<WATCHING-MOVIES 313545675>)
 CASH-ON-HAND:                      24943.4
 HORIZON-DISTANCE:                  40
 HORIZON-TIME:                      NIL
 LOCATION:                          #<OFFICE LOTUS-POINT 313525137>
 DEFAULT-SPEED:                     3
 LAST-TIME-LOCATION-UPDATED:        1474.7799
 CURRENT-SPEED:                     0
 DIRECTION-OF-MOTION:               NIL
 LAST-TIME-TIREDNESS-UPDATED:       1500.0
 TIREDNESS-RATE:                    0.17
 NORMAL-WAKE-TIME:                  800
 NORMAL-BEDTIME:                    2400
 WOKE-UP-AT:                        901
 AWAKE-ASLEEP-STATE:                :AWAKE
 SLEEPING-RENEWAL-RATE:             0.3
 TIREDNESS:                         64.2
 DEFAULT-WAKING-GET-TIRED-RATE: 0.17
 NEED-FOR-MONEY:                    4
 MY-HOME:                           #<HOME ABBIES-BY-THE-SEA 313525467>
 MY-CAR:                            #<FANCY-CAR RED-PORSCHE 313531756>
 WALK-RUN-STAMINA:                  2>
```

Figure 6.1 Instance of the concept "person" in Main Street

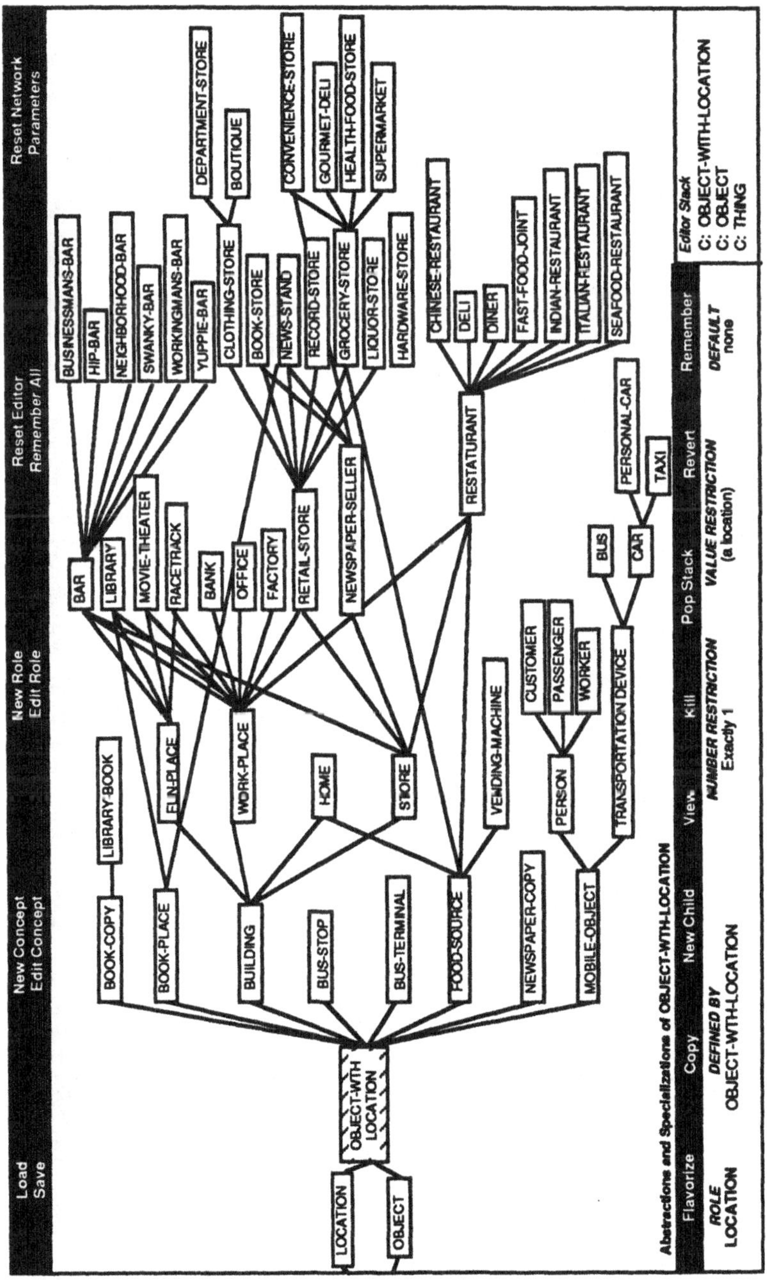

Figure 6.2 Portion of the hierarchical domain model

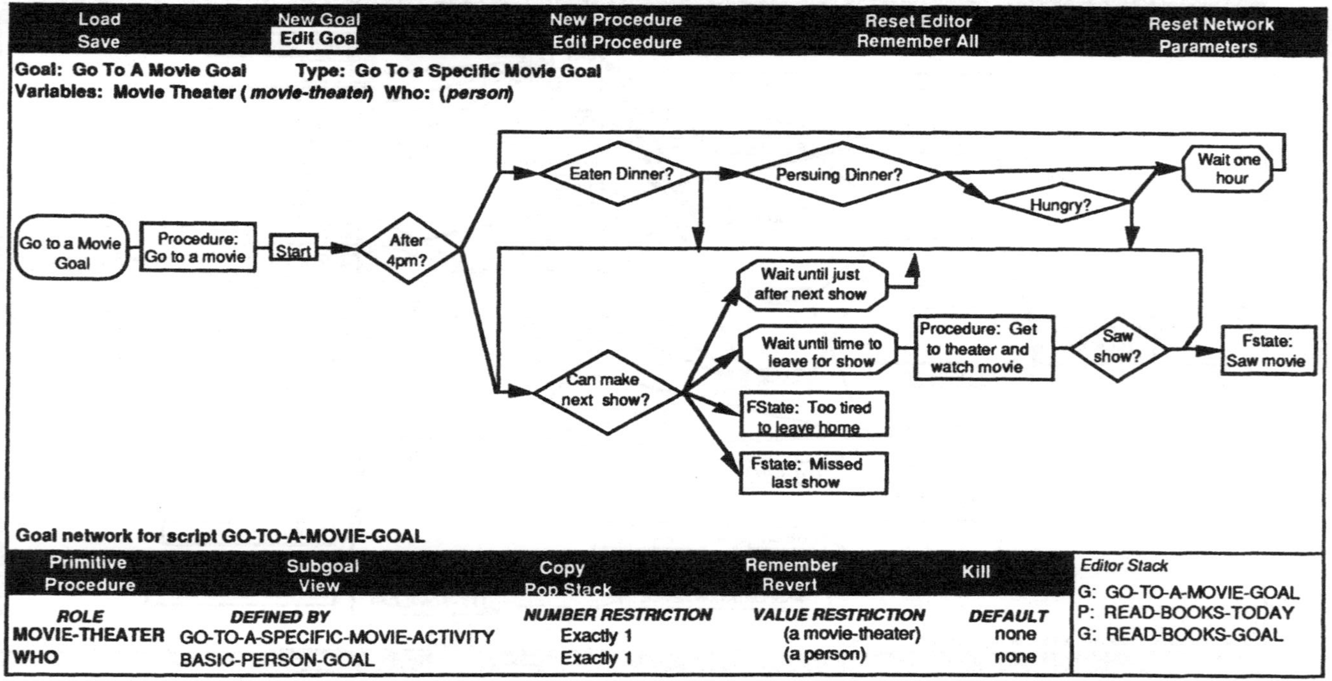

Figure 6.3 Goal/procedure network for going to a movie

The simulation itself is driven by the goal/procedure networks (GPP). When the agents in the simulation are instantiated, they are given a set of top-level goals; for example instances of PERSON get goals such as MAINTAIN-ENERGY-LEVEL and SATISFY-INTEREST, and instances of STORE get the goal MAINTAIN-OPEN-CLOSED-STATE. When the goal is instantiated, its goal procedure plan is executed. The GPP can execute activities, evaluate decision nodes, and spawn independent subgoals. Figure 6.3 shows the GPP for going to the movies. Hexagons are goals, squares are procedures, and diamonds are decision nodes.

The goal type, GO-TO-A-SPECIFIC-MOVIE-GOAL, is a concept in the domain hierarchy. The variables in the goal are the slots on this concept, MOVIE-THEATER and WHO, shown in the bottom box in the picture of the screen in Figure 6.3.

6.1.2 *The selection algorithm*

I have chosen a generation task which takes advantage of the kinds of information in Main Street and the incremental generation capabilities of Spokesman. The task is to generate biographical descriptions of the characters. These biographies include the current state of the characters at the moment in the simulation when the biography is generated; general knowledge about the characters, such as their skills, interests, and job; and some of their experiences up to the current point in the simulation. The overall organization of the biographies is centered around topics: current-status, work, movies, books, TV. The Text Structure and text in Figure 6.4 show an example of a biography for the character Abbie.[77] The following rather simple selection algorithm was used to determine what information to include:

```
Given a person and a topic list
For each topic
    Collect "interesting" information about that person related to that topic
    Build the Text Structure for that information
    When other objects are mentioned,
            look for interesting information about them
            if possible
                    add it to the Text Structure
            otherwise
                    put it on a list and try to add it later
    Send what is planned to the LRC
Go on to the next topic
```

[77] This text is the output of Spokesman, with the exception of which pronouns are used; because of a lack in the underlying representation in Main Street, the pronouns in this example are realized as "it" and "its", rather than "she" and "her" (the sex of the characters is not represented, so Spokesman uses the default, neuter). I discuss this problem in more detail in §7.3.2.

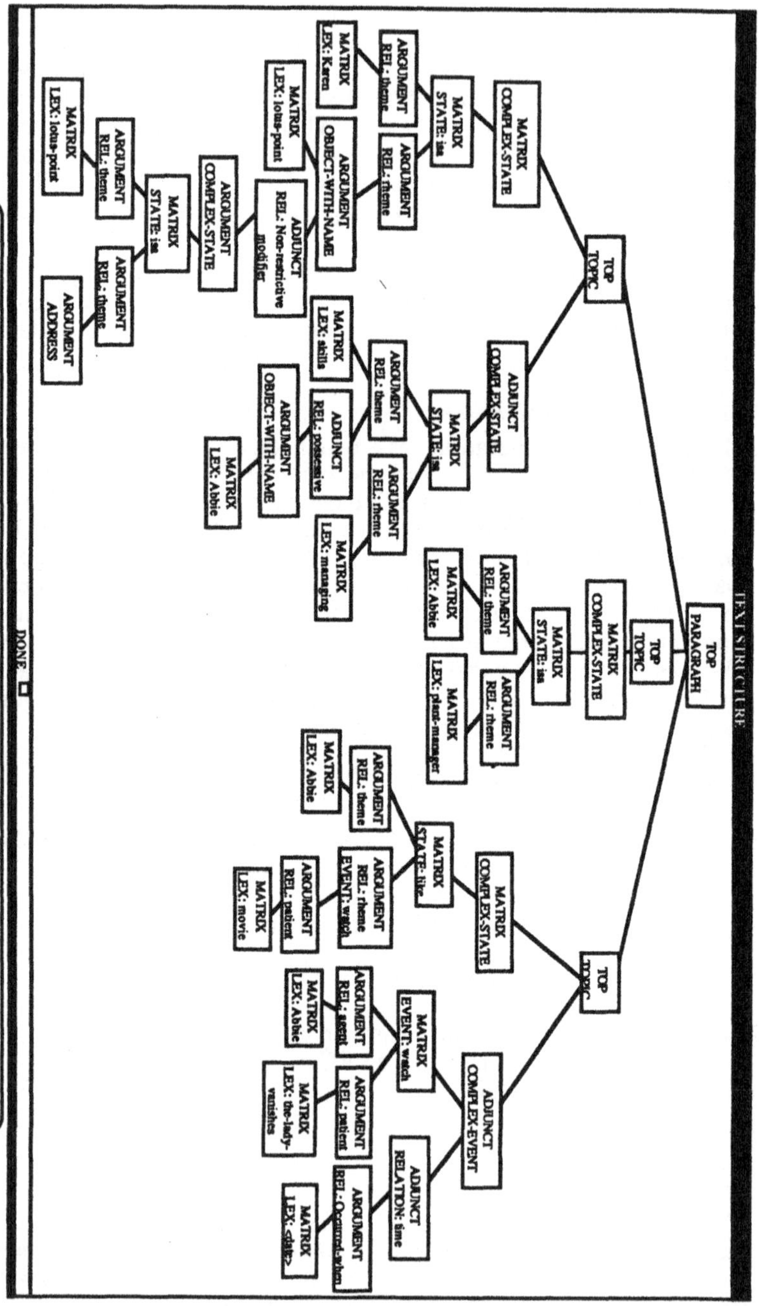

Figure 6.4 Text Structure and Text

Note the paragraph in Figure 6.4 reflects only the first three topics on the list, current-status, work and movies, and does not include all of the possible information on these topics. My goal in working in this domain has been to look closely at more interesting phenomena at the expense of completeness; this is a complementary approach to my work in the military domains, where the focus has been on broader coverage at the expense of deep analyses of interesting constructions. Clearly, even using this selection algorithm, more information could be considered for all of the topics; I have artificially limited the consideration to focus on certain kinds of problems. Moreover, more complex selection algorithms would make the information available at different moments and allow for more considered organization of the material. While the architecture presented here allows for these possibilities, I have chosen to use the simplest and sparest selection routines in order to focus on the Text Structure itself.

6.1.3 *A walk through*

The example I will walk through in detail is the last two sentences of the biographical description shown in Figure 6.4: *Abbie likes watching movies. She watched "The Lady Vanishes" on Sun 07-May-89 7:20 PM.* As we begin this portion of the utterance, we are at the top of the loop of the selection algorithm, with the person #<PERSON ABBIE 313526034> and the topic *MOVIES*. The next step is to collect "interesting" information about that person related to that topic and add it to the Text Structure. (We discuss how "interesting" is determined below.)

As I described in Chapter Five, the system uses predefined mappings from object types both for the alternative ways of *expressing* the object and for determining associated information to use in *elaborating* the object. It is the second of these that we use to collect information to express in the biography.

Figure 6.5 shows the elaboration class for instances of the concept "person". I have also repeated a portion of the instance "Abbie" and highlighted those parts of both the instance and the class that relate to our current topic, *MOVIES*.

As described in more detail in §5.2, each choice in the elaborating information class has a label (the first element) and three fields: the result object, a salience function, and a subject area. The system first collects the choices related to the topic by looking at the SUBJECT-AREA field (in this case there is only one), and then evaluates the result object field to return the object that will be expressed if this choice is taken. In this case, the function MOVIE-INTEREST returns the movie-watching object from the person's interest field, since one exists (shown in Figure 6.6), and the triple function builds a triple of self (#<person Abbie>), the slot INTERESTS, and the WATCHING-MOVIES instance.

```
#<PERSON  ABBIE  313526034
 BELIEFS:                        ((CAR-LOCATION . 105))
 NAME:                           ABBIE
 SKILLS:                          (#<MANAGING 313545576>)
 JOB:                            #<PLANT-MANAGER 313525223>
...
 INTERESTS:
    (#<EATING-FOOD 313545604> #<READING 313545625> #<WATCHING-TV 313545640>
    #<DRINKING 313545652> #<GOING-OUT-TO-BARS 313545666>
    #<WATCHING-MOVIES  313545675>)
 ..>
```

```
(define-elaborating-information-class (concept 'person)
 (location  :result-object (triple self 'location)
            :salience default-inclusion-check
            :subject-area *current-status*)
 (job  :result-object (triple self 'job)
       :salience default-inclusion-check
       :subject-area *work*)
 (skills  :result-object (triple self 'skills)
          :salience default-inclusion-check
          :subject-area *current-status*)
 (employment-history    :result-object (triple self 'employment-history)
                        :salience default-inclusion-check
                        :subject-area *work*)
 (movies   :result-object (triple self 'interests (movie-interest self))
           :salience likes-movies
           :subject-area *movies*)
 (books  :result-object (triple self 'interests (reading-interest self))
         :salience likes-reading
         :subject-area *books*)
 (tv   :result-object (triple self 'interests (tv-interest self))
       :salience likes-tv
       :subject-area *tv*) )
```

Figure 6.5 Elaborating information class for "person"

To determine whether this information is "interesting" in this context, the system first checks the table of objects referenced in the discourse so far to avoid repeating information, and then it evaluates the function in the salience field to determine whether the object is interesting (in this case, the function "likes-movies" simply checks that there is an object of type WATCHING-MOVIES in the interests slot of the person).

```
#<WATCHING-MOVIES 313545675
 CONCEPT-NAME:          WATCHING-MOVIES
 INTENSITY:             5
 EXPERIENCES:           (#<WATCHING-MOVIE-EXPERIENCE 321763542>)
 PREFERENCES:           ((:DRAMA 7) (:COMEDY 5) (:COPS-N-ROBBERS 3)
                           (:POLITICAL 3) (:ART 3) (:SCI-FI 5) (:HORROR 5))
 CARE-ABOUT-QUALITY: 5 >
```

Figure 6.6 Instance of "watching movies"

Once the information is selected, it needs to be added to the Text Structure. At this point, the only available place to add the information is as the matrix to the topic node. The restriction on this node (See §5.2.1.3) is PROPOSITION; since all topic information collected at this level is some fact about the person in the simulated world, it is guaranteed to be a proposition, so we do not make an explicit check. However, checking would be a simple matter of using the mapping and realization class shown in Figure 6.7 to ascertain that one of the choices in the class (the one shown) has a result of type PROPOSITION.

```
(define-mapping (role ':interests)
  triple-to-realization-class-table
  (:class-name like-activity
  :arguments (tri-object self) (tri-value self))))

(define-realization-class like-activity (person activity)
 (:result  'proposition
  :body    (complex-state-tree
              :matrix ( :state like
                        :theme person
                        :rheme activity
                        :restrictions (argument-restrictions (theme object)
                                             (rheme activity)))))
```

Figure 6.7 Mapping and realization class

Once the object is placed in the Text Structure, the mapping and realization class (shown in Figure 6.7) are used to expand the Text Structure. Note that the mapping for triple objects is determined by their relation field (in this case the role INTERESTS). This is described as a "two-step mapping" in §5.4.2 because the first step is a mapping from the triple object itself and the second uses the tri-role (the relation) slot to get the triple-to-text-structure table entry for the value of that slot. (The mechanisms and resource objects used to expand the Text Structure were discussed in more detail in §5.2.)

The resulting Text Structure is shown in Figure 6.8. As in the previous diagrams, each box is a node in the Text Structure; the bold label at the top of the box is the structural relation to its parent and the one on the bottom is its relation to its children. The second label is the contents of the node and the third is the restrictions. Restrictions may either be stipulated by the routine that builds the node or determined by the contents of the node. For example, the restriction PARAGRAPH on the root of the Text Structure in Figure 6.8 was stipulated when it was built; the structure of the biography being generated guarantees that the subnodes (the topics) will each dominate multiple propositions that may be realized as one or more sentences. In the case of the complex-state node, the restrictions are determined by what categories of adjuncts the semantic category of the matrix will allow. The restrictions on the argument nodes of the matrix are set by the choice in the realization class

(Figure 6.7). They ensure that the selectional restrictions of the verb "like" will not be violated.[78]

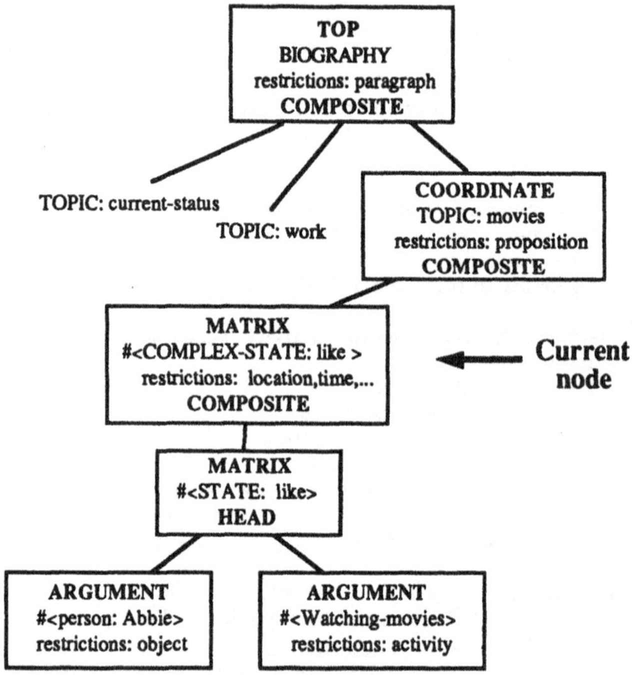

Figure 6.8 Text Structure

Once the Text Structure has been expanded, it is traversed: extensions are considered at composite nodes, and leaves are expanded until they bottom out at LEX objects (which contribute lexical heads to the utterance). The current position (at the beginning of the traversal) is the node complex-state. Since there is no information directly related to our triple and none pending on the OPTIONAL-INFORMATION-TO-BE-INCLUDED list, no extensions are possible and the traversal continues, through the state node to the first argument, #<person Abbie>. Since this node is a leaf, the first step is to see if it can be expanded. Figure 6.9 shows the domain mapping for person and the class of alternatives available. As I described in §5.2.3, the perspective class (also shown in Figure 6.9) gathers together the alternative semantic categories that the object may be

78 "Like" clearly allows other types of arguments, since one can "like dogs" or "like Peter". I am being deliberately agnostic at this point as to whether these are multiple meanings of "like" (as many lexical semanticists would argue), which would mean they had different selection classes in this framework, or if there is just one meaning (and one selection class) and the choices were distinguished by the semantic categories of the arguments. I am currently leaning toward the second; however, lexical ambiguity and type coercion are topics for future research.

expressed as and annotates them with the criteria for distinguishing among them. By bundling the surface resources into semantic categories and grouping those into predefined sets of alternatives, the text planner is prevented from choosing combinations of resources that are not expressible in the language. (For a more complete discussion of the semantic categories and their motivations, see Chapter Four.)

```
(define-mapping (concept ':person )
  class-to-realization-class-table
  (:class-name INDIVIDUAL-NAMED
  :arguments ((name self)))

  individual-to-realization-class-table
  (:class-name INDIVIDUAL
   :arguments ( )) )


(define-perspective-class INDIVIDUAL-NAMED (name)
 ((return-typed-complex-object 'unique-object-proform '*you*)
  :context-features (hearer))

 ((return-typed-complex-object 'named-object name)
  :context-features (introduce known))

 ((return-typed-complex-object 'named-object name)
    :context-features (subsequent-reference))

 ((return-typed-complex-object 'instance-of-a-kind self)
  :context-features (introduce unknown-in-context))

 ((return-typed-complex-object 'unique-individual self)
  :context-features (subsequent-reference unknown-in-context))

 ((return-typed-complex-object 'definite-set name)
  :context-features (known)
  :operators ((multiplex))))
```

Figure 6.9 Mapping for "person"

In this case the third (highlighted) choice is taken, since Abbie has already been mentioned in the utterance. (The decision of whether or not to pronominalize this reference will not be made until the mapping to the linguistic specification, when the complete context is available.) The contents of the node is replaced with a Text Structure object of type NAMED-OBJECT and a leaf node with the name "Abbie" is added as its child. (See Figure 6.11.)

Since our current position is a composite node, the next step before the traversal continues is to see if there is any information related to Abbie. However, since we began by collecting the information related to Abbie on the topic *movies*, there is nothing new to add here.

Traversal continues through the LEX node, which will remain a leaf, to the second argument of the STATE, watching-movies. Again, we first need to expand this node. The mapping for the object and the realization class are shown in Figure 6.10 Since this node is restricted to object of type activity, the second choice in the realization class is chosen.

```
(define-mapping (concept ':watching-movies)
  class-to-realization-class-table
  (:class-name event-relation
  :arguments ( *current-person*
               'watch
               (build-typed-complex-object
                    'sample-of-a-kind (build-lex-leaf 'movie))))))

(define-realization-class EVENT-RELATION ( obj1 event obj2)
(:result-type proposition
 :body (complex-event-tree
          :matrix ( :event event
                    :agent obj1
                    :patient obj2
                    :restrictions (argument-restrictions
                         (agent object) (patient object))
          :time 'past))
(:result-type activity
 :body (complex-activity-tree
          :matrix ( :event event
                    :patient obj2
                    :restrictions (argument-restrictions
                         (patient object))))))
```

Figure 6.10 Mapping for "watching movies"

The resulting Text Structure after the expansion of the two arguments is shown in Figure 6.11.

Having made the selection for the WATCH-ACTIVITY and extended the Text Structure, we will shortly begin traversing the tree, but first, we will determine whether the Text Structure can be extended. As I described in the original description of the selection algorithm, the mention of an object triggers the consideration of any related information. In this case, the underlying object of the current node is an instance of WATCHING-MOVIES (shown in Figure 6.6). The elaborating information class[79] (shown in Figure 6.12) is used to determine if there is any related information that might be included here. In this case, there may be previous movie experiences recorded in this object that are appropriate to mention.

[79] Again, in order to keep the selection algorithm simple, this choice only picks one experience to include (the first on the list which is the most recent). There may, in fact, be numerous movie experiences recorded and a more sophisticated selection algorithm should choose among them or group them. Since one experience is sufficient to make the point here, I have limited the elaboration choice.

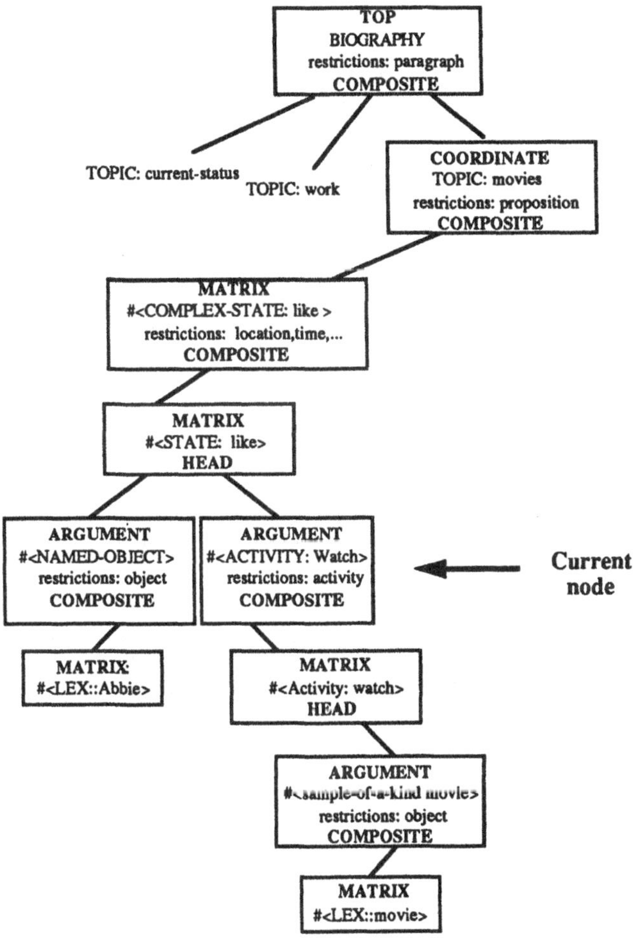

Figure 6.11 Text Structure

```
(define-elaborating-information-class (concept 'watching-movies)
  (one-experience   :result-object (car (experiences self))
                    :salience default-inclusion-check
                    :subject-area *movies*))
```

Figure 6.12 Elaborating information class for "watching movies"

The result object picks the first of the experiences and determines whether it is relevant here. The subject area (*movies*) is the current topic, and the default-inclusion-check finds that the result object is not NIL (that is there was in fact an experience object in the experiences slot). Next it must check whether the object can be added to the current position in the Text Structure. To do this it uses the mapping and realization class for the object. The object WATCHING-MOVIE-EXPERIENCE and its mapping are shown in Figure 6.13.

```
#<WATCHING-MOVIE-EXPERIENCE
  CONCEPT-NAME:     WATCHING-MOVIE-EXPERIENCE
  OCCURRED-WHEN:    620.9501
  MOVIE-SEEN:       #<MOVIE THE-LADY-VANISHES 313657765>>

(define-mapping (concept ':watching-movie-experience)
 class-to-realization-class-table
  (:class-name event-relation
   :arguments (  *current-person*
                 'watch
                 (movie-seen self)) ) )
```

Figure 6.13 Mapping for "movie-watching-experience"

The mapping is to the same realization class as the movie-watching object: event-relation (shown in Figure 6.10). The three arguments are the person watching the movie (*current-person*[80]), the relation WATCH, and the value of the MOVIE-SEEN slot of the movie-watching-experience object. The result types of each choice in the realization class are checked to see if they are compatible with the current position. However, the current position is the ACTIVITY watch, which can only take a location, time, or manner, and the only expressions of the movie experience are a proposition and an activity. Therefore, the object cannot be added at this point, so it is put on the ADDITIONAL-INFORMATION-TO-BE-INCLUDED list, which will be checked at other composite nodes to determine whether the information can be added later.

The next point in the Text Structure traversal is the matrix ACTIVITY, which is a head node, so no information can be attached, and the traversal continues to its argument, SAMPLE-OF-A-KIND. This node is expanded similarly to the NAMED-OBJECT argument. Again, the possibility for adding the MOVIE-WATCHING-EXPERIENCE is considered; however, since propositions can be adjuncts to objects only if one of the arguments of the proposition is the same as the argument (i.e. for a relative clause), it cannot be added in.

[80] Note that the movie-watching-experience object does not contain the information of who did the watching, but rather relies on the context of this object in the program as a whole. This is problematic when any consumer of this information (such as a text generator) needs to manipulate this object independently of its context. I have used a global variable (*current-person*) to compensate for this lack, but this is clearly inadequate, since the system may be talking about more than one person. The correct fix is to add a slot to the movie experience object for the experiencer. The problem of relying on context and not explicitly recording relevant information is pervasive in this and most (if not all) the application programs I have worked with. Finding these lacks is another way text generation can help an application program under development to be more robust and general.

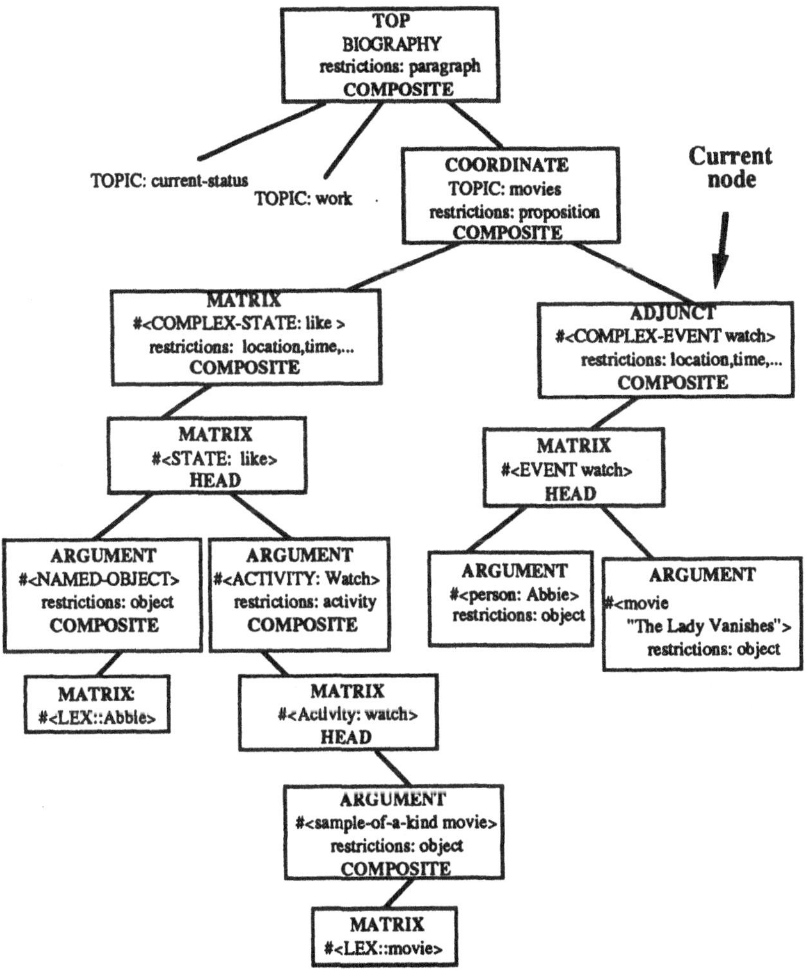

Figure 6.14 Text Structure

The traversal continues up the tree until it reaches the topic node. Again the ADDITIONAL-INFORMATION-TO-BE-INCLUDED list is checked and the possibilities for adding the MOVIE-WATCHING-EXPERIENCE are considered. At this node the restriction is PROPOSITION, so there the MOVIE-WATCHING-EXPERIENCE can be added. Figure 6.14 shows the addition and expansion of this object.

Again the next step is to consider whether there is any related information that can be added in. Figure 6.15 shows the movie-watching-experience object and its elaborating information class.

```
#<WATCHING-MOVIE-EXPERIENCE
   CONCEPT-NAME:         WATCHING-MOVIE-EXPERIENCE
   OCCURRED-WHEN:        620.9501
   MOVIE-SEEN:           #<MOVIE THE-LADY-VANISHES 313657765>>

(define-elaborating-information-class (concept 'watching-movie-experience)
  (time  :result-object (triple self 'occurred-when)
         :Salience default-inclusion-check
         :subject-area *movies*) )
```

Figure 6.15 Elaborating information class for "movie-watching-experience"

The "interesting" criteria are checked: this information has not been expressed before, there is a value in the occurred-when slot, and the subject area is *movies*, and the next step is to see if it can be added into the Text Structure.

```
(define-mapping (role 'occurred-when)
 triple-to-text-structure-table
  (:class-name time-relation-triple
  :arguments ((tri-object self)
              (tri-role self)
              (make-ms-time time-integer (tri-value self))))
 individual-to-specification-table
  (:template-name return-realization-function
  :arguments (mumble::pp+on)))

(define-realization-class TIME-RELATION-TRIPLE (object relation time)
 (:result-type  proposition
 :body  (complex-state-tree
                    :matrix (  :state isa
                               :theme object
                               :rheme time)))
 (:result-type  time
 :body  (relation-tree
           :head relation
           :argument time
           :related-to object)))
```

Figure 6.16 Mapping for "occurred-when"

The current node (the WATCH event) is a composite node with restrictions time, manner, or location. We can see from the mapping and realization class shown in Figure 6.16, that the information on the time of the movie-watching experience can be added to the current node. The resulting Text Structure is shown in Figure 6.17.

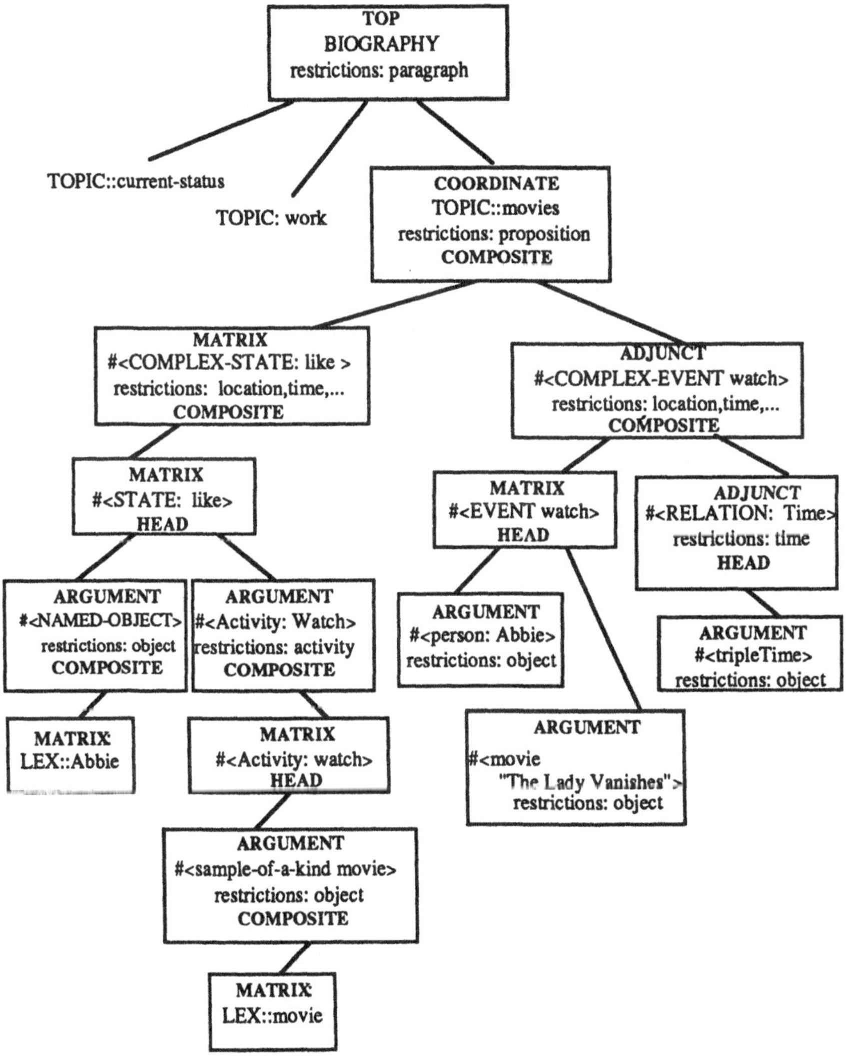

Figure 6.17 Final Text Structure

The traversal continues through the leaves of this subtree, expanding them as it did its sister node, the matrix COMPLEX-STATE. No additional information is added and the traversal eventually reaches the topic node. At this point the entire subtree will be sent to the next phase of the text planner, where the linguistic specification is built, and, if more topics are on the topic list, the selection and composition components of the text planner will continue as it has for the *movies* topic.

6.2 Text Structure and portability

There are generally two approaches to achieving portability. One is to build peripheral components that can automatically or semi-automatically acquire the knowledge needed to port to a new domain. The second is to modularize the system so that the components that are not domain specific are kept separate from those that are, and to try to maximize the amount of knowledge in the more general components. In the long term, a combination of these approaches will certainly be needed. In the work presented here, we have concentrated on the latter. For example, by taking advantage of the fact that most of language is not particular to any domain, we have isolated the linguistic realization component and used the Text Structure to capture abstract linguistic generalizations.

In this section, I show how the Text Structure and the mapping mechanism increases the portability. To make the point clearer, I contrast the current approach with an earlier one in which we connected an application program to the linguistic realization component (LRC) Mumble-86, using a special-purpose text planner to handle the mapping from one to the other. In a paper entitled "From Water to Wine: Generating Natural Language Text from Today's Application Programs" (McDonald & Meteer 1988), we presented the input specification language to Mumble-86, which provided "a means of compensating for the semantic deficits of linguistically naive underlying application programs without compromising principled grammatical treatments in natural language generation."[81] This architecture is shown in Figure 6.18. The "text planning" component in this architecture (indicated with diagonal lines) was tailored specifically to the ALBM application ("AirLand Battle Management") and its underlying knowledge representation, KEE™.

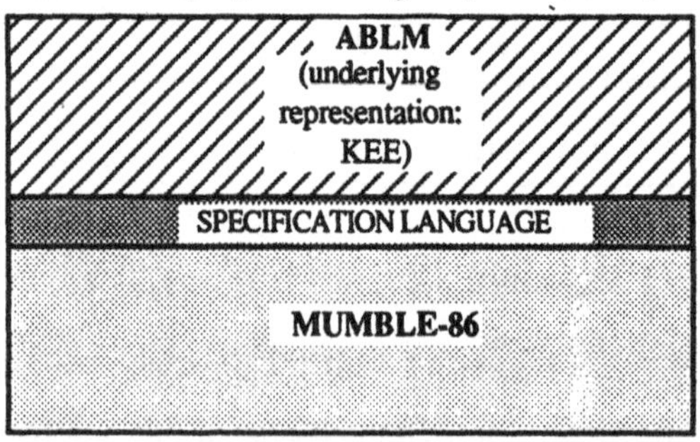

Figure 6.18 1988 Architecture: interfacing to Mumble-86

While the specification language modularizes the generation process so that the linguistic component is isolated from the application program, using the LRC directly requires the developer to be aware of the very low-level linguistic

[81] McDonald & Meteer 1988, p.41.

details that the LRC requires. For example, the specification of a noun phrase requires that information about number, person, and determiner be included. Furthermore, there is no way to ensure that a particular specification built by a text planner will actually be expressible by the linguistic component. For example, there is nothing to prevent a planner from composing a specification combining a completive event with a duration (e.g. *"the plane landed for ten minutes"). The specification language itself also fails to capture certain generalizations about what features can co-occur in language and what is expressed by certain combinations of features. For example, a single noun phrase with a definite article indicates that the entity is known (e.g. "the dog"); however if a proper name is used, the article is omitted even when the entity is known (e.g. "Fluffy").

A related problem is that while this architecture was a successful means of working directly with Mumble-86, it left a great deal of work to be done by the interface component, most of which must be built specifically for each application. In working with any application program, there will always be a great deal that is specific to that application, from the utilities that know how to access objects and their properties in the application's knowledge representation language[82] to the words and phrasings particular to the domain. However, there are also many more generalizations across applications/domains than are covered by the LRC, as noted above. Our approach in developing a text planner for the current system was again to modularize, separating what is general to language from that which is specific to an application. The architecture of the resulting system, Spokesman, is shown in Figure 6.19. The general knowledge used by the text planner resides in the TEXT PLANNER CORE; the domain specific portions of the text planner are again indicated by diagonal lines.

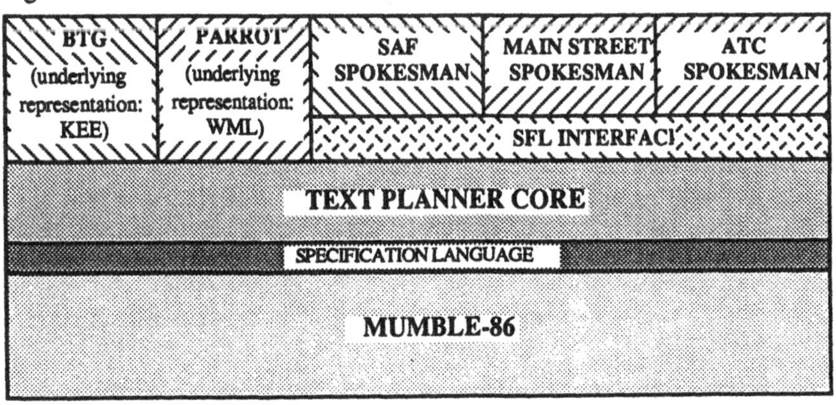

Figure 6.19 1992 Architecture: the Spokesman Generation System

[82] We assume that any application program will at least have some frame-based, taxonomic knowledge representation language defining the types and relations in the application. We discuss the implications of these assumptions later in the book.

The BTG (Block Text Generator) is the direct descendent of the original interface to ALBM in which we produced Operations Orders (OPORDs) from a representation of a battle plan in KEE™ (examples in §3.2 and §5.2). Parrot is a paraphraser that takes as input the output of the IRUS-II (Weischedel *et al.* 1989) understanding component, which is intensional logic representations of queries in the World Model Language (WML).

The three other applications in the figure that Spokesman has generated text for all use the same knowledge representation language, the Simple Frame Language (SFL, Abrett *et al.* 1989): the Semi Automated Forces (SAF) project, which is a component of DARPA's SIMNET battle simulation program at BBN (examples in §5.2-4); Main Street, which is a simulation program developed by Glenn Abrett (examples in §6.1); and Air Traffic Control (ATC), an internal research and development project at BBN on simulating communication among multiple agents. Following our overall approach of modularizing those portions of the system that are shared, we built a subsystem for interfacing with the representation language that contains all the routines for accessing objects in SFL and for handling what is common to all SFL-based applications, such as the root concept THING.

For frame-based hierarchical knowledge representations, such as SFL, Spokesman can generate descriptions of the definitions of object types and their attributes directly from the knowledge base without needing any application specific information. It takes advantage of the frame structure of the types to organize the information, and creates words from the symbolic names of the frames and slots. The following paragraph was generated just using the application independent components of the system: the SFL INTERFACE component, the CORE TEXT PLANNER, and the LRC.

> *A car is a transportation-device. The default speed of a car is a speed. The direction-of-motion of a car is a direction. ... Taxi and personal-car are specializations of a car.*

This kind of sharing will become more common as knowledge representation languages become standardized and are distributed community-wide, as LOOM is being now (MacGregor & Brill 1989).

6.2.1 *Interfacing to an application program*

As we discussed earlier, Spokesman is essentially an *object-oriented* program in that the routines for mapping from one level to the other are specialized for the type of object being mapped, just as generic methods in CLOS or Flavors are specialized for different classes or flavors in those object-oriented programming languages.[83] Each mapping function is a table which, when given an object, will walk up the KB hierarchy until it finds a routine associated with that object's type or a type it inherits from. If that routine is a template,[84] it will

[83] At the time that Spokesman was implemented, there were no platform independent object-oriented languages, such as CLOS. The same functionality is implemented in Spokesman using tables to associate types with routines for manipulating them.

[84] A "template" in this system is essentially open code which takes as arguments elements from one level of representation and returns elements of the next level of representation. For

execute the template; if it is a class of alternatives, it will select one and execute that. This process is shown schematically in Figure 6.20. There are different tables for the mappings between each level of representation in Spokesman, and, in some cases, different tables depending on the context defined by representational level.

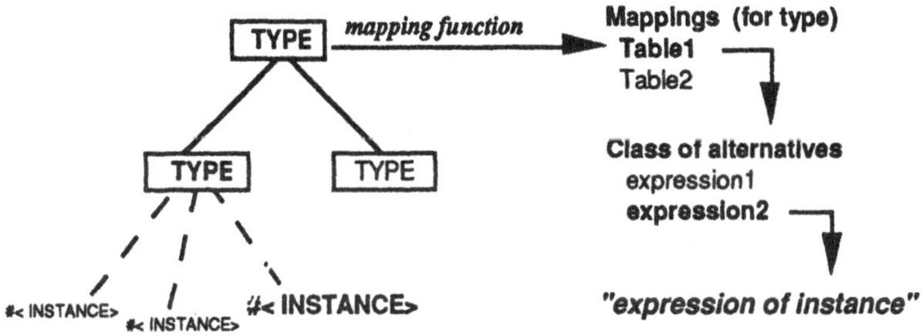

Figure 6.20 Mappings

One of our goals has been to isolate what is common to a language (though not necessarily all languages) from what is particular to the application the generator is speaking for. In particular, we wanted both to capture the generalizations available from the co-occurance of features in the linguistic specification and ensure that the specifications that are built are expressible in language. Within the text planner, these generalizations are captured in the Text Structure, which is used to compose the text.

As we have seen, there is a great deal that is common to all generation tasks and even across related applications, and these portions of the generator can be isolated into application independent components. However, the actual connection between the types and entities in the domain must be done for each specific application. Since most language systems require some sort of taxonomic domain knowledge to specify their semantics and most AI systems also have a central knowledge base, it is common to connect such systems through the knowledge base (KB). There are essentially three ways to do this:

(1) *Maintaining a separate domain model.* Some language systems maintain their own domain model, independently of the application it is working with (e.g. JANUS, Weischedel *et al.* 1989). Porting to a new domain means translating the application's domain model (if it has one) to the representation language of the language system (Bobrow *et al.* (1990) describe ways of doing this semi-automatically.) This method works for applications that are relatively static, such as databases, where the values may change, but the types and relations are static. However, in evolving applications, the effort to maintain two knowledge bases becomes difficult.

example, a Text Structure template takes objects from the application program and builds a Text Structure subtree, and a specification template takes a text structure node and builds a linguistic specification.

(2) *Integrating a portion of a language-specific domain model into the application's knowledge base.* Another approach is to integrate a portion of a domain model used by the language system into the knowledge base of the application system. For example, the Penman generation system (Mann 1983) uses an "upper model" KB which sits above the KB of the application system (Bateman 1990). The theoretical implication of this approach, i.e. that all of the things in the world are subsumed by some linguistically relevant concept, is appealing. However, in practice, knowledge bases of existing applications are rarely so conveniently organized as to be able to be partitioned so neatly. The organization of the KB generally grows out of the needs of the application, which do not necessarily include linguistically interesting distinctions, such as object and event, and these will not necessarily be maintained. Furthermore, this approach still does not handle domain-specific idiosyncrasies. For example, in the ATC domain, the concept PILOT inherits from PERSON, however, when addressing a pilot, a controller would not use the pilot's name, but rather the flight ID of the plane he is flying (we return to this example in the next section).

(3) *Using the applications knowledge base directly.* The approach used in Spokesman is to create mappings directly from the application's KB to the routines or sets of alternatives in the text planner for expressing those objects. This approach has the advantage of being able to handle idiosyncrasies in the KB and in language more easily. However, like all of these approaches, it does place an onus on the developers of the application's KB completely and explicitly to represent the knowledge. We return to this point in Chapter Eight; first we will describe how the connections work in Spokesman.

In determining the mappings from the application program objects to the resources in the text planner we have two goals: one is to pick an appropriate level in the KB of the application to associate a particular resource and the other is to select a resource that will allow its expression to vary appropriately in the contexts that entity can appear.

We can illustrate this by contrasting with our earlier work (McDonald & Meteer 1988). Figure 6.21 shows a mapping from an instance in the ALBM system,[85] the 53RD-MECHANIZED-DIVISION, to a specific template, ARMED-FORCES-UNIT-NAME, for building the linguistic specification for expressing that instance:

[85] In this version of the ALBM system, instances of military units were simply symbols rather than structured, typed objects. This is why the arguments are included with the mapping, since they are not otherwise explicitly represented. In later versions of ALBM, military units were represented as instances of types, so that this information could be parameterized somewhat and mappings were only needed for the different kinds of units; this still numbered in the tens however, since there were very few organizational levels represented.

```
(define-default-specification '53rd-mechanized-division
  :template-name armed-forces-unit-name
  :arguments ("53rd" "Mechanized" "Division"))

(define-specification-template armed-forces-unit-name (number type size)
  (let ((K (make-a-kernel 'np-common-noun size))
        (B (make-a-bundle 'general-np)))
    (set-bundle-head B K)
    (neuter-&-third-person B)
    (singular B)
    (no-determiner B)
    (add-specializing-description
      (property-realized-as-an-adjective number) B)
    (add-specializing-description
      (property-realized-as-an-adjective type) B)
    B))
```

Figure 6.21 Mapping and template from 1988 system

Since the mapping in this example is for a particular instance, there is no generality captured by the mapping and there needs to be a separate mapping for every instance of a military unit in the system. Furthermore, the template only produces a single specification; there is no provision for choosing among alternative resources for realizing the element (except for grammatically required pronominalization and elision, which occur within the LRC).

In contrast, the example in Figure 6.22 uses a parameterized mapping associated with the type TANK-COMPANY, since all tank companies have the same range of expressions. The mapping in this case has three tables. The first is used in the stage where the text structure is built and the object being mapped is an instance of the class TANK-COMPANY. The mapping function is a realization class for individuals with names. It takes two parameters, one the concept TANK-COMPANY and the other the name, which is kept in the UNIT-NAME slot of the instance. The second table is also used in the Text Structure construction phase, and it is used when the concept itself is being expressed (as in"2/TB is a tank company"). The third table is used in the later stage of processing that builds the specification from the text structure and again is used when the concept itself is being expressed.

In addition to a finer granularity in the mapping in Spokesman, the mapping functions themselves have alternative resources to choose from. In this example, the realization class in the first mapping, INDIVIDUAL-NAME, is used for any individual that is referred to by a name and provides the alternative realizations "you", "2/TB", "the tank company", etc. which are chosen among depending on the context.

```
(DEFINE-MAPPING-TABLES (concept 'TANK-COMPANY)
  class-to-text-structure-table
  (:realization-class INDIVIDUAL-NAME
   :arguments ((concept self) (unit-name self )))

  individual-to-text-structure-table
  (:realization-class INDIVIDUAL
   :arguments ((concept self)))

  individual-to-lexical-resource-table
  (:specification compound-noun
   :arguments ("tank" "company" )))
```

Figure 6.22 Mapping from Spokesman

6.2.2 Capturing differences between domains

In what we have presented so far, the focus has been on taking advantages of similarities within language and among applications to isolate domain independent components from those that need to be specific to the application program. However, there are some things that are intrinsically domain specific, both in what information is expressed and in how it is expressed. A generation system that is to produce realistic texts in a domain must allow the developer to specialize routines at all levels of the generation process. There are several examples of this in our latest domain, Air Traffic Control, which is a simulation of the communication between controllers and pilots. Spokesman is used to display this communication (which occurs between the simulated agents as passed message objects) in the sublanguage of English specific to controller/pilot interactions. The following is an example of the text produced by the system (AC: approach controller; TC: tower controller; P: pilot):

AC: *United 506, descend to 5000 feet, fly heading 100*
P: *5000 feet, heading 100, United 506*
AC: *Delta 1704, reduce speed to 190 knots, descend to 2300 feet, fly heading 360*
P: *heading 360, 2300 feet, Delta 1704*
AC: *Delta 1704, contact Tower 126.55*
P: *ok , Delta 1704, good day*
P: *Regional tower, Delta 1704, 5 miles out for runway three five right*
TC: *Delta 1704, regional tower, cleared to land runway three five right*
P: *roger, three five right*

One example of a domain specific expression is the way pilots are addressed in this domain. Rather than using the pilot's name, the controller addresses the pilot using the flight ID of the plane the pilot is flying — in effect he addresses the plane; similarly, pilots address controllers using their function (e.g approach, tower). In SPOKESMAN, this is handled using the mappings. Rather than using the mapping for PERSON, which pilot inherits from, a text structure mapping specific to the concept PILOT is set up which uses the realization class for named entities (shown in Figure 6.23), but it puts the aircraft instance rather than the pilot instance in the resultant Text Structure node, which is marked as a lexical leaf. In the next phase of the generation process, which maps from the text structure to the linguistic specification, the mapping from the aircraft to the lexical resource is used which combines the airline and the plane's ID number into a flat phrase.

```
(DEFINE-MAPPING-TABLES (concept 'pilot)
  class-to-text-structure
   (:realization-class INDIVIDUAL-NAME
     :arguments (self (build-lex-leaf (my-aircraft self)))
   ))

(DEFINE-MAPPING-TABLES (concept 'aircraft)
  class-to-text-structure
   (:realization-class INDIVIDUAL-NAME
    :arguments (self self))

  individual-to-text-structure
   (:realization-class INDIVIDUAL
    :arguments ((build-lex-leaf self) ))

  object-to-lexical-resource
   (:mapping-function flat-phrase
    :arguments (      (airline self)
                      (mumble::number-word (flight-id self)))
  ))
```

Figure 6.23: Domain specific mappings

Another example is what information is included in the utterance. Some of the information being passed between pilots and controllers is necessary for the simulation, for example when the controller is giving orders, since this information is used by the pilot agent to change the speed, altitude, etc. of the aircraft. However, some information that is conventionally communicated is not used by the simulation system and therefore is not represented in the communication object.[86] For example, when the pilot initially contacts a controller he gives some information about his location to the controller. If he's calling approach, he gives his previous and target altitudes ("Out of 10,000 for 7000") and if he's calling tower he gives his distance from the airport and target runway ("Five miles out for runway three five right"). While in real life this information may help the controller distinguish this plane on his radar screen, in the simulation it is assumed the controller can read the information directly (and it does appear on actual controller screens). Therefore, it is not necessary to include this information in the simulation. However, we need to include it to make the conversation sound realistic. In this case, the we use a domain specific template to select the information needed and construct a text structure representation of it. This template is shown in Figure 6.24:

[86] Some might argue that this is a flaw in the simulation; however, it is such a common occurrence that language requires more than is represented in today's systems that these situations must be handled by the generator in order to make their output realistic.

```
(define-text-structure-template pilot-contact-tower (speaker to plane)
 (let* ((runway (runway (flight-plan plane)))
       (distance (make-distance
                  (distance-from-runway plane runway)))
       (target-runway (build-subordinate-relation-object
                       'for runway plane))
       (dist-out (build-composite-modifier
                  (build-lex-leaf 'out)
                  (cons 'restrictive-modifier distance))))
  (build-coordinate-tree
   'atc-transmission
   (list to speaker dist-out target-runway)
   self)))
```

Figure 6.24: Domain specific Text Structure template

Once the Text Structure has been constructed, the domain specific actions are completed and the later stages of the generation process can be handled by more general, domain independent routines. This modularization isolates the more idiosyncratic actions in the earlier stages of the process, leaving the later stages to be handled by more general operations.

7 Alternative Architectures

The goal of this chapter is to survey the work in natural language generation in order to place my work with respect to others in the field. The focus of this discussion will be the problem of expressibility and how other systems either address it directly, avoid it, or ignore it (the "plan and pray" approach).

By its very nature, the generation process involves a change in the terms in which information is represented. The situation from which the generator is producing the text is represented in the terms of the application program. The final utterance must be in the surface terms of the language. It is this change that creates the problem of expressibility. As the generator is selecting and composing the information to be expressed, it must make sure that there are resources in the language for realizing that information. In this chapter, I look at how different generation systems address or avoid the problem of expressibility. There are three general approaches:

(1) Those that simply organize kernel clauses, thereby limiting the competence of their generation systems: McKeown, Mann & Moore, Hovy.

(2) Those that relax some of the processing constraints adopted in my approach, in particular, efficiency, and let the system backtrack and change decisions: Mann & Moore, Nirenburg, Gabriel.

(3) Those that are not necessarily concerned with modelling the process at all, but rather focus just on achieving competence (e.g. in particular, the systemic approaches: Mann & Matthiessen, Bateman) or on principled planning (Appelt).

The section is organized into two parts. In the first, I look at systems which follow the traditional two-component architecture: text planning and linguistic realization. In the second, I look at the less-traditional architectures.

7.1 Traditional two-component systems

The first set of systems I will look at follow the traditional division of the generation process into two components: text planning and linguistic realization.

7.1.1 *McKeown's TEXT*

McKeown (1982, 1985b) focuses on the strategic ("what to say") rather than the tactical ("how to say it") side of natural language generation. She addresses how to choose what information to include and how to organize that information to produce paragraph length texts in response to users' queries about an underlying knowledge base. Her system TEXT uses its knowledge about "discourse strategies" (represented in predefined schemas) and a representation of focus (following Sidner, 1983) to specify the paragraph. The tactical (linguistic) component, which realized the specification, was a functional unification grammar.[87]

McKeown uses the observation/assumption that people use certain discourse patterns to express certain discourse goals. Therefore, for each "communicative goal" the system might have, there is a corresponding schema representing a discourse strategy, for instance "define", "describe", and "compare". TEXT uses the particular type of query (there are a limited number in the system) to choose the appropriate schema and to circumscribe a portion of the knowledge base, called the "relevant knowledge pool". For example, the query "What is a ship?" selects the "definition" schema and puts all the information associated with the concept "ship" from the data base in the knowledge pool.

The schemas are made up of "rhetorical predicates" such as "identification", "attribution", "analogy". (She uses all of Grimes' (1975) and William's (1983) predicates and adds three of her own, for a total of twenty-three. It is unclear why she thought these were the best.) The schemas, implemented with an ATN, specify the order of the predicates and whether they are obligatory, optional, or repeatable. The rhetorical predicates may themselves be schemas whose terms are rhetorical predicates, making the entire system recursive (although this was not fully taken advantage of in the TEXT system). Thus the order of the predicates determines the order in which the information is expressed in the final text.

The individual rhetorical predicates select the information (i.e. building the "propositions" to be communicated). If there is a choice of rhetorical predicate (and thus a choice of resulting proposition), or if a predicate could build more than one proposition given the information available in the knowledge pool, then the system uses focus considerations to choose among the propositions. It uses both a representation of "immediate focus" (the object being talked about) and a set of focus constraints which enforce local coherence (keep the topic from shifting randomly).

Once the ordered set of propositions is determined, the structures returned by the dictionary are individually translated into the input notation for a functional unification grammar (Kay 1979), with the help of dictionary entries associated with the predicates. They are then sent through a functional unification grammar to produce the final text. Each proposition contributes one sentence.

One of the major drawbacks of TEXT is that it is severely limited: there are a small number of query types and associated discourse strategies (three, in fact)

[87] TEXT's planning component was later connected to a version of Mumble (circa 1984), resulting in a considerable speed up of the system (Rubinoff 1986).

and the schemas are not very flexible. It is hard to see how the system would scale up to handle general discourse, where the possibilities for organizing information are not as structured as definitions and comparisons. However, it is a fully implemented system which runs from an substantial (albeit simplistic) underlying program. It addresses the problem of where organizing strategies come from when what is behind the generator is merely a data base. Furthermore, the text that is produced by the system is far more sophisticated than one might expect. Consider the following example:[88]

> A ship is a water-going vehicle that travels on the surface. Its surface-going capabilities are provided by the DB attributes DISPLACEMENT and DRAFT. Other DB attributes of the ship include MAXIMUM_SPEED, PROPULSION, FUEL (FUEL_CAPACITY AND FUEL_TYPE), DIMENSIONS, SPEED_DEPENDENT_RANGE and OFFICIAL_NAME. The Downes, for example, has MAXIMUM_SPEED of 29, PROPULSION of STMTURGRD, FUEL of 810 (FUEL_CAPACITY) and BNKR (FUEL_TYPE), DIMENSIONS of 25 (DRAFT), 46 (BEAM) and 438 (LENGTH) and SPEED_DEPENDENT_RANGE of 4200 (ECONOMIC_RANGE) and 2200 (ENDURANCE_RANGE).

This text is produced by the "definition" schema which instantiates four rhetorical predicates: identification, evidence, attributive, and particular illustration, each contributing one sentence to the paragraph. While the use of actual terms from the knowledge base (in upper case) and complete lists of all attributes in the second two sentences is a bit awkward, the structure of the text is fairly good, with complex noun phrases, conjunctions, and discourse connectives (e.g. "for example"). This raises some questions about exactly how the system actually works. The earlier description of McKeown's system in terms of schemas that organize rhetorical predicates, each of which returns a proposition, with the propositions in turn each contributing a single sentence, seems too simplistic to account for the example paragraph. For instance, how does it combine information into conjunctions ("the attributes DISPLACEMENT and DRAFT"), or choose between an adjective ("water-going") and a relative clause ("that travels on the surface"), and how does it choose to use such discourse connectives as "other" (in sentence two) or "for example" (sentence three)?

A further question, more to the point in the context of this work, is how does TEXT ensure expressibility. The text planner is choosing and organizing information blindly, i.e. with no explicit consideration for the linguistic resources available; there are no options for backtracking if any parts of the plan built by TEXT and handed to the realization component do not work—it is just assumed that they will (the "plan and pray" method). Why doesn't this cause a problem?

The answer is that there is in fact much more careful engineering and limiting of possibilities than is apparent on the surface. There are two places in the system where a great deal of special-purpose work goes on: one in the

[88] McKeown 1985b, p. 211. The items that appear in upper case are lexicalizations computed directly from the knowledge representation, rather than requiring their own lexical entries in the dictionary.

construction of "propositions" for a chosen rhetorical predicate, and the other in the "dictionary" that translates from the propositions to the functional specification which is input to the linguistic component (the functional unification grammar).

As described earlier, the rhetorical predicates in the schema are responsible for going to the relevant knowledge pool and finding a proposition which fulfills that rhetorical predicate. On closer inspection, the "propositions" that are returned are not a standard-form expression composed of a predicate and arguments, or even a logical form with operators. Rather they are special-purpose structures represented in a "message formalism" that already implicitly encodes not only the information, but also how the information should be organized when it is expressed. McKeown defines a "predicate semantics", which essentially establishes a set of templates that will be filled for each predicate. A predicate will have more than one template associated with it if it can be instantiated by different data types. In TEXT, there are ten rhetorical predicates, many of which can be instantiated with different types, for a total of twenty-six different templates. These templates solve part of the problem by limiting the possible ways information can be combined in a proposition.

For example, the following template is for the "identification" predicate. (1) shows the template used by this rhetorical predicate, (2) shows an instantiation of it, and (3) shows the sentence that was produced from it:[89]

(1) (identification <entity> <super-ord> (restrictive <attr-name> <attr-value>) (non-restrictive <attr-name> <attr-value>)

(2) (identification SHIP WATER-VEHICLE (restrictive TRAVEL-MODE SURFACE) (non-restrictive TRAVEL-MEDIUM WATER) (non-restrictive FUNCTION TRANSPORTATION)

(3) A ship is a water-going vehicle that travels on the surface.

Note that "restrictive" and "non-restrictive" have very special (non-standard) definitions: non-restrictive attributes are attributes of the parent of the entity (and thus all the children of that parent will have that attribute); restrictive attributes are attributes of the entity itself (and thus distinguish it from its siblings). Note, however, that the "non-restrictive" attributes have the same relation to the superordinate as the "restrictive" attributes have to the entity; both kinds of attributes are restrictive, they just restrict different entities. This similarity is not captured in the template, as it would be in a more general, compositional approach.

The terms in the templates for propositions, such as "restrictive" and "non-restrictive" in the above template, not only indicate special relations among the parts of the template, but also translate directly into cues for how the information should be realized:

In the TEXT system, a restrictive modifier (i.e. one that restricts the class of items the entity refers to) calls for the use of a relative clause. A

[89] McKeown, 1985a, p. 210 and 227.

non-restrictive modifier (i.e. that describes all instances of the class that the entity denotes) results in the selection of an adjective.[90]

This is a rather arbitrary rule (and counter-intuitive, since adjectives are usually considered restrictive modifiers); however, the terms "restrictive" and "non-restrictive" are *only* used in the template for the predicate "identification". They ensure that the first sentence of a definition will be in the form "an *x* is a (*m*) *y* that has property *z*", without affecting how other modifiers used by other predicates will be realized. This special-purpose machinery goes a long way towards making the text sound good; however, it means that the system doesn't have a way to express these relations outside of the context of the template, since it relies on the terms in the template to control realization decisions.

This brings us to the second place in which specialized processing goes on in the TEXT system: the "dictionary". Dictionary entries associate predicates with the so-called "deep structure"[91] for each proposition and lexical items for the tokens. The entry itself is a Lisp function that builds the specification that drives the functional unification grammar (FUG). In fact, very little is left for the grammar to do: the specification encodes lexical item, part of speech, and all grammatical features, (definiteness, plurality, etc.). Nearly the only decisions left are between active and passive (based on focus information) and subject-verb agreement.

The dictionary entries themselves are quite powerful, as is evident from the relationship between the input propositions and the output texts in many of TEXT's examples. In the following instance, the entry function actually adds an example that wasn't in the original proposition:

Proposition: (evidence based-db TORPEDOE (TARGET-LOCATION UNDERWATER) (SOME-TYPE-OF DEPTH))

Text: "The torpedo's underwater capabilities are provided by the DB attributes under DEPTH (for example MAXIMUM_OPERATING_DEPTH)."[92]

The entry functions are also responsible for filling in any grammatical information that will be needed by the realization component (the FUG). As evidenced by the following quote, the operations rely on the limitations of the system, rather than attempting to be general.

> *Use of indefinite is always made for this particular construction ["an underwater target location"], since it is assumed that this proposition would not be generated if target location were already mentioned.*[93]

Such an assumption could not be made if all of the places each construction could be used had not been predicted in advance.

90 McKeown, 1985a, p. 158.

91 Note again, that McKeown's terminology is non-standard: "deep structure" has little to do with Chomsky's original (1957) use of the term or how linguists use it today. I suspect it was the ability of the grammar to apply "transformations" such as active-passive that lead McKeown to call the input to the grammar a "deep structure".

92 McKeown, 1985a, p. 210.

93 McKeown, 1985a, p. 167.

McKeown herself recognizes the dangers inherent in using unrestricted Lisp code in the dictionary entries to make decisions.

> *Another effect of hand-encoding is that the dictionary designer is free to encode as complex (or as ad-hoc) translations as he likes. This means that the generated text can be made to appear arbitrarily complex.*[94]

She mentions both problems of the time and effort in producing special-purpose entries and the problem of putting syntactic decisions in the hands of the dictionary rather than the linguistic realization component. According to McKeown, all the syntactic features had to be spelled out in the dictionary entries because the actual realization component used by TEXT was not powerful enough to handle the complexity of the constructions produced by the system. However, it is not clear that a more powerful realization component could have been made use of in TEXT. Since many of the linguistic decisions in the system are stipulated rather that reasoned about, such as the choice of an adjective over a relative clause or the indefinite described above, the input to the linguistic component still would have needed many syntactic features spelled out.

In summary, the main drawback of McKeown's system is that it is not compositional. Templates control all of the decisions, from the overall organization of the text (the discourse schemas) to the organization of information within propositions (the templates used by the rhetorical predicates), to how the propositions are expressed (the functions in the dictionary entries). There are no general rules about how units could independently combine outside of their prescribed context. This lack of compositionality obviates the problem of expressibility, but it also limits the competence of the system.

7.1.2 *Derr & McKeown*

The lack of compositionality of the utterances in McKeown's original system is addressed to some degree in later work with a different application program, a student advisory expert system that was being developed at Columbia University. In a paper by Derr & McKeown (1984), they describe a more powerful realization component which uses focus and shared arguments to combine propositions into complex utterances.

The linguistic component combines the functional grammar of McKeown's earlier system with a definite clause grammar (Pereira & Warren 1983). This allows them to use the more functional and less syntactic terms of the functional grammar (e.g. protagonist [agent], goal, and focus) and to replace the expensive unification with the simpler and more efficient operations over the logical forms of the DCG implemented in Prolog.

"Propositions" in this work are simple predicate–argument structures, rather than the templates described above. Each would produce a simple sentence on its own. The following proposition would be expressed as "The student gave

94 McKeown, 1985a, p. 162.

the answer." The arguments are (in order) protagonist, goal, beneficiary, and focus:

```
(prop   (pred (give, past)
        arg (student, singular)
        arg (answer, singular)
        arg (nil)
        arg (student, singular)))
```

The paper says nothing about where these propositions come from. There is an implicit assumption that the system works with a McKeown-style text planner, but this is not explicitly stated anywhere in the paper.

A more serious problem is that the only operation shown for combining propositions involved checking whether two arguments were EQUAL, such as rules which conjoin sentences with the same focus. Nothing is said about other relations among propositions or a relation between a proposition and an argument of another proposition. While Derr & McKeown might extend their analysis to allow combinations based on relations among relations that are expressible as explicit lexical connectives, it is unclear as to whether they could as easily extend it to relations expressed structurally, for example purpose clauses (see Huettner, Meteer, and McDonald 1987), or to more integral forms of modification, such as adverbs and adjectives.

Again, the expressive power of the system must be limited to the combinations of clauses so that it could be assured that the set of propositions input to the system would be guaranteed to be expressible.

7.1.3 *Mann & Moore*

Mann & Moore (1981) also addressed the problem of combining propositions into complex sentences in their system, KDS (Knowledge Delivery System), which produced multi-paragraph text describing procedures (such as fire emergency procedures). KDS used what I call "optimization", that is evaluating and changing intermediate structures within the generator during initial generation. They began with the following assumptions: (1) there was a lack of isomorphism between the size and organization of objects in the underlying program and those in a text and (2) a restriction that the input to the generation component be in sentence-sized chunks. They then used a unique "fragment and compose" paradigm to produce complex sentences which were cohesive with the surrounding text.

Their first phase, the "fragmenter" module, delimited the content of the utterance. It first extracted the relevant information from the underlying knowledge base using the goals of the utterance, and then broke the information into "propositional units" (each of which would produce a kernel clause). The second phase, organizing the units, involved three modules, the "Problem Solver", the "Knowledge Filter", and the "Hill Climber". First, the units produced by the "Fragmenter" were given a gross organization by the "Problem Solver" module and filtered to delete any repetitious or inferable information by the "Knowledge Filter" module. Next the "Hill Climber" attempted to compose complex protosentences from simple ones by applying a set of aggregation rules, which corresponded roughly to English clause combining rules, for example the following "Common Cause" rule (shown in the "informal notation" which appeared in the paper):

Whenever C then X
Whenever C then Y ⟶ Whenever C then X and Y

Note that this organization of units is done at what is generally considered the text planning level, in contrast to Derr & McKeown (described above) who combine units in the linguistic realization module.

Once a set of protosentences was determined, KDS used a set of preference rules to judge the relative quality of the resulting units; then it repeatedly improved the set of protosentences on the basis of those judgements, always using local judgements and hill climbing to a locally optimal solution. The use of a hill climbing approach guarantees that, while the "optimal solution" may not be found, it will avoid the combinatorial explosion of a full search of all the possibilities.

Once the final set of protosentences is determined, they are handed off one by one to a sentence generator which uses a simple context-free grammar to produce surface forms. Subsequent references are handled by a special "Referring-phrase Generator" which keeps track of what objects have been referred to and how the references were expressed.

As in the other systems described so far, the internal integrity of the individual propositions is not changed. They are only arranged with connectives put between them (coordinate and subordinate conjunctions) Since each proposition is realizable as a clause, any combination of the propositions will also be realizable. Again, expressibility is ensured, but with a cost to the expressiveness of the system.

There are several other problems with KDS's approach. First, once the original information has been fragmented into kernels, the original relations among the kernels are lost. The aggregation rules must consequently use shared arguments and predefined templates to combine the kernels into sentence-sized chunks, rather than making use of the underlying coherence relations that were there in the first place. Second, the preference rules use a quantitative measure of evaluation and are stated independently of any linguistic context. The score assigned to a particular construction or combination of units does not consider which rules have been applied in nearby sentences. Consequently, intersentential relations cannot be used to evaluate text for more global considerations. Third, since an intermediate representation of the text rather than the final form is being evaluated, the interdependence of future decisions cannot be taken into account.

In KDS, as in TEXT and the later work of Derr & McKeown, the goal of the generation system was to produce text in the well-defined context of a particular application program. While the text that these systems produced was adequate for their tasks, it does not reflect the full expressiveness of language in general.

This is in part due to the limitations of the applications program each system worked with and in part due to the architecture, which separates the choice of propositions and information on what resources are available to realize these propositions.

In the next section, I look at a similar architecture in a system with much broader goals: to be a domain independent generation system.

7.1.4 *Penman*

The PENMAN generation system, developed at the Information Sciences Institute in Los Angeles, is one of the most comprehensive generation systems ever developed. It has two main components:[95] a text planner (Hovy 1988), which is based on Rhetorical Structure Theory (RST) (Mann & Thompson 1987), and a systemic grammar-based linguistic component, NIGEL (Mann & Matthiessen 1985).

Penman's text planner is very similar to those we have already seen in this section. The linguistic component, however, is quite different. In fact, it is this component that ensures that the plan will be expressible. Nigel uses a *grammar-directed* control structure, grammar directed in which the order of the decisions and what information they take into consideration is determined by the grammar[96]. The message produced by the text planner is passive: the grammar is traversed and the message and other knowledge sources queried at decision points. While this ensures expressibility, i.e. that a grammatical utterance will be produced, it does not ensure that the utterance will convey the entire message. If there is something unexpected in the message, it won't break the system; it simply won't be included in the utterance.

We will look briefly at the text planner and realization component, and conclude with some of their more recent work.

7.1.4.1 *The text planner* Penman's text planner is essentially a top-down, hierarchical planner (following Sacerdoti 1977) which uses a formalized version of the relations of RST as the elements of its plans. As I discussed earlier (§2.2.4), Hovy's RST-based text planner defines text structuring as the process of organizing units at the clause level and above. In fact, Hovy makes similar assumptions about the input as Mann & Moore in KDS, i.e. that it is comprised of independent kernels that must be chunked into sentences; KDS, however, goes to some length to fragment the input into these kernels while Hovy simply assumes they exist in this form initially:

[95] Early architectures for Penman (Mann 1983) included a revision component, but it was never implemented and was not included in the latest documentation of the system (Penman Group 1989). This recent documentation also indicated that the text planner was optional, which was not the case earlier. They have defined an input specification language (Sentence Plan Language, SPL) which allows applications to build the input to the grammar component directly for simple utterances, or so that users can design their own text planning component.

[96] This is in contrast to a message-directed control structure where the order of decisions, etc, is controlled by the representation of the message. This distinction is discussed in more detail in Chapter One (Section 1.2.2.1) and in McDonald, Meteer, & Pustejovsky (1987).

> *Assuming that input elements are sentence- or clause-sized chunks of representation, the permutation set of the input elements defines the space of possible paragraphs.*[97]

Both Mann & Moore and Hovy recognize the inefficiencies of brute force approaches to organizing kernels and go to some lengths to avoid having to attempt all possible organizations of kernels: KDS uses a hill-climbing algorithm and Hovy uses the schemas of RST to organize the units.

The schemas of RST are smaller and thus lead to much more composition than those used by McKeown. Each schema captures one rhetorical relation (e.g. purpose, elaboration; there are about 20 in the theory) and has two parts, a nucleus and a satellite.[98] Each schema also has constraints on what the nucleus and satellite can be and on what the intended effect of the schema is, which are defined in terms of belief and goal operators (following Cohen & Levesque 1985). Schemas nest recursively, from the top level, which spans the entire text, to the leaves, which are clause-sized units. As with the other systems we have looked at in this section, there is no attempt to consider the possible resources for realizing the leaves; each is ensured to be expressible since each is a proposition.

7.1.4.1 *The linguistic realization component* Penman's linguistic component, NIGEL, is an implementation of a systemic grammar and has one of the greatest competences of any linguistic component. The systemic school of linguistics (Halliday 1985) is particularly adaptable to natural language generation because it takes a functional approach which views language as a resource offering a set of choices to the speaker (Fawcett 1988, Bateman 1988). Systemic functional linguistics divides language, not along the structural lines of syntax and semantics, but along functional lines, into three independent lines of analysis:

- ideational: the content of the utterance and the organization of the speaker's experience in terms of processes, things, qualities, etc.
- interpersonal: the relation of the speaker and hearer (aspects of speech act theory appear here)
- textual: organization and cohesion of text, that which allows it to flow smoothly.

The grammar is a network of "systems", each of which represents a minimal choice point where one feature must be selected from a set of valid alternatives. There are independent lines of traversal through the network for each of the three functional lines of reasoning, each contributing features to the overall specification of the utterance. As a result, a structural syntactic unit is specified cumulatively, rather than all at once, and is contributed to by all three lines.

NIGEL uses a "chooser" (or choice expert) to decide between features in a system. Each of these choosers queries the "demand expression" for that

97 Hovy, 1988, p.164.

98 In the original design of RST, there could be multiple satellites with one nucleus. Hovy made the nucleus/satellite binary in the text planner to make the computation simpler.

particular utterance (built by the planner as its "text plan") and a terminological knowledge base representing the phenomena in domain of discourse. In the current implementation, the demand expression is represented in first order logic and the knowledge base in NIKL.

While this approach captures the flavor of generation as a decision-making process, it is not attempting to model the process itself. Since the features are collected through multiple passes through the grammar, it cannot incrementally generate the text left to right, as people do. Their focus is achieving the competence that people display in their use of language, and not with the actual production characteristics.

Furthermore, NIGEL's implementation, which puts the grammar in control of the processing, is particularly inefficient. For example, when determining the features of a noun phrase, the system asks "Is there a color attribute?", "Is there a size attribute?", etc. even when there are no such attributes for the head of the phrase in the demand expression. A second problem is that Nigel cannot use the linguistic context of an utterance to make decisions. This is problematic since it is unclear how obligatory pronominalization such as that controlled by c-command, for instance, can be handled without left context.

A final problem is that NIGEL is only a sentence generator, and so it must rely on the text planner to group the input into sentence-sized chunks. But since the text planner works without any knowledge of the available linguistic resources, it must be conservative in how it groups elements. As we saw earlier, the current text planner uses the approach of combining only propositions, which can be guaranteed to have a realization as clauses.

In the context that NIGEL is used, i.e. as a linguistic component for a conservative text planner, much of the power of the systemic approach is underutilized. Other systemic-based systems handle all of the generation process, from the decision to speak to the final text (e.g. Fawcett 1981). In more recent work, Bateman and Paris (1989) are looking at how a text planner could have more control over the linguistic resources, in particular how register (the level of formality and detail) can influence the utterance.

7.2 Non-traditional architectures

In the approaches we have seen so far, the processing has been divided into two sequential components (text planning and linguistic realization) with a strict sequencing of the activities: selecting the information, organizing the units, linguistically realizing the units. Any changes in decisions were made within a decision module, where I use "decision module" to be a component where decisions of the same kind are made. All of these approaches have had to restrict the expressive power of their text in order to ensure that what was planned would be expressible in language. The following systems recognize that this restriction is a problem and attempt to address it through their architectures. Appelt views language generation as a part of planning, and looks at what is necessary to plan language and actions from first principles. Nirenburg *et al.* treat natural language generation as general problem solving and use a blackboard architecture that allows conflicting decisions to be changed; Gabriel optimizes intermediate levels of representation; Danlos controls for interactions among decisions through a "discourse grammar" that stipulates the possible combinations of sentence structures.

7.2.1 *Appelt*

Appelt was one of the first to break away from the traditional two-component approach, arguing that planning language and action were essentially the same process:

> *Human language behavior is part of a coherent plan of action directed toward satisfying a speaker's goals.... Thus, the planning at each level [from planning an illocutionary act to deciding to communicate an intention to refer] involves consideration of both linguistic rules and goal satisfaction. The distinction between 'what' and 'how' [what to say and how to say it] then becomes merely two points on a continuum between goal-satisfaction and rule-satisfaction.*[99]

Appelt takes a more sophisticated view of utterances as actions in a plan than Cohen & Perrault (1979) or Allen & Perrault (1980). His approach recognizes that the complexities and subtleties of language allow the speaker to fulfill multiple goals with a single utterance. For example, an instruction to do something includes both the instruction and verbal pointings (references) to the objects necessary to carry it out. In turn these references can both refer to an object and convey additional information or emotional attitude towards it.

Appelt's planning system KAMP ("Knowledge and Modalities Planner") plans actions/utterances from first principles using formal logic of "knowledge and action" (following Moore, 1980). The system begins with a set of axioms about the state of the world, knowledge about both physical and linguistic actions: their preconditions and effects, and knowledge about the agents: their beliefs and goals. The plan is developed using a procedural net where each node has a possible world associated with it and the arcs are the actions that transform one world into another. The deduction system proves whether the goals are satisfied in a particular world. Specific critics are used to evaluate the plan, looking for particular interactions between goals. The net is hierarchical with each successive level representing less abstract plans, with more particular steps filled in.

The value of this work is not as a planner and generator: KAMP only produced one complex sentence and took nearly an hour to do that. Planning from first principles takes far too much time to expect to do it in an interactive situation. However, in order to make the assumptions necessary to abbreviate the reasoning process, we need to know what is behind those assumptions. Appelt's work contributes to those foundations.

[99] Appelt, 1985, in Grosz *et al.* 1986, p.502.

7.2.2 *Nirenburg*

Nirenburg *et al.* (1989) argue against strict serialization of decisions in generation, and opt instead for a very general and powerful architecture, a blackboard controlled by an agenda, which lets decisions be made opportunistically. In essence, they treat natural language generation as general problem solving:

> *Natural language generation planning is naturally interpretable as search with constraints in a complex space of realizations for the various (pragmatic, discourse, referential, lexical, syntactic) meaning types.*[100]

While they keep the same basic set of decision types as other generation systems, they make three major changes to the traditional serial decision approaches:

- They put virtually all of the decision making into the "text planner" (with the exception of content delimitation, which they do not yet address, and morphology, which they term "realization").
- They relax the constraints on the ordering of the decisions. (Though ordering is not completely free, since the control structure is agenda based and different decision types have different base priority levels.)
- They let any decision that has been made be changed if it conflicts with another decision.

Their generation system, DIOGENES, uses a blackboard architecture with agenda-style control, where each decision module operates independently and posts its results on the blackboard. While the actual processing is independent, the modules can share information via the blackboard. There are five decision-making modules in DIOGENES:

Text Structuring: determining the order of propositions, the discourse relations among them, and the sentence boundaries;

Lexical Selection: choosing the open class words;

Syntactic Selection: choosing syntactic structure for the clauses and choosing closed class lexical items;

Coreference Treatment: using anaphora, deixis, and ellipsis where appropriate;

Constituent Ordering: establishing the order of syntactic constituents in a sentence.

While the ordering of the decision making in these modules is not fixed, it is not completely free either, since the control structure is based on an agenda with priorities. Each of the different decision types (i.e. the decisions made in each module) has a different base priority level, which produces an initial default ordering. So initially, text structuring decisions are made before lexical selection decisions, which are made before syntactic structure decisions; this

[100] Nirenburg, Nyberg, & Defrise, 1989, p.11.

ordering is not maintained, of course, since decisions may be retracted and other decisions remade.

There are currently two processes in DIOGENES for changing the agenda: "obviation", eliminating an item that is no longer needed, such as lexical selected for an item that the syntactic decision component has decided to elide; and "retraction", changing a decision, which retriggers items on the agenda with new input. The designers are currently in the process of developing more sophisticated prioritizing heuristics that can choose the most appropriate agenda item (the one most likely to produce an efficient solution) and take into account the cost of retracting a decision.

There are two main problems with this approach. The first is its inherent inefficiency. Once one decision is changed, all other decisions depending on it must be rechecked. If any of those have to be retracted, then another search for the decisions depending on the changed ones must be made, and so on. Circular alterations are prevented stipulatively, by placing an upper bound on the number of conflict resolution attempts. They admit this may result in "a loss in stylistic quality of the output", but do not address what happens if it results in an ungrammatical or incoherent text.

The second problem is that modularizing the decisions ignores their inherent interconnectivity. For example, when information which is grouped into "sentences" independently of lexical or syntactic decisions, as it is in DIOGENES, then there is no guarantee that the information will be expressible as a sentence in the target language (in English there must be at least one proposition—state or event—that can be realized with a verb as the matrix clause to make the sentence grammatical). Also there is no guarantee that the lexical items and syntactic structures later chosen for the elements that have been grouped will be legally combinable into a single sentence in the language.

It is not modularization, *per se*, that is the problem here, but rather that the modularization is according to what are typically areas of study, instead of according to what constraints the decision types impose on other decision types. A reorganization of the decision modules that, for example, did not attempt to combine organizing the information with determining sentence boundaries, but rather let the boundaries be a side effect of syntactic choices, would be more effective.

7.2.3 *Gabriel*

Gabriel (1988) focuses on the production of written text, which he calls "deliberate writing" in contrast to casual writing or speech:

> *Deliberate writing: When I sit down to write several paragraphs of English text for an audience which I cannot see and which cannot ask me questions, and if I care that the audience understands me perfectly the first time, I am engaged in 'deliberate writing.*[101]

[101] Gabriel, 1988, p. 1.

Like Nirenburg, above, Gabriel treats all of generation as a planning problem, uses independent processing modules for different types of decisions, and an agenda-style control mechanism. His system, Yh (short for Yackity Hack), consists of a set of experts, each of which has a description and a procedure that will be executed when it is invoked. The descriptions are compared to the current situation with a pattern matcher and the one with the best match is invoked. The descriptions not only contain information about what actions the expert will take (what goals it will accomplish), but also the preconditions for when it can be invoked and "preferences" and "influences" that affect the strength of the match. The application of the system is writing documentation for Lisp programs.

Yh starts out with a description of the initial state (a set of facts to explain) and the goal state (the textual explanation of those facts) and tries to find a sequence of experts that will transform the initial state to the goal state. There are three stages to the process (each an item on the agenda): (1) coarse planning, (2) plan execution, and (3) revision ("observation-expert activation"). The first stage orders the facts and partitions them into "sentences"; this is the initial plan for the generation of the text. In stage two, a set of experts uses this plan to build the first draft, represented as a syntactic surface structure with lexical items inserted. This structure is annotated with what information is expressed by each phrase and what situation description caused it to be created. As these experts are operating, a set of critics are noting improvements that might be made. While some of these critics operate immediately (such as those that collapse conjoined phrases), most are entered on the agenda. In the third stage, these agenda items are executed, "revising" the text. There is a claim in Gabriel's later paper (1988) that critics can also alter the initial plan (by "moving facts between planning islands"). However, no account is given of how the effect of those changes would be taken into account, or whether the system could go back and replan in general.

The text produced by Yh is quite good. In fact, Gabriel successfully surprises his readers by integrating text produced by Yh into the description of the program Yh is generating from and then only afterwards indicating it was produced by the generator (the program being described is a Lisp implementation of the "Dutch National Flag" problem):

> *The flag is represented by a 1-dimensional, 0-based array of n elements, FLAG. There are three array markers, L, M, and R, standing for Left, Middle, and Right, respectively. L and M are initialized to 0; R is initialized to n-1.*
>
> [...two more paragraphs...]
>
> *The above three paragraphs are written by Yh from an internal representation that captures exactly what is in the above code plus comments.*[102]

[102] Gabriel, 1981, p. 102; 1987, p. 29.

Gabriel's approach is more similar to what I call "revision" in §2.2.3 (and close to what people do when they revise texts) than other systems that optimize (e.g. Mann & Moore, Mellish), since he leaves the changes until after the system has completed all of its operations except for the final reading out of the text. However, Gabriel is still operating over an intermediate representation, not the text itself. The "transformations" (which he explicitly states are unrelated to Chomsky's) are Lisp procedures that can change any aspect of the structure, from surface structure changes (e.g. active to passive) to changes in lexical items (e.g. "iguana" to "green reptile"). Some actions are local to a clause, such as the active–passive change, and it is unclear why these wait until after all surface structure for the entire text is generated. Others are a bit more global, such as those controlling anaphora or those that look to see if two noun phrases are too "similar" to avoid ambiguity.

While the use of optimizing transformations does improve the text to some degree, most of the fluency is captured by the initial experts, which have very particular kinds of knowledge. For example, once it is determined that one of the data structures to be described is an array, then an "array expert" is invoked. This expert not only knows what information should be included (the name, length, base, etc), but also what sentence structures will express this information ("the <array> represents <something>", "the <array> has n elements", "the <array> is n dimensional").

In fact it is assumed that these initial experts will always produce grammatical, understandable text. This is another example of the "plan and pray" approach, where, as in McKeown's work, there is careful engineering in the initial stages where the information is chosen and detailed experts that are guaranteed to transform correctly that information into grammatical text.

7.2.4 *Danlos*

Danlos defines generation as the mapping between meaning and form and she takes this definition literally. She isolates elements of meaning and then looks at the possibilities for expressing those elements. Her overall goal seems to be to make the mapping between the two as direct as possible.

Danlos also argues against the traditional distinction between text planning and linguistic realization. In particular, she argues that serially ordering decisions is inadequate, that in fact decisions are interdependent and therefore any ordering will prove inadequate.

In her work she isolates three decision types: lexical selection, the choice between passive and active, and the ordering of clauses. Using examples such as the following set,[103] she shows that all possible combinations of these decisions are not possible.

Mary was killed by John. She was shot.

[103] All of the example sets are made up (presumably by Danlos) and all of the judgements are based on intuition (presumably Danlos's). This presents a basic methodological weakness throughout the work. An additional problem may be that Danlos's native language is French, not English, which may account for some of the awkwardness of her examples.

Mary was killed. She was shot by John.
Mary was shot by John. She was killed.
* Mary was shot. She was killed by John.[104]

However, instead of letting decisions interact or incompatible decisions be changed, as in the architectures of Nirenburg and Gabriel, Danlos forces all decisions to be made at once. She defines a "discourse grammar" that lists all possible combinations of sentence types for each discourse relation. Each rule of the grammar captures a particular setting of the parameters, so that selecting the rule in effects binds all the parameters at one time. According to Danlos, "The selection of a discourse structure amounts to making decisions on the ordering of the information, the number of sentences, and their form." The following shows a portion of a discourse grammar for a "direct causal relation":

(1) (active <ACT>). (active <RESULT>)
(2) (active <RESULT>). (active <ACT>)
...
(6) (passive-the-agent <RESULT>) . (active <ACT>)
...
(15) (passive-the-agent <ACT>). [relative-subject (active <RESULT>)].

Danlos developed these fifteen structures by listing all the possible parameter settings for two clauses related by the "direct causal" relation, i.e. the order of the two sentence types ACT and RESULT, whether they are two separate sentences or combined into one, and whether each clause is active, passive with agent, or passive without agent. She determined that of the thirty-six possibilities given these three parameters, only the fifteen listed in the grammar are allowed by the language and the rest are not. Of course this grammar doesn't include all the possible forms for all verbs. For example when Danlos includes the ergative ("the glass broke") as a possibility for the RESULT, several more rules are added to this set. The grammar also doesn't address how any information might be added to these simple clauses and what effect that has on the structures. The potential combinatorial explosion of possibilities when all verb types and possible combinations are included isn't addressed. While this approach may work for the examples she has tried, it is unclear that it will be able to expand to all the needed cases without being combinatorically intractable.

In effect, Danlos has provided a *stipulative* answer to the problem of expressibility. Rather than exploring why some sentence combinations are better than others, she ensures that the combinations deemed awkward are not generated by simply listing all the legal cases and requiring the choice to be taken from that set. However, this ignores the fact that decisions in generation are not made randomly. For example, a simple model of focus would allow sentence (1) below and disallow sentence (2):

(1) John shot Mary. He killed her.
(2) * John shot Mary. She was killed by him.

104 Danlos uses "*" to indicate sentences that are awkward, not strictly ungrammatical, as is the conventional use by linguists.

A simple focus model, such as McKeown's (1985b), states that the focus is placed in the subject position in the sentence when possible and that the focus is not gratuitously changed from one sentence to the next, that is any focus shift must be explicitly marked. With this general rule, sentence (2) would never be generated. There would be no need explicitly to exclude it and others like it from the language.

7.3 Summary

One of the most important differences among architectures of generation systems is whether or not they follow the traditional two-component architecture with a text planner and linguistic realization component. In the first section of this chapter, I looked at systems that do adopt this architecture: McKeown, Derr & McKeown, Mann & Moore, and the Penman group (Hovy, Mann, Matthiessen, etc.). All of these systems attempt to select and organize the information to be communicated in the terms of the application program, independently of the component which determines what linguistic resources will be used for expressing the information. In all cases, in order to achieve expressibility, these systems had to limit the linguistic competence (e.g. the ability to vary their expression and to use the full range of constructions that the language provides). They limit expressiveness in two ways:

- careful engineering of the selection and composition of the information to ensure it will be within the competence of the system (usually done with predefined templates);
- limiting the compositionality of the system to only organize elements that are realizable as clauses, which have little or no constraint on their composition.

The second set of systems I looked at appreciated the problems of the two-component architecture and built systems that tried to avoid these problems (though it is not clear that Danlos and Gabriel actually did avoid them). However, in all cases there was a resulting inefficiency caused mainly by allowing the system to backtrack and remake decisions, but also in not appreciating the inherent dependencies among types of decisions.

The approach I present in this work keeps the division into two components (and the accompanying efficiency of being able to modularize decisions and make decisions indelibly). However, I lessen the difference between the vocabularies of the two modules by using an abstract linguistic representation in the text planner that creates a bridge from the terms of the application program to the linguistic terms of the resources for expression.

8 Conclusion

I have described the problem of generation as taking information couched in one representation, that of the application program, and expressing it in a very different representation, natural language. In previous approaches to generation, and in particular to text planning, the utterance was composed in the terms of the application program and then that "plan" was passed to the linguistic component which chose the resources for realizing the plan. This approach leaves a *gap*: these systems have no principled way of ensuring that the message composed is expressible in the language, that is that the linguistic component has resources for expressing the plan. Therefore, they had to limit the expressiveness of the system overall so that the composition of the utterance in the planner would not violate the rules of composition in the language. (Chapter Seven discusses the various kinds of limitations these systems imposed.)

This work addresses the problem of expressibility directly: how can we constrain the actions of a text planner to ensure that it will not compose an utterance that cannot be realized and can still make use of the full expressive power of language? I have answered this problem by designing an intermediate level of representation, the Text Structure, which is used by the text planner in composing the utterance. This intermediate level of representation bridges the "generation gap" between the representation of the world in the application program and the linguistic resources provided by the language.

The terms and expressions in the Text Structure are abstractions over the concrete resources of language. They provide the text planner with composite terms that define the possible combinations of features that express semantic categories, such as instance-of-a-kind and definite-set. By providing the text planner with a set of semantic categories, rather than letting it choose from the individual features that make up the categories, it is prevented from choosing a set of features that is not realizable. The abstractions in Text Structure further constrain the composition of the utterance by defining what kinds of constituents can be extended and how the semantic categories can compose.

8.1. Methodology

The problem of trying to bridge two very different representations is not unique to natural language generation. Instances of the problem occur in vision, where three-dimensional objects must be recognized from a two-dimensional array; speech recognition, where discrete words must be recognized from a continuous acoustic signal; compilers, where a high-level language must be translated into a machine language; and, in fact, wherever two independently developed components must communicate. The use of intermediate levels of representation is common to many of the approaches to these problems.

Speech, vision, and natural language understanding and generation share the further problem that they are constrained on one side by the world. We cannot "rework" natural language to make it easier to translate into, the way we might rework the microcode of our machine language, no more than we can change the color of a tree to make it easier to identify in a forest.

The method that I used here for defining the intermediate level of representation was to push from two directions, text planning and linguistic analysis. This is the appropriate methodology for designing such representations. We must abstract over what is concrete and fixed (in this case, the surface resources of the language) and also take into consideration the process that uses those abstractions (in this case, composing a message from the underlying objects). In designing the Text Structure, I worked from the language side by both analyzing a large number of revisions of text which showed how a single text could vary, and applying the work of several linguists whose extensive analysis contributed to developing a set of semantic categories that reflect the surface forms. From the other direction, I developed a text planner which produced text for a number of different domains, giving me experience in working with a variety of underlying representations and applications.

8.2 Summary of the contributions

As I have already described in this chapter, and throughout this book, the greatest accomplishment presented here has been the identification of the problem of expressibility in text generation and its solution: the design of the Text Structure, an intermediate representation used in text planning. However, there are other contributions this work makes as well. I focus here on what I see to be the most important: an efficient architecture for generation and an implemented generation system, Spokesman, which produces text for many different application programs.

8.2.1 *An architecture for generation*

The computational model of the generation process presented in Chapter One accounts for what I see as the most interesting properties of natural language generation, using the characteristics of human language production in people. I repeat those properties here:

- A generator must be *efficient*. Given today's processor speeds, it should at least be able to produce text as fast and continuously as people can talk. Therefore, the algorithm should be closer to linear than exponential.

- A generator must be able to *produce continuous, connected text.* Therefore, it must be able to begin uttering words before all of the details of the entire utterance have been determined.
- A generator must be able to produce text that is *grammatical and understandable*; and it must be competent in the language. While it need not have the complete coverage of the language (it's not clear any individual has such coverage, or that we even know what it is), it must be capable of a large subset.
- However, the text it produces need not be optimal text. The generator can use a revision component to assess its own output, decide how to improve it, and revise it by regenerating the text.
- The generator should be independent of the application program. The same mechanisms should work regardless of the topic of the text being produced or the particular application program the generator is working with. (This is not to say we cannot establish minimal requirements for an application program for generation.)
- The same architecture must be capable of working in written or spoken mode; that is, it should be able to both generate competent text in a single pass and revise that text to produce quality written text.

These characteristics have led me to an architectural design with the following properties:

- *Multiple levels of representation* from the application program objects to the final text, each successively less abstract and more linguistic.
- *Progressive refinement*: the text planner begins by building an abstract representation of the utterance and filling in details conservatively as it passes through the levels.
- *Message driven control*: the representation of the utterance at each of the levels controls the processing.
- *Indelible processing*: once a decision is made it cannot be retracted.

The architecture of Spokesman reflects these design properties. It has five levels of representation from the application program to the final text. The representation used by the text planner for composing the utterance, the *Text Structure*, is an abstraction over the concrete resources that gets successively more refined through the *linguistic specification* of the utterance, where lexical heads are finalized and classes of syntactic structures are determined; to the *surface structure*, where the constituents are linearized, to the *word stream*, where morphology, capitalization and pronominalization are applied to produce to final *text*.. Each of these representations drives the processing that builds the next level of representation; they control the order of the decisions through their structures and what actions are taken through the objects that populate those structures. And finally, all of the decision making throughout is indelible; that is, no decisions are changed and there is no backtracking.

8.2.2 *The Spokesman generation system*

The SPOKESMAN generation system is an implementation of the architecture described above. It is *domain independent*, that is the knowledge structures in the system are not dependent on any particular application, and is currently being used in several applications at BBN. Not only do the applications differ in the style of the text produced, but also in the kinds of representations that drive the generation. I have described the text-planning component of the system in detail in Chapter Five (details of the linguistic component are available in Meteer *et al.* 1987); here I show samples of the systems capabilities in its various domains:

- The Main Street simulation program is the most recent of Spokesman's domains, and the one I am doing the most experimental work with. The following is a sample of some of that work in progress:[105]

  > Karen 10:49 AM: Karen is at International-conglomerate, which is at 1375 Main Street. Karen's skills are managing and cooking. Karen likes watching movies.

- In the DARPA funded Semi-Automated Forces (SAF) Project[106] (Ceranovicz *et al.* 1988), Spokesman produces Operations Orders (OPORDs) from a domain model represented in a NIKL-based frame representation called SFL ("Simple Frame Language") and a goal-procedural network represented in TARL ("Tactical Action Representation Language", Abrett *et al.* 1989). The following is an example of an OPORD produced by Spokesman. The Friendly Situation paragraph uses the military units hierarchy, terrain information, and mission task objects to produce an overview of other units with respect to the current command post; the Mission and Execution use the instantiation of the goal procedure net representing the missions assigned to these units:[107]

  > OPERATIONS ORDERS FOR D/1 TB
  >
  > 1. FRIENDLY SITUATION
  >
  > C/1 TB is to the east and its mission is to attack Objective GAMMA from ES646905 to ES758911 at 141423 Apr. A/1 TB is to the south. B/1 TB and HHC/2 are to the east.
  >
  > 2. MISSION

[105] The subsequent references to Karen in this paragraph would normally be pronominalized by the system; however, since gender is not represented explicitly anywhere in the underlying application, the system currently uses the pronoun "it". In deference to Karen, I turned off the pronominalization until the underlying system can be expanded to include this information.

[106] SAF is part of DARPA's SIMNET project, contract number MDA972-89-0600. See MacLaughlin & Shaked, 1989, for a complete description of the integration between Spokesman and SAF.

[107] "TB" is an abbreviation for Tank Battalion. The initial letter refers to which subordinate is being referred to and the number following the slash is the number of the tank battalion, e.g. C/1 TB is the 3rd company of the 1st Tank Battalion; A/1 TB is the 1st company of the 1st tank battalion. HHC is the headquarters unit.

D/1 TB'S mission is to defend Area of Responsibility ALPHA at 141420 Apr. The approach route is Route 1 from ES702809 to ES739864.

3. EXECUTION

a. 1/D/1 TB

March along Route P1. First change to a line formation at ES731852 and then go to ES738865.

b. 2/D/1 TB

March along Route P1. First change to a line formation at ES731852 and then go to ES737866.

c. 3/D/1 TB

March along Route P1. First change to a line formation at ES731852 and then go to ES730864.

- Also in the SAF Project, Spokesman produces simulated radio messages from information packets sent to a Symbolics workstation from a battle simulation executing on a Butterfly™.

A/74 TB has spotted a platoon of 3 vehicles at ES700800.

A/74 TB's fuel level is 80%.

- In the mission analysis and order preparation phases of the AirLand Battle Management Project,[108] Spokesman produces descriptions of military tasks from underlying Task Objects represented in the object-oriented frame language KEE: (See Meteer, 1989c, for further details.) The following is a portion of an OPORD produced for ALBM:

2. MISSION

10th Corps defend in assigned sector to defeat the 8th Combined Arms Army.

3. EXECUTION

a. 52nd Mechanized Division

(1) Conduct covering force operations along avenues B and C to defeat the lead regiments of the first tactical echelon in the CFA in assigned sector.

(2) Detach 1 battalion task force.

(3) Defend along Avenues B and C to defeat the follow on regiments of the first tactical echelon in the MBA in assigned sector.

b. 313th Separate Mechanized Brigade

...[109]

- In ALBM's Soldier Machine Interface (SMI), Spokesman produces textual responses to natural language queries as well as preparing the labels on dynamic menu items whose underlying objects are complex networks rather than simple values.

108 Sponsorship of ALBM is by the Defense Advanced Research Projects Agency, the US Army Ballistic Research Laboratory, and the US Army Center for Communications, contract number DAAA15-87-C-0006.

109 The Execution paragraph continues as in a. for all units organic to the corps, which, depending on the scenario, will be five or six units with between three and five tasks each. A full opord runs about a page.

Q: Which units are organic to the 23rd Mech Div?

A: The following units are organic to the 23rd Mech Div: 3-52 Mech Brigade, 52nd Aviation Brigade, ...

- For frame-based hierarchical knowledge representations, such as SAF and the Main Street simulation, Spokesman generates descriptions of the definitions of types ("concepts" in SFL terms) and their attributes from the knowledge base. The system takes advantage of the frame structure of the types to organize the information and creates words from the names of the frames and slots, so that it can produce descriptions for new knowledge bases (KB) with no changes to the general algorithm. The following description of the KB in Main Street was generated using the unchanged code written for SAF with no special interface mappings or adjustments to the algorithm. The system will walk through the hierarchy, producing several pages of such descriptions:

  A car is a transportation-device. The default speed of a car is a speed. The direction-of-motion of a car is a direction. Taxi and personal-car are specializations of a car.

- The Parrot paraphraser uses Spokesman to generate paraphrases of queries understood by the IRUS-II understanding system. Paraphrases are generated from the internal representation in the understanding component, which is a hybrid of intensional logic and a taxonomic domain model. As shown in the following examples, the paraphrases are semantic rather than literal parrots of this input: they may use different lexical items and resolve the pronominal references (MacLaughlin 1989).[110]

  Query: List the ships in San Diego.

  Paraphrase: List the vessels in San Diego.

  Query: What was their previous overall readiness?

  Paraphrase: What was the previous readiness of the vessels in San Diego?

- Spokesman produces cooperative and diagnostic responses, as well as paraphrases, in the JANUS Seamless Interface System.[111] Responses are produced from structures from the data base being queried and diagnostic responses from internal structures of the parsing component. In the following excerpt taken at the RADC AI Tech Fair, November 15-16 1988, the text in all capitals was typed by the user and analyzed by the IRUS-II understanding component (Weischedel *et al.* 1986); the text in quotes was produced by the Spokesman Generation System:[112]

  DISPLAY THE C1 BLUE SUBS THAT ARE M1 ON ASW.

  Paraphrase:

110 See Meteer & Shaked (1988) for a discussion of paraphrasing strategies and how they can be used effectively in interfaces.

111 Sponsored by DARPA as part of the Strategic Computing Natural Language Project, contract number N00014-85-C-0016.

112 Abbreviation Key: C1 and M1 are navy readiness ratings; ASW: anti-submarine warfare.

"Display the C1 blue submarines which are M1 on antisubmarine warfare."
Text Response:
"The following have been displayed: Puffer, William H Bates, and Diego Garcia."

SELECT THEM.
Paraphrase:
"Select the C1 blue submarines which are M1 on antisubmarine warfare."
Text Response:
"The following have been selected: Puffer, William H Bates, and Diego Garcia."

WHICH COMMANDERS HAVE BEEN DEPLOYED TO THE PACIFIC OCEAN?
Diagnostic Response:
"I don't understand how commanders can be deployed."

8.3 What does this work have to say to AI in general?

While the details of the work described here are particular to generating natural language, the architectural arguments are applicable to the design of any computational system. In §8.1, I discussed the appropriateness of the methodology of designing an intermediate level of representation using abstractions found by pushing from both sides, the source and the target. Two other architectural arguments made here are (1) the use of specialized architectures over general techniques and (2) the influence of natural language generation on issues in knowledge representation.

8.3.1 *Choosing the right technique*

I have shown in this work that choosing the right vocabulary can make planning in a limited domain a efficient task. It is a general principle for designing systems that the power of the technique should fit the task at hand. An overly powerful technique results in a "weak" method, that is it will trivially work, but we learn very little from it and it will be wasteful because it has to be powerful enough to handle a lot of cases that will never appear.

An example of this is in the control structure of generation systems: some people construe the problem of choice in generation as search (Nirenburg, Patten). Rather than exploring the strong constraints that language itself provides, they use a general-purpose technique which is unnecessarily powerful, and thus inefficient, for the task.

8.3.2 *Knowledge representation*

I have already argued the importance of the careful design of representational levels within the generator. Here I look at what research in language generation has to say to knowledge representation in general. As I discussed in Chapter One, and as the following quote from Woods makes clear, what knowledge is represented and how that knowledge is represented can either limit or facilitate the capabilities of a system:

In computer science, a good solution often depends on a good representation. For most applications in artificial intelligence, the choice of representation is especially important, since the possible choices are more diverse and the forcing criteria are less clear. ... The representational primitives, together with the system for their combination, effectively limit what systems can perceive, know, or understand.[113]

Any system that has the goal of explaining its actions must explicitly represent the information that is required by language. A trivial case of this is shown by the following example of text that was generated in the Main Street domain:

> Karen is at International Conglomerate, which is at 1375 Main Street. Its skills are cooking and managing.

The "it" in the second sentence refers back to Karen, but because the application program does not explicitly represent the gender of people, the system cannot pronominalize correctly. As people, we know that "Karen" is female because it is a woman's name ("Kyle" or "Ashley" would be more difficult), and if we personally knew Karen we wouldn't have any trouble choosing a pronoun. However, programs don't have this general world knowledge, nor this ability to infer the information without explicit rules.

Folding information into the names of objects is one of the most common flaws in the representations I have worked with. In Main Street, instances of cars have names such as "green-jag" and "red-porsch", but no slots for color or car make; instances of homes have names such as "Karen-and-macks" or "Vals-cape-cod", but no slots for owners, occupants, or house type. Military units in the military domains often have their unit ID, size (e.g. division) and type (e.g. mechanized) folded into their names. In all of these instances, the information in the name is not needed by the processing in the application program, and therefore it did not occur to the developer to make it explicit in the representation. However, in order to talk about these objects, this information needs to be broken out where the generator can get at it independently. There is always the fallback of treating the name in the application as a canned phrase, but we don't always want to include the color of a car every time we refer to it, nor do we always want to include the type of house. Furthermore, the owner information on houses needs to be represented explicitly in order to generate the possessive correctly, as in "Val's cape cod".

Attempting to generate text from these representations very quickly finds their flaws: you can't talk about what's not represented. Furthermore, working on potential target texts can give you clues to what is interesting to represent that might not already be there and some ideas for how to represent that information. For example, the semantic categories for events in the Text Structure (e.g. transition, state, process, transition, result) can contribute to the way actions are represented in simulations and other application programs, thus allowing these various perspectives on the event be expressed by the generator.

All of the applications that Spokesman has produced text for are knowledge-based systems with some taxonomic representations of the types of entities in

[113] Woods, 1984, p .45.

the system. This requirement is part of the data-directed architecture: information must be explicitly represented in the underlying system in order to be expressed in the text produced by the generator. The positive result of this constraint is that we are assured that the text produced is an accurate description of what is represented in the underlying system (a property termed "fidelity" by Swartout (1990)). However, it also means that the quality of the text is directly dependent on the quality of the information represented. We found that in adding text generation capabilities to our systems, we were forced to make the representation of the information more consistent and complete. The following are some of the heuristics we found useful in determining what information to represent and how to represent it in the knowledge base:

(1) *Representing information explicitly, rather than implicitly.* Properties of an object that are not used directly in the application often folded into the name of the object. For example, military unit names ("23.mech.batt") encode the ID number, type, and size of the unit. In order to use general routines for constructing the full name of the unit ("23rd Mechanized Battalion") or to refer to the unit in some other way ("the lead battalion"), this information must be represented explicitly in the slots of the unit, not just in its name.

(2) *Introducing more levels into the concept hierarchy.* Often a flat organization for concepts in the hierarchy is all that is necessary for the application's own use. However, intermediate nodes in a hierarchical representation capture important generalizations that can be used by the text generation system. For example, COMPANY-MARCH, PLATOON-MARCH, COMPANY-WITHDRAWAL, and PLATOON-WITHDRAWAL are all types of MANEUVER ACTIONS in the SAF application. However, without an intermediate node grouping the various kinds of marches as distinct from the various kinds of withdrawals, the generator needs a separate routine to handle each of these actions, even though the English word for the action (i.e. "march" or "withdraw") is the same regardless of the size of the group (i.e. "platoon" or "company") executing the action.

(3) *Using specific types, rather than generic data structures such as string or number as the values of slots.* Generic data structures carry no particular meaning outside their context, whereas a typed object can use a behavior associated with that type to indicate how it should be expressed. For example, if a vehicle object has a slot named SPEED whose value is an integer and another slot named FUEL-CAPACITY whose value is also an integer, there needs to be a way to determine that the measure for speed is in terms of miles per hour and that fuel capacity is in terms of gallons, since the English will require a head noun for the integer value even if the application doesn't need the information. By making these values instances of type SPEED and FUEL-CAPACITY, respectively, then this information of how to express the integer is always available.

8.4 Future excitements

One of the greatest rewards of this work has been the new ideas and directions for work that have opened up as a result. Text Structure was designed to solve a very real and practical problem in text planning that has great theoretical import: expressibility. However, in addition, it has provided a stepping stone to a whole new set of problems, many of which were not clearly describable without it. In this section, I discuss some of the new and exciting problems my solution has let me talk about more concretely.

8.4.1 *Lexical choice*

Lexical choice has received little serious attention in generation research, as Marcus (1987) pointedly told the natural language research community at the last TINLAP (Theoretical Issues in Natural Language Processing). In our defense, this is not terribly surprising given the lack of sophistication in the application programs generators have had to work with; subtle word choice has simply not been necessary and the motivation for making subtle choice has not been present. But as programs become more sophisticated, the issue of how to choose lexical items must be addressed.

In the approach to generation described here, lexical choice is assumed to be one of the earliest decisions made, as it is the most constraining decision and carries most of the content. Furthermore, it is assumed that the choice of lexical head cannot be made independently of the choice of semantic category being expressed by the constituent the lexical item heads nor of the arguments to that head. This requires the reference knowledge of the lexicon to be in the same terms as the semantic categories in the Text Structure.

In Chapter Four I described how the work of lexical semanticists such as Pustejovsky and Talmy influenced the development of the semantic categories in Text Structure. This work could also be used in developing a lexicon for generation. For example, Pustejovsky's integrated theory of lexical semantics explores the internal structure of lexical items from a computational perspective. He has developed a theory of "Event Structure" for describing verbs and a theory of "Qualia Structure" for nouns and modifiers. This work allows us to explore in more detail the interaction between combinations of words, and provides insight into why, for example, a "long book" refers to how long it takes to read the book, whereas a "long stick" refers to its physical length. If we want to modify the physical size of a book, we must say a "big book" or a "thick book". This kind of reasoning is essential for lexical selection in generation.

8.4.2 *Selection of information*

Another area that is not addressed directly in this work is the selection of what information to include. Again, the existence of the Text Structure and its vocabulary in terms of abstract linguistic resources offers interesting possibilities for exploring selection from a new perspective. Specifically, I would like to explore how the availability (or lack) of resources for expression affects the choice of what to say. For example, does the availability or familiarity of some term influence how an object is described, and, once some choices are made, how much do the constraints influence the choice of what else to include?

8.4.3 *Revision*

Finally, I would like to return to the problem that first inspired me to do this work: the problem of revision. The work presented here has made great inroads into the problem of how to describe the variations in surface form that I found in my analysis of revisions and does so at a sufficiently abstract level to capture general kinds of changes that occur (as I describe in Chapter Three). While there is still a great deal of work to be done to cover all of the revision I found in my data, we will soon be able to turn the focus from describing *how* such changes could be made to *why* the changes are made.

Bibliography

Abrett, G., Burstein, M., & Deutsch, S. (1989), "Tarl: Tactical Action Representation Language, an environment for building goal directed knowledge based simulation", BBN Technical Report No. 7062, BBN Systems and Technologies, Cambridge, Massachusetts.

Allen, J.F. & Perrault, C.R. (1980), "Analyzing Intention in Utterances", *Artificial Intelligence*, vol. 15, 143-178, reprinted in Grosz *et al.*, 1986, pp. 441-458.

Appelt, D.E. (1985), "Planning English Referring Expressions", *Artificial Intelligence*, vol. 26, 1-33.

Bateman, J.A. (1988), "From systemic-functional grammar to systemic-functional text generation: Escalating the exchange" *Proceedings of the AAAI-88 Workshop on Text Planning and Generation*, St. Paul, Minnesota, August 25 1988, pp.123-134.

— (1990), "Upper Modeling: Organizing Knowledge for Natural Language Processing", in Proceedings of the 5th International Workshop on Natural Language Generation, Pittsburgh, Pennsylvania.

— & Paris, C.L. (1989), "Phrasing a text in terms the user can understand", *IJCAI-89*, Detroit, Michigan, pp.1511-1517.

Beaugrande R. de (1984), *Text Production: Toward a Science of Composition,* Ablex Publishing Corporation, Norwood, New Jersey.

Beaugrande R. de & Dressler, W. (1981), *Introduction to Text Linguistics*, Longman, London.

Bienkowski, M.A. (1986), *A Computational Model for Extemporaneous Elaborations,* Cognitive Science Laboratory Technical Report 1, Princeton University, Princeton, New Jersey, September.

Block, R. (1988), "Can a 'parsing grammar' be used for natural language generation?" in M. Zock & G. Sabah (eds), *Advances in Natural Language Generation*, Pinter Publishers, London, Vol. 1, pp.53-62.

Bobrow, R., Resnik, P., & Weischedel, R. (1990), "Multiple Underlying Systems: Translating User Requests into Programs to Produce Answers", *Proceedings of the 28th Annual Meeting of the Association for Computational Linguistics,* Pittsburgh, Pennsylvania.

Bock, K. (1987), "Exploring Levels of Processing in Sentence Production" in Kempen (ed.), *Natural Language Generation*, Martinus Nijoff Publishers, Dordrecht, pp. 352-363.

Bunt, H. (1988), "Discontinuous Phrase Structure Grammar and its use in sentence generation" in M. Zock & G. Sabah (eds.), *Advances in Natural Language Generation*. Pinter Publishers, London, vol. 2, pp.1-26.

Cargano, D. & Iordanskaja, L. (1989), "Content Determination and Text Structuring in Gossip" in *Extended Abstracts presented at the Second European Natural Language Generation Workshop*, Edinburgh, April 6-8, pp.15-22.

Ceranovicz, A., Downes-Martin, S., & Saffi, M. (1988), *Simnet Semi-Automated Forces Version 3.0: A Functional Description,* BBN Technical Report No. 6939, BBN Systems and Technologies, Cambridge, Massachusetts.

Chomsky, N. (1957), *Syntactic Structures*, Mouton & Co., The Hague,

Cohen, P. & Feigenbaum, E. (1982), *The Handbook of Artificial Intelligence*, Vol. 3, William Kaufman, Inc., Los Altos, California.

Cohen, P.R. & Levesque, H.J. (1985), "Speech Acts and Rationality", *Proceedings of the 23rd Annual Meeting of the Association for Computational Linguistics*, Chicago, Illinois, pp. 49-59.

Cohen, P.R. & Perrault, C.R. (1979), "Elements of a Plan-Based Theory of Speech Acts", *Cognitive Science* 3(3), pp.177-212, reprinted in Grosz *et al.*, 1986, pp.423-440.

Conklin, E. (1983), "Data-driven Indelible Planning of Discourse Generation Using Salience", unpublished Ph.D.Thesis, Department of Computer and Information Sciences, University of Massachusetts, Amherst, Massachusetts.

Cullingford, R.E. (1986), *Natural Language Processing: A Knowledge-engineering Approach,* Rowman & Littlefield, Totowa, New Jersey.

Dale, R. (1988), "Generating Referring Expressions in a Domain of Objects and Processes", unpublished Ph.D. Thesis, University of Edinburgh.

— (1989), "Cooking up Referring Expressions" in *Proceedings of the 27th Annual Meeting of the Association for Computational Linguistics*, Vancouver, British Columbia, June 26-29, pp.68-75.

Danlos, L. (1987), "Conceptual and Linguistic Decisions in Generation" in *Proceedings of Coling-84*, Stanford University, Palo Alto, California, July 2-6 1984, pp.501-504.

— (1987), *The Linguistic Basis of Text Generation,* Cambridge University Press, Cambridge.

Davey, A. (1974), *Discourse Production*, Edinburgh University Press. Edinburgh.

Derr, M.A. & McKeown, K.R. (1984), "Using Focus to Generate Complex and Simple Sentences", *Proceedings of Coling-84,* Stanford University, Palo Alto, California, July 2-6 1984. pp.319-326.

Dik, S.C. (1988), "Concerning the logical component of a natural language generator" in M. Zock & G. Sabah (eds), *Advances in Natural Language Generation*, Pinter Publishers, London, Vol. 1. pp.73-91.

DiMarco, C. & Hirst, G. (1988), "Stylistic Grammars in Language Translation", *Proceedings of Coling-88*, Budapest, pp.148-153.

Fawcett, R.P. (1981), "Generating a sentence in systemic functional grammar" in M.A.K.Halliday & J.R. Martin (eds), *Readings in Systemic Linguistics*, Batsfords Academic and Educational Ltd, London, pp.146-184.

— (1988), "Language generation as choice in social interaction" in M. Zock & G. Sabah (eds), *Advances in Natural Language Generation*, Pinter Publishers, London, Vol. 2. pp.27-50.

Fodor, J.A., Bever, T. & Garret, M. (1974), *Psychology of Language: An Introduction to Psycholinguistics and Generative Grammar*, McGraw-Hill, New York, New York.

Francis, W.N. (1958), *The Structure of American English*, The Ronald Press Company, New York, New York.

Gabriel, R. (1981), "An Organization for Programs in Fluid Domains", unpublished Ph.D. Thesis, Department of Computer Science, Stanford University, Palo Alto, California.

— (1988), "Deliberate Writing" in D.McDonald & L.Bolc (eds), *Natural Language Generation Systems*, Springer-Verlag, New York, New York.

Garrett, M.F. (1975), "The Analysis of Sentence Production", *Psychology of Learning and Motivation*, Vol.98, pp.133-177.

Goldman, N.M. (1975), "Conceptual Generation" in R. Shank (ed.), *Conceptual Information Processing*, Elsevier, North-Holland, pp.289-372.

Grimes, J.E. (1975), *The Thread of Discourse*, Mouton, The Hague.

Grimshaw, J. (1988), "On the Representation of Two Kinds of Noun", Presented at Theoretical Issues in Computation and Lexical Semantics Workshop, Brandeis University, April 1988.

— (1991), *Argument Structure*, MIT Press, Cambridge, Massachusetts.

Grosz, B.J. & Sidner, C.L. (1986), "Attention, Intentions, and the Structure of Discourse", *Computational Linguistics*, Vol.12, No. 3, pp.175-204.

—, Webber, B., & Spark Jones, K. (1986), *Readings in Natural Language Processing*, Morgan Kaufmann Publishers, Los Altos, California.

Hajicova, E. (1983), "Topic and Focus", *Theoretical Linguistics*, Vol. 10, pp. 268-276.

Hale, K. & Keyser, J. (1987), "On Principles of Grammatical Projection from the Lexicon", Lexicon Project Working Papers, Center for Cognitive Science, MIT, Cambridge, Massachusetts.

Halliday, M.A.K. (1985), *An Introduction to Functional Grammar*, Edward Arnold, London.

Hayes, J. & Flower, L. (1980), "Identifying the Organization of Writing Processes" in L.Gregg & E. Steinberg (eds), *Cognitive Processes in Writing*, Lawrence Erlbaum Associates, Hilldale, New Jersey, pp. 3-30.

Hirschberg, Morton A. (1987), "AirLand Battle Management", *Proceedings of the 1987 IEEE International Conference on Systems, Man, and Cybernetics,* October 1987, pp.1042-1043.

Hobbs, Jerry R. (1982), "Towards an Understanding of Coherence in Discourse" in W. Lehnert & M. Ringle (eds), *Strategies for Natural Langauge Processing,* Lawrence Erlbaum Associates, Hilldale, New Jersey, pp.223-244.

Horacek, H. (1988), "The application of unification for syntactic generation in German" in M. Zock & G. Sabah (eds), *Advances in Natural Language Generation,* Pinter Publishers, London, Vol. 1. pp.63-72.

Hovy, E.H. (1987), "Generating Natural Language Under Pragmatic Constraints", unpublished Ph.D. Thesis, Yale University, New Haven, Conneticut, March 1987.

— (1988), "Planning Coherent Multisentential Paragraphs" in *Proceedings of the 26th Annual Meeting of the Association for Computational Linguistics,* Buffalo, New York, June 7-10 1988, pp. 163-169.

— (1991), "Approaches to the planning of Coherent Text" in C. Paris, W. Swartout, and W. Mann (eds), *Natural Language Generation in Artificial Intelligence and Computational Linguistics,* Klewer Academic Publishers, Boston, Massachusetts, pp.83-102.

—, McDonald, D.D., Young, S. (eds) (1988), *Proceedings of the AAAI Workshop on Text Plannings and Realization,* St. Paul, Minnesota, August 1988.

Huettner, A.K., Meteer, M.W., & McDonald, D.D. (1987), "Constraints on the Generation of Adjunct Clauses" in *Proceedings of the 25th Annual Meeting of the Association for Computational Linguistics,* Stanford University, Palo Alto, California, July 1987.

Iordanskaja, L., Kittredge, R., and Polguere, A. (1991), "Lexical Selection and Paraphrase in a Meaning-Text Generation Model" in C. Paris, W. Swartout and W. Mann (eds), *Natural Language Generation in Artificial Intelligence and Computational Linguistics,* Klewer Academic Publishers, Boston, Massachusetts. p. 293-312.

Jackendoff, R. (1978), "Grammar as Evidence for Conceptual Structure" in M.Halle, J.Bresnan, & G.Miller (eds), *Linguistic Theory and Psychological Reality,* MIT Press, Cambridge, Massachusetts, pp. 201-228.

— (1983), *Semantics and Cognition,* MIT Press, Cambridge, Massachusetts.

Jacobs, P. (1985), "A Knowledge-Based Approach to Language Production", unpublished Ph.D. Thesis, Computer Science Division, University of California at Berkeley, Report No UCB/USC 86/254, August 1985.

— (1987), "KING: A knowledge-intensive natural language generator" in G. Kempen (ed.), *Natural Language Generation,* Martinus Nijoff Publishers, Dordrecht, pp. 219-231.

Joshi, Aravind K. (1985), "How much context-sensitivity is required to provide reasonable structural descriptions: Tree Adjoining Grammars" in D.Dowty, L.Karttunen, and A. Zwicky, (eds), *Natural Language Processing: Psycholinguistic, Computational, and Theoretical Perspectives*, Cambridge University Press, Cambridge, pp.206-250.

— (1987), "The Relevance of Tree Adjoining Grammar to Generation" in G. Kempen (ed.), *Natural Language Generation*, Martinus Nijoff Publishers, Dordrecht, pp. 233-252.

Kay, Martin (1979), "Functional Grammar" in *Proceedings of the 5th Annual Meeting of the Berkeley Linguistic Society*, University of California, Berkeley, pp.142-158.

Kegl, Judy (1987), "The Boundary Between Word Knowledge and World Knowledge" in Y. Wilks (ed.) *Theoretical Issues in Natural Language Processing*, Lawrence Erlbaum Associates, Inc., Hillsdale, New Jersey, pp.22-27.

Kempen, Gerard (ed) (1987), *Natural Language Generation*, Martinus Nijoff Publishers. Dordrecht.

Kintsch, W. (1985), "Text Processing: A Psychological Model" in Van Dijk (ed.), *Handbook of Discourse Analysis*, Vol. 2, Academic Press, London, pp. 230-243.

Kittredge, R., Korelsky, T., and Rambow, O. (1991) "On the need for Domain Communication Knowledge", *Computational Intelligence* 7(4).

Longacre, R.E. (1979), "The Paragraph as a Grammatical Unit" in T. Givon (ed), *Syntax and Semantics, Vol. 12: Discourse and Syntax*, Academic Press, New York, New York, pp. 115-134.

MacGregor, R. & Brill, D. (1989), *The LOOM Manual*, Technical Report, USC/Information Sciences Institute, Marina del Rey, California.

MacLaughlin, D. (1989), "Parrot: The Janus Paraphraser", BBN Technical Report, No. 7139, BBN Systems and Technologies, Cambridge, Massachusetts.

— & Shaked, V. (1989), "Text Generation in Semi-Automated Forces", BBN Technical Report No. 7092, BBN Systems and Technologies, Cambridge, Massachusetts.

Mann, W.C. (1983), "An Overview of the Penman Generation System" in *Proceedings of the National Conference on Artificial Intelligence*, pp. 261-265. Also available as USC/ISI Technical Report RR-83-114. Marina del Rey, California.

— & Matthiessen C. (1985), "Nigel: A Systemic Grammar for Text Generation" in R. Freedle (ed.), *Systemic Perspectives on Discourse: Selected Theoretical Papers of the 9th Intl. Systemic Workshop*, Ablex Publishing Corporation, Norwood, New Jersey. Also available as USC/ISI Technical Report RR-83-105. Marina del Rey, California.

— & Moore J.A. (1981), "Computer Generation of Multiparagraph English Text", *American Journal of Computational Linguistics*, 7 (1), Jan-Mar, pp. 17-29.

— & Thompson, S. (1987), "Rhetorical Structure Theory: Description and Construction of Text Structures" in G. Kempen (ed.), *Natural Language Generation*, Martinus Nijoff Publishers, Dordrecht, pp. 279-300.

Marcus, M.P. (1987), "Generation Systems Should Choose Their Words", *Proceedings of Theoretical Issues in Natural Language Processing-3*, New Mexico State University, Las Cruces, New Mexico, January 7-9, pp.211-214.

Marr, D. (1982), *Vision*, W.H. Freeman and Company, San Fransisco, California.

Matthiessen, C. & Thompson, S. (1987), "The Structure of Discourse and Subordination" in J.Halman & S.Thompson (eds), *Clause Combining in Discourse and 'Subordination'*, John Benjamins Publishing Company, Amsterdam.

McCoy, K.F. (1988), "Reasoning on a Highlighted User Model to Respond to Misconceptions", *Computational Linguistics*, 14 (3), pp.52-63.

— & Cheng, J. (1991), "Focus of Attention: Constraining what can be said next" in C. Paris, W. Swartout, and W. Mann (eds), *Natural Language Generation in Artificial Intelligence and Computational Linguistics*, Klewer Academic Publishers, Boston, Massachusetts, pp.103-124.

McDonald, D.D. (1980), "Natural language production as a process of decision making under constraint", unpublished Ph.D. Thesis, MIT, Cambridge, Massachusetts.

— (1984), "Description Directed Control", *Computers and Mathematics* 9(1). Reprinted in Grosz *et al.* (eds), *Readings in Natural Language Processing*, Morgan Kaufman Publishers, Los Altos, California, 1986, pp.519-538.

— (1988), "Modularity in Natural Language Generation: Methodological issues" *Proceedings of the AAAI-88 Workshop on Text Planning and Generation*, St. Paul, Minnesota, August 25 1988, pp.91-98.

— (1991), "On the Place of Words in the Generation Process" in C. Paris, W. Swartout, and W. Mann (eds), *Natural Language Generation in Artificial Intelligence and Computational Linguistics*, Klewer Academic Publishers, Boston, Massachusetts, pp.229-248.

— & Meteer, M.W. (1988), "From Water to Wine: Generating Natural Language Text from Today's Applications Programs", *Proceedings of the 2nd Conference on Applied Natural Language Processing*, University of Texas at Austin, February 9–11 1987, pp.41-48.

— & Meteer, M.W. (1990) "The Implications of Tree Adjoining Grammar for Generation" presented at the 1st International Workshop on Tree Adjoining Grammar: Formal Theory and Application, Germany, August 1990.

—, Meteer, M.W., & Pustejovsky, J.D. (1987), "Factors Contributing to Efficiency in Natural Language Generation" in G. Kempen (ed.), *Natural Language Generation*, Martinus Nijoff Publishers, Dordrecht, pp. 159-182.

McKeown, K.R. (1982), "Generating Natural Language Text in Response to Questions about Database Queries", unpublished Ph.D. thesis, University of Pennsylvania, Philadelphia, Pennsylvania.

— (1985a), *Text Generation*, Cambridge University Press, Cambridge.

— (1985b), "Discourse Strategies for Generating Natural Language Text", *Artificial Intelligence*, vol. 27, pp. 1-41.

Melchuk, I. (1988), *Dependency Syntax: Theory and Practice*, State University of New York Press, Albany, New York.

Mellish, C. (1988), "Natural Language Generation from Plans" in M. Zock & G. Sabah (eds), *Advances in Natural Language Generation*, Pinter Publishers, London, Vol. 1, pp.131-145.

Meteer, M.W. (Vaughan) (1985), "The Writing Process as a Model for Natural Language Generation", Master's Thesis, University of Massachusetts, Amherst.

— (1988), "Defining a Vocabulary for Text Planning" *Proceedings of the AAAI-88 Workshop on Text Planning and Generation*, St. Paul, Minnesota, August 25, 1988, pp. 115-122.

— (1989a), Review of *Advances in Natural Language Generation*, M. Zock & G. Sabah (eds) *Computational Linguistics*, 15 (2), pp.120-122.

— (1989b), *The SPOKESMAN Natural Language Generation System*, BBN Technical Report 7090.

— (1989c), "Block Text Generation in ALBM", ALBM Technical Report.

— (1991), "The Implications of Revisions in Natural Language Generation" in C. Paris, W. Swartout, and W. Mann (eds), *Natural Language Generation in Artificial Intelligence and Computational Linguistics*, Klewer Academic Publishers, Boston, Massachusetts, pp.155-178.

— (Vaughan) & McDonald, D.D. (1986), "A Model of Revision in Natural Language Generation" in *Proceedings of the 24th Annual Meeting of the Association for Computational Linguistics*, Columbia Univerisity, New York, New York, pp. 90-96.

— , McDonald, D., Anderson, S., Forster, D., Gay, L., Huettner, A., Sibun, P., (1987), *Mumble-86: Design and Implementation*, UMass Technical Report 87-87, 173 pgs.

— & Shaked, V. (1988), "Strategies for Effective Paraphrasing", *Proceedings of COLING-88*, Budapest, Hungary, pp. 431-436.

Moore, J.D. & Paris, C.L. (1989), "Planning Text for Advisory Dialogues", *Proceedings of the 27th Annual Meeting of the Association for Computational Linguistics*, Vancouver, British Columbia, June 26-29, pp. 203-211.

Moore, R.C. (1980), "Reasoning about knowledge and action", SRI International AI Center Tech. Note No.191, Menlo Park, California.

Nirenburg, S., Lessor, V. & Nyberg, N. (1989), "Controlling a Language Generation Planner", *Proceedings of IJCAI-89*, Detroit, Michigan, pp.1524-1530.

—, McCardell, R., Nyberg, E., Werner, P., Huffman, S., Kenschaft, E. and Nirenburg, I. (1988), *Diogenes-88*. Technical Report CMU-CMT-88-107, Center for Machine Translation, Carnegie Melon University, Pittsburgh, Pennsylvania.

— & Nirenburg, I. (1988), "A Framework for Lexical Selection in Natural Language Generation", *Proceedings of Coling-88*, Budapest, Hungary, pp.471-475.

—, Nyberg, E., Defrise, C. (1989), *Text Planning with Opportunistic Control*, Technical Report CMU-CMT-89-113, Center for Machine Translation, Carnegie Melon University, Pittsburgh, Pennsylvania

Paris, C.L. (1987), "The Use of Explicit User Models in Text Generation: Tailoring to a User's Level of Expertise, unpublished Ph.D. Thesis, Department of Computer Science, Columbia University, New York, New York.

— (1988a), "Planning a Text: Can we and how should we modularize this process?", *Proceedings of the AAAI-88 Workshop on Text Planning and Generation*, St. Paul, Minnesota, August 25 1988, pp.55-62

— (1988b), "Tailoring Object Descriptions to a User's Level of Expertise", *Computational Linguistics*, 13 (3), pp.64-79.

Patten, T. (1988), *Systemic Text Generation as Problem Solving*, Cambridge University Press, Cambridge.

Penman Natural Language Group (1989), *The Penman User Guide*, ISI Technical Report, Information Sciences Institute, Marina del Rey, California

Pereira, F.C. & Warren, D.H. (1983), "Parsing as Deduction" in *Proceedings of the 21st Annual Meeting of the Association for Computational Linguistics*, Cambridge, Massachusetts, pp.137-144.

Pierrehumbert, J.B. (1980), "The Phonology and Phonetics of English Intonation", unpublished Ph.D. Thesis, Department of Linguistics, MIT, Cambridge, Massachusetts.

Pike, K. (1967), *Language in Relation to a Unified Theory of the Structure of Human Behavior*, Mouton, The Hague.

Polanyi, L. (1986), *The Linguistic Discourse Model: Towards a Formal Theory of Discourse Structure*, BBN Technical Report No. 6409., BBN Laboratories, Cambridge, Massachusetts.

— & Scha, R. (1984), "A Syntactic Approach to Discourse Semantics" in *Proceedings of the International Conference on Computational Linguistics*, Stanford University, Palo Alto, California, July 2-6, pp. 413-419.

Pustejovsky, J.D. (1988), "Event Semantic Structure", Computer Science Technical Report, Brandeis University, Waltham, Massachusetts.

— (1991), "The Generative Lexicon", Computational Linguistics, 17 (4), pp.409-441.

Quirk, R. & Greenbaum, S. (1975), *A Concise Grammar of Contemporary English*, Harcourt Brace Jovanovich Inc., New York, New York.

Rubinoff, R. (1986), "Adapting Mumble: Experience with Natural Language Generation", *Proceedings of AAAI-86*, Philadelphia, Pennsylvania, Morgan-Kaufmann. pp.1063-1068.

Sacerdoti, E. (1977), *A Structure for Plans and Behavior*, North Holland, Amsterdam.

Schabes, Y., Abeille A., & Joshi A. (1988), "Parsing Strategies with 'Lexicalized' Grammars: Application to Tree Adjoining Grammars" in *Proceedings of Coling-88*, Budapest, Hungary. pp.578-583.

Shieber, S. & Schabes, Y. (1990), "Generation and Synchronous Tree-Adjoining Grammar", *Proceedings of the 5th International Workshop on Natural Language Generation,* Pittsburgh, Pennsylvania.

Sidner, C. (1983), "Focusing in the Comprehension of Definite Anaphora" in M. Brady & R. Berwick (eds), *Computational Models of Discourse*, MIT Press, Cambridge, Massachusetts, pp. 267-330.

Stefik, M. (1981), "Planning with Constraints (MOLGEN: Part 1)", *Artificial Intelligence*, vol. 16, pp.111-140.

Strunk, W. & White, E.B. (1979), *The Elements of Style*, 3rd edition, Macmillan Publishing Co. New York, New York.

Suthers, D. (1988), "Providing Multiple Views of Reasoning for Explanation" in *Proceedings of the International Conference on Intelligent Tutoring Systems*, Montreal, June.

Swartout, W. (1990), " Evaluation Criteria for Expert System Explanation", Presented at the AAAI-90 Workshop on Evaluating NL Generation Systems.

Talmy, L. (1987), "The Relation of Grammar to Cognition" in B. Rudzka-Ostyn (ed.), *Topics in Cognitive Linguistics*, John Benjamins.

Thompson, H. (1977), "Strategy and Tactics: a model for language production", *Papers from the 13th Regional Meeting, Chicago Linguistics Society*, pp.651-668.

Webber, B. (1988), "Discourse Deixis: Reference to Discourse Segments", *Proceedings of the 26th Annual Meeting of the Association for Computational Linguistics*, Buffalo, New York, June 7-10 1988, pp.113-122.

Weischedel, R., Bobrow, R., Ayuso, D.M. and Ramshaw, L. (1989), "Portability in the Janus Natural Language Interface" in *Speech and Natural Language*, Morgan Kaufmann Publishers Inc., Los Altos, California, p.112-117.

— , Walker, E., Ayuso, D., de Bruin, J., Koile, K., Ramshaw, L., Shaked, V. (1986), "Out of the Laboratory: A case study with the IRUS natural language interface" in *Research and Development in Natural Language Understanding as part of the Strategic Computing Program*, BBN Labs Technical Report No. 6463, pp.13-26.

Williams, W. (1983), *Composition and Rhetoric*, Heath, Boston.

Woolf, B.P. (1984), "Context Dependent Planning in a Machine Tutor", unpublished Ph.D. Thesis, Department of Computer and Information Science, University of Massachusetts, Amherst, Massachusetts.

Wong, W. C. & Simmons, R. (1988), "A Blackboard Model of Text Production with Revision", *Proceedings of the AAAI-88 Workshop on Text Planning and Generation*, St. Paul, Minnesota, August 25 1988. pp. 99-106.

Woods, W.A. (1984), "Knowledge Representation: What's Important About It?" in N. Cercone (ed.), *The Knowledge Frontier: Essays in the Representation of Knowledge*, Springer-Verlag, New York, New York, 1987. pp.44-79.

Wyrick, J. (1984), *Steps to Writing Well: A Concise Guide to Composition*, Holt, Rinehart, & Winston, New York, New York.

Yazdani, M. (1987), "Reviewing as a Component of the Text Generation Process" in G. Kempen (ed.), *Natural Language Generation*, Martinus Nijoff Publishers, Dordrecht, pp. 183-190.

Zock, M. & Sabah G. (eds.) (1988), *Advances in Natural Language Generation*, Pinter Publishers, London.

Index